# Change and Development— Latin America's Great Task

PRAEGER SPECIAL STUDIES IN
INTERNATIONAL ECONOMICS AND DEVELOPMENT

# Change and Development— Latin America's Great Task

REPORT SUBMITTED TO THE
INTER-AMERICAN DEVELOPMENT BANK

# Raúl Prebisch

**Published in cooperation with the
Inter-American Development Bank**

PRAEGER PUBLISHERS
New York • Washington • London

The purpose of Praeger Special Studies is to make specialized research in U.S. and international economics and politics available to the academic, business, and government communities. For further information, write to the Special Projects Division, Praeger Publishers, Inc., 111 Fourth Avenue, New York, N.Y. 10003.

PRAEGER PUBLISHERS
111 Fourth Avenue, New York, N.Y. 10003, U.S.A.
5, Cromwell Place, London S.W.7, England

Published in the United States of America in 1971
by Praeger Publishers, Inc.

Library of Congress Catalog Card Number: 74-146892

Printed in the United States of America

# FOREWORD

This report originated with a suggestion made by the President of Colombia, Dr. Carlos Lleras Restrepo, at the ninth meeting of the Board of Governors of the Inter-American Development Bank, held in Bogotá in April, 1968. In an address at the opening session of that meeting, President Lleras expressed his concern over the failure of the Latin American countries to achieve targeted rates of development and recommended that the Bank take the initiative in carrying out an in-depth "evaluation of the true significance of international assistance to Latin America during the last decade or so; an evaluation . . . of what can and must be done to correct defects at the national level and those of external cooperation." In making this suggestion, President Lleras anticipated subsequent widespread concerns, which have resulted in a number of useful reports that draw conclusions based on the results of economic development and international assistance programs of the past decade and which evolve policy guidelines designed to accelerate the process of economic expansion in the developing countries.

It is no mere coincidence, nor a preoccupation with marking the endings of decades, that the Pearson, Tinbergen, Rockefeller, Jackson, Peterson, and Prebisch Reports all appeared at about the same time. There can be no question that during the 1960's advocates of greater internationalization of development gained considerable ground. This is exemplified by the expanded activities of multinational agencies contributing to development and the establishment of such new instruments of cooperation as the Inter-American Development Bank and the regional banks in Africa and Asia. In the developing countries, in turn, the goal of economic progress has taken deeper root in the community and in the platforms of various political groups, serious efforts have been made to overcome obstacles to growth, and the instruments and techniques of progress have been improved.

Nevertheless, the major indicators show that the gap in economic well-being between the rich and poor countries is still widening and, worse yet, that greater sectors of population in the developing countries continue to subsist in conditions of extreme poverty. At the same time, national and international political circumstances and even social values have been changing in both developed and backward countries. Scientific and technological progress has resulted in new achievements which exceed the boldest predictions made only a few years ago, while at the same time it offers increasingly promising means of attacking the problems of underdevelopment.

Furthermore, while such progress helps to bring countries together, it also encourages the spread of rising expectations.

In addition, based to a greater or lesser extent on changes in the fundamental economic conditions of the various countries, production and population patterns are being altered rapidly, aggravating old problems or creating new ones. This framework of changing circumstances, the growing pressure of unfulfilled development aspirations at both international and national policy levels, and the widespread awareness that much remains to be done in order to bring about a more orderly expansion of world economic well-being, based on accelerated growth in the developing countries, undoubtedly sparked these various analyses of past development experiences and searches for more effective guidelines for the future. Hopefully these concerns will lead to greater knowledge, and above all to a greater will to act.

The report contained in this volume is confined to the development experience of one region: Latin America. Although developing countries in different areas have much in common, from the standpoint of socioeconomic factors and the tasks and challenges which they face, certain differences exist among them which, apart from theory, exert a strong impact on specific policy guidelines. Even among countries in a single region, these differences are significant, and, as the report notes, within the similarity of Latin American problems are concealed differences that are important to a detailed analysis of individual national situations. Thus this study of the Latin American development scene should prove a useful supplement to the efforts made by other institutions on the international scene.

In carrying out this study, the Bank was fortunate to have the valuable cooperation of Dr. Raúl Prebisch, Director of the Latin American Institute for Economic and Social Planning, who had the primary responsibility for preparing the report. The valuable experience gained by Dr. Prebisch in leading an entire generation of thinkers and men of action in fostering Latin American economic development has been enhanced by his work within the international framework as the first Secretary-General of the United Nations Conference on Trade and Development (UNCTAD).

Dr. Prebisch's report transcends the original principal purposes of the study. He does not confine himself solely to the problem of financing; rather, he carries out an evaluation of overall development strategies. External financial assistance constitutes but one chapter in a broader look at Latin American problems, a view which makes a significant contribution to the comprehensive analysis of regional problems and which avoids uniform or simplistic solutions, such as that the root of problems lies only in the behavior of external factors. The report seeks to analyze Latin America's problems within a context of internal and external forces whose interaction determines the limitations which hinder Latin America's development.

The report highlights one of the factors that will be of growing concern over the next decade: the dualism that unfortunately still persists throughout Latin America between the modern part of the economy and the traditionally backward one, as well as the implications of this dualism for the full use of currently misemployed or unemployed labor. From this standpoint, the report presents a new perspective in the study of regional development strategies, which makes it possible to identify and analyze problems properly, according to the sectoral progress, such as the modern sector of the economy, or the backward sector, where a high percentage of the active population still maintains very low productivity levels, by seeking to correlate these situations in order to achieve an authentic integration of the various sectors of our community.

The report goes beyond the simple interplay of technical and quantitative relations to carry the discussion of current problems to the very heart of political and social conflicts in the hemisphere. The document expresses the firm conviction that it is impossible to discuss regional problems, much less to find adequate solutions to them without transcending economic problems in order to solve social and political conflicts. All of these form part of a single complex phenomenon. Accordingly, the report explicitly goes into a basic element which is often omitted from more easily handled, strictly technical schemes: that is, what is involved in economic development in essence is sociocultural change.

The preparation of this report coincided with the close of the first decade of activities of the Inter-American Development Bank. For its part, within the framework of its field of action, the Bank has initiated a reexamination of its past experience in order to find guidelines that will enable it to contribute still more effectively to the development of its member countries. At the meeting of the Board of Governors held at the end of April, 1970, in Punta del Este, Uruguay, much of the discussion was aimed at evaluating the Bank's past experience. The Bank's traditional round table was specifically devoted to this purpose. At the meeting a publication entitled *Una década de lucha por América Latina,* in which Bank staff members and others examine the experience of the Bank in its various aspects, was distributed. The Prebisch Report will undoubtedly provide our Bank with the broad grasp of regional socioeconomic development problems that will facilitate the evaluation of specific Bank activities.

We are certain that this report will not only assist our executives and experts in their continuing task, but also that it will help all those concerned with the development of Latin America to achieve a better understanding of actual conditions in the hemisphere. It is also our hope that at both national and international assistance levels, the observations made by Dr. Prebisch will contribute to a greater commitment to action and to a formulation of policies better designed to cope with the problems and challenges of underdevelopment.

Felipe Herrera
May, 1970

# PREFACE

A first version of "Change and Development—Latin America's Great Task," the report prepared by Dr. Raúl Prebisch, Director-General of the Latin American Institute for Economic and Social Planning, for the Inter-American Development Bank, was presented to the Bank's Board of Governors at its eleventh annual meeting in Punta del Este, Uruguay, in April, 1970. A number of changes were subsequently made in the format and in some of the statistical data. They do not alter the essence of the report. The only substantive change in this printed edition is the addition of a foreword by Mr. Felipe Herrera, President of the Bank.

The final Spanish version was prepared in June and July, 1970, as was its English translation, which is the work of Dorothy Hayes de Huneeus, who has been for many years a translator for the UN Economic Commission for Latin America and an assistant to Dr. Prebisch.

In this edition, certain chapters have been improved through the elimination of tables and graphs, many of which have been moved to a statistical appendix which also includes the tables used to support the projections.

The eight original chapters were maintained in substantially the same order but were grouped into five major parts to provide a clearer separation of the subjects and problems examined.

Part I is a general introduction to the topics of Latin American development and its problems. It discusses the dynamic insufficiency of our economy, examines the need to accelerate development and the obstacles working against it, and reviews alternatives in development and international cooperation.

Part II contains three chapters in which the problem of the dynamic insufficiency of the Latin American economy is examined and corrective measures are proposed. The first chapter examines population growth and the occupational structure of the labor force. The second describes the pace of development and its external limitations. The third chapter proposes possible remedies for dynamic insufficiency and examines, in turn, the distortions in the occupational structure, the pace of development, and the need for capital formation and international financial cooperation in order to accelerate development. The chapter closes with a section on political techniques and skills for promoting development.

Part III entitled "International Cooperation and Dependence," analyzes a number of problems affecting Latin America's relations with the rest of the world, and cooperation among the Latin American countries themselves. It reviews international financial cooperation and the importance of the multilateral approach; the flow of international financial resources; the continuity and conditions of financial cooperation; foreign private investment; the recommendations of UNCTAD; and the problems of trade preferences. It closes with a critical examination of the current status of international cooperation in Latin America, especially from the standpoint of the regional common market.

Part IV, entitled "The Economic System and Its Transformation," consists of two chapters. The first examines the structural foundations of the economic system and its operation, with emphasis on the historical conflict between expediency and foresight in political decision-making. This is followed by a description of dilemmas posed by advances in science and technology, in terms of government action and the market mechanism, as well as capital formation, foreign trade, and population. It also discusses the problems of adapting present technology to conditions in Latin America, and governments' intervention to redress social inequalities. The chapter then offers reflections on strategy and planning and examines experiences in this field.

The second chapter of Part IV is entitled "Beyond the Economic System." In this chapter the paramount problems analyzed throughout the report are carried beyond the merely economic plane and are examined in terms of the political and moral issues that are the central concerns of our time. A number of grave and provocative questions are raised in the hope that their discussion will highlight a cardinal need; that from the present turmoil and effervescence in our region an authentically Latin American system of thought will emerge.

Part V reviews basic conclusions and summarizes the principal contributions which the author has endeavored to make toward solving the problems of economic and social development in Latin America.

## ACKNOWLEDGMENTS

I wish to place on record here my warm gratitude to all the staff members of the Latin American Institute for Economic and Social Planning and of ECLA who so effectively collaborated in the preparation of this report.

In the Institute, Ricardo Cibotti, Benjamín Hopenhayn, and Francisco Giner de los Ríos devoted long days to working with me on the critical revision of the entire text, suggesting changes which have helped to clarify it or to give it more force and precision. They also assembled a number of comments and suggestions formulated by several staff members (whose names are mentioned later in the present note) and helped me to incorporate them duly in the text. Mssrs. Cibotti and Hopenhayn collaborated with me in drafting the Conclusions which constitue Part V of this report, and Francisco Giner de los Ríos undertook the editing of the whole study.

In Chapters 2 and 3, José Ibarra—seconded by Danilo Astori and Pedro Sainz—was responsible for preparing the statistical material and the labor force projections, in the latter of which Esteban Lederman and Angel Fucaraccio (of LADECE) collaborated. The Universidad Católica de Chile kindly placed a system of computers at the disposal of this group.

Manuel Balboa, of ECLA, had exemplary patience with me. We carefully discussed the statistical material for Chapter 3, the methods applied, and the conclusions reached. He also made valuable comments which I have incorporated into the text. In all this work the staff of ECLA's Latin American Center for Economic Projections—in particular Eligio Alves, Mario La Fuente, and Arsenio Aguirre—participated directly.

Norberto González, of the Institute, using material supplied by the Economic Development and Research Division of ECLA and by the above-mentioned Projections Center, formulated with scrupulous care the projections relating to foreign trade, foreign capital investment, and domestic saving, and collaborated with me very closely in the analysis of the results and the drafting of Chapter 4. In this work he was actively assisted by Juan Ayza, Pedro Esparza, Gerard Fichet, Viera Ostojic, and Bernard van der Wolf.

In Washington, David Pollock gave me constant help, both in the search for information and through frequent discussion of topics dealt with in the report.

The comments and criticisms formulated by various colleagues in ECLA and the Institute in connection with different sections and chapters of the report were most stimulating. Apart from the names already listed in the foregoing paragraphs, I hope I shall be forgetting nobody in mentioning Cristóbal Lara, William Lowenthal, José Medina Echavarría, Jacobo Schatan, Héctor Soza, Oscar J. Bardeci, Aldo Solari, Fernando Pedrão, Jesús González, Carlos de Mattos, and Octavio Rodríguez.

In connection with the statistical aspects of the report, I should like to offer my appreciative thanks to Jorge Espinoza (IDB), who undertook the preparation of most of the graphs in Washington, and Mario Movarec (ECLA), who prepared those relating to the terms of trade. Gladys Reyes (ECLA) and her team were as efficient as ever in helping with the graphs constructed in Santiago, and so was the ECLA/ Institute Statements Pool, in the case of the tables.

It would be very difficult—without risking omissions that I should find it hard to forgive myself—to cite the names of all those who were responsible for the actual typing and reproduction of the text. I have asked Mercedes Bonhomme, Supervisor of the Institute's Secretarial and Typing Pool, and Juan Enrique Hernández, Supervisor of the ECLA/Institute Documents Reproduction Unit, to transmit to all the personnel who worked under their competent and tireless direction my sincere thanks for the hard work they did in meeting a grueling deadline.

Last, I should like to say how grateful I am to Bodil Royem, who devoted so much time and energy to helping me in Washington with the transcription of the original drafts of many chapters, and to Marjorie Fones, who did the same work in Santiago; for both of them this involved deciphering my handwriting.

In the preparation of the whole document a team of collaborators, coordinated at my request by Enrique Iglesias, was available. This team produced supporting material in the shape of extremely useful papers on the various topics covered by the report, which will be published as annexes in a second volume now in course of preparation.

The steadfast cooperation of senior IDB officials and technical experts from the Bank's Division of Economic and Social Development could be relied on at all times. In the course of the preparatory work, distinguished specialists belonging to academic circles in Latin America and the United States, and to ICAP, made valuable contributions to the discussion of particular aspects of the research work. A list of papers and their authors is given below.

## Special Papers Prepared by Institute and ECLA Experts

Cristóbal Lara Beautell
>    Regional Development: Disparity and Dilemma

Jacobo Schatan
>    Employment and Income in the Dynamics of Latin American Agriculture

Héctor Soza
>    Industrial Planning and International Economic Integration
>    Main Problems of Industrial Development in Latin America

ECLA/Institute
    The External Bottleneck and the Shortage of Savings in Latin America:
    Analysis of Problems and Some Solutions

Ricardo Cibotti and Oscar J. Bardeci
    A Critical Approach to Planning in Latin America

Aldo Solari
    Reflections on Youth in Latin America

Papers Prepared in Washington

Enrique Iglesias
    The Scale and Nature of the External Financing Problem
    The Quality of Cooperation
    Strengthening Multilateralism
    Contributions to the Mobilization of Domestic Resources
    IDB Policies in the 1970's
        In the preparation of these papers use was made of notes and
    comments furnished by Eduardo Figueroa and Felipe Pazos as part of
    their valuable cooperation.

David Pollock
    Comparisons Between the Pearson and UNCTAD Reports

David Pollock, Nicolas Bruck, and others
    Trade Trends and Policies

Jorge Marshall
    Problems of Private Financing in Latin America
    Defects of Public External Financing
    Coordination of Financing
    Linking Up Aid
    Compensatory Financing
    The Two-Gap Model
    Absorption Capacity
    Financing for Integration
    The Organization of Public External Credit

Leonard D. Steed (with the collaboration of Eduardo Zalduendo)
    The Mobilization of External Financial Resources in Latin America

Felipe Paolillo
    Critical Reflections on Financial Assistance to Latin America

Ronald Müller
    The Political Economy of Direct Foreign Investment

Dear President Herrera,

I have pleasure in presenting herewith the report you asked me to submit in my capacity as Director-General of the Latin American Institute for Economic and Social Planning. You were perfectly right: the problem of mobilizing internal investment resources cannot be approached as a separate issue, but must be dealt with in the context of economic and social development; and the aim of the report is to present that context, in accordance with your wishes and, I think, with what the President of the Republic of Colombia, Mr. Carlos Lleras Restrepo, had in mind when he broached the idea at the meeting of the Board of Governors of IDB in Bogotá.

On my return to Latin America after an absence of six years—during which I continued to strive, at the international level, for the solution of some of its major problems—I find myself filled with concern, but more firmly convinced than ever of the region's great development potential. Thus we Latin Americans are faced with a colossal task that can be put off no longer.

Fraught with difficulties as it is, this task of bringing about change and development in Latin America is at the same time imperatively necessary and passionately absorbing. I note with great interest, and also, I confess, with much fellow-feeling, all that is being done in some of the countries of the region. The struggle is, and must be, a grim one; the more so, inasmuch as it is being waged with steadfast determination to preserve certain basic values which must be placed on a firmer and broader footing.

Encouraging moves are being made, both at the national and at the inter-Latin American level, of which I have no need to remind you, Mr. President, active as you have been in promoting these and other measures of vital importance for the region's development.

In preparing this report I have enjoyed the valuable cooperation of ECLA staff members whose names are given in the note of acknowledgment appearing in the document. And, of course, the staff of the Institute have been my assiduous collaborators. I suspect that these latter have been influenced not only by the magnetism of the subject, but also by the wish to take this means of showing the Inter-American Development Bank, and you personally, their appreciation of the support you have given our institution.

First and foremost, I should like to lay special stress on what the collaboration of Enrique Iglesias has meant to me. During the past months—a longer period than I had expected—I have frequently discussed with him the ideas presented in this report, and he has offered me most constructive suggestions. Moreover, he was responsible for the technical reports on the mobilization of internal financial resources which will appear in another volume. A separate list of some of the titles of these papers is given in advance.

I should also like to place on record my great appreciation of the services of Mr. Pedro Irañeta, a high official of the Inter-American Development Bank, who, together with his collaborators, spared no effort to facilitate my work.

In conclusion, I should like to repeat what I have already said on another occasion of my gratitude to you and to the members of the Board of Executive Directors of the Bank for the confidence you have reposed in me. Whatever opinion you may form of the content of this report, it cannot but reflect the deep and sincere convictions of one who has put the major interests of Latin America before every other consideration that short-term circumstances might suggest.

To you, Mr. President, I am particularly indebted for the help you have given me—by posing questions, listening, and propounding suggestions—in the elucidation of my ideas on that attractive intellectual plane of discussion from which you have never departed, despite your heavy load of responsibilities.

Accept, Mr. President, the assurances of my highest consideration and my personal regard.

Raúl Prebisch

Mr. Felipe Herrera,
President,
Inter-American Development Bank,
Washington, D.C.

# CONTENTS

PART I:    THE DEVELOPMENT OF LATIN AMERICA
AND ITS PROBLEMS

# LIST OF TABLES

# LIST OF FIGURES

## LIST OF TABLES IN THE APPENDIX

# LIST OF FIGURES IN THE APPENDIX

# LIST OF ABBREVIATIONS

| | |
|---|---|
| AID | (United States) Agency for International Development |
| DAC | (United Nations) Development Aid Committee |
| ECLA | Economic Commission for Latin America |
| FAO | (United Nations) Food and Agriculture Organization |
| GATT | General Agreement on Tariffs and Trade |
| IA-ECOSCO | Inter-American Economic and Social Council |
| IBRD | International Bank for Reconstruction and Development |
| ICAP | Inter-American Committee on the Alliance for Progress |
| IDB | Inter-American Development Bank |
| ILO | International Labor Organization |
| IMF | International Monetary Fund |
| LADECE | Latin American Demographic Center |
| LAFTA | Latin American Free Trade Association |
| LAIESP | Latin American Institute for Economic and Social Planning |
| OAS | Organization of American States |
| OECD | Organization for Economic Cooperation and Development |
| SCLAC | Special Committee on Latin American Cooperation |
| UNCTAD | United Nations Conference on Trade and Development |
| UNDP | United Nations Development Program |

Observe, brother Sancho, that this adventure and those like to it are not adventures of isles, but at crossroads, from which nothing is to be gained but a broken head or the loss of an ear. Be patient, for adventures will occur to us whereby I will make you not only a governor, but something greater still.

Cervantes, Don Quixote, trans. J. M. Cohen (Baltimore: Penguin Classics, 1968), p. 80.

PART I THE DEVELOPMENT
OF LATIN AMERICA
AND ITS PROBLEMS

# 1

## THE LACK OF THE REQUIRED DEGREE OF DYNAMISM

### Spurious Absorption of Manpower

This report is geared to action. For the Latin American countries can no longer put off the decision to take deliberate steps to influence the course of their economic and social development if they are to overcome serious handicaps which the passage of time is more likely to aggravate than to remedy.

In reality, the region has not as yet been able to cope with the contradictions which the march of science and technology brings in its train along with the far-reaching possibilities of human welfare that it opens up.

These contradictions, whose implications have become increasingly apparent in the last two decades, include the inconsistency between the population explosion and the factors limiting capital formation. For this and other reasons, only a part of the economically active population is productively absorbed. A very high proportion constitutes redundant manpower in the rural areas, where the surplus labor force has been and still is large; and the migrants from the rural areas who constantly pour into the bigger towns merely shift the scene of their redundancy.* In their new environment, they needlessly swell the motley ranks of the services sector, in which a substantial proportion of the natural increase in the urban labor force itself is also skirmishing for jobs. Thus the result is a spurious rather than a genuine absorption of manpower, if not unemployment pure and simple.

This phenomenon is characteristic of the Latin American economy's lack of the required degree of dynamism. Its rate of development has been too slow to meet the peremptory demands deriving from the population explosion, and a huge amount of human potential is wasted in one way or another, to the

---

*In the present report, the terms "redundant" and "redundancy" will be applied to the manpower that could be dispensed with, even on the basis of the techniques in current use, without a resulting decrease in production of goods and services. With technical progress, of course, the redundant labor force tends to grow larger, and in order to absorb it the rate of development must be speeded up.

detriment of economic growth, equitable income distribution, and social harmony.

Disparities in income distribution date back for centuries in Latin America, and privilege is deeply rooted in the region's history. During the phase of outward-looking development which preceded the world depression of the 1930's, no solution of the problem was forthcoming; on the contrary, the increases in income which development brought in its train, and which in many countries were substantial, were concentrated in the few hands that already held land and wealth in their grasp. Since then, in the phase of development which has continued up to the present time, the effects of the process have undeniably been more widely spread out; although it is also true that new patterns of concentration of wealth and income have emerged. Those at the top of the social pyramid have conspicuously prospered; the urban middle strata, too, have increased in size and have raised their level of living, although less than might have been the case, and far from enough to satisfy their growing consumption aspirations. But the benefits of development have hardly touched the broad masses relegated to the lower income strata. The percentage of the population represented by the last-named groups may possibly have diminished, although precise data to substantiate such an assertion are lacking. In any event, they still constitute as much as about 60 percent of Latin America's total population, both in rural and in urban areas, although the proportions vary from one country to another. They would seem to have decreased in relative terms; but at the same time the gap between the lower and upper strata has widened.

Nor is this all. The advances made in mass communication techniques—almost inconceivable in bygone days—are giving rise to new phenomena, the scope of whose implications defies prediction. The broad masses of Latin America's rural population, formerly cut off by the illiteracy which debarred them from access to books and newspapers, are swiftly becoming receptive to the radio and the television, which bring them nearer and nearer to the beguiling mirage of city life. Beguiling at first, only to prove later on a hotbed of tormenting frustration: the frustration bred of social marginality in the larger towns.* It is not just a matter of consumption aspirations. There is something of greater social and political significance. The rural and urban masses are awakening to consciousness of their long-forgotten dignity as human beings, of their pathetic relegation to ways of life long left behind by the peoples of the developed countries.

The social integration of these stranded masses is of primary importance. It is a question of fair distribution. Let there be no misunderstanding, however. Redistribution measures alone will not suffice. The income distribution pattern is defective, and could undoubtedly be amended to some extent in existing circumstances. But there will be no

---

*The serious phenomenon of urban marginality originates largely in the cities themselves. But it has been greatly aggravated by the exodus of rural population, mainly people who in one way or another were socially integrated in their places of origin. There is a manifest link between the increase of marginality and the incapacity of urban activities to absorb the population increment in productive employment.

substantial and lasting improvement unless the rate of development is speeded up.

Economic considerations are not necessarily at variance with social needs, but when growth is sluggish, distribution is almost always unsatisfactory. The practice of social equity calls for a vigorous rate of development, as well as for the political art of distribution, a delicate business in itself.

## The Occupational Structure and the Waste of Human Potential

It is common knowledge that the migration of manpower from the countryside to the towns has always been a spontaneous product of development, whatever the economic and social system in force; and equally well-known is the importance of the dynamic role that industry, construction, and mining* are called upon to play in the productive absorption of the labor force from the rural areas. In Latin America they have failed to do their part in this respect, at any rate during the last two decades. Only two countries are exceptions to the rule, and for very different reasons in each case.

If the production of goods in all these nonagricultural activities absorbs fewer people than it should, and employment in services increases disproportionately, a serious imbalance inevitably supervenes: the proportion of the labor force that wishes to consume such goods expands beyond all reasonable bounds, while the proportion that produces them shrinks to an abnormal extent.

The scale on which this is happening is truly disconcerting; an approximate idea of it can be obtained from a glance at Figure 22 (see Chapter 4), which clearly shows how the proportion of the economically active population working in the industry group steadily declines instead of rising, whereas the opposite is the case in the services sector, where the spurious absorption of redundant manpower occurs, and part of the labor force is left jobless altogether. It is essential to correct this distortion of the occupational structure by reversing the trends described.

The mere correction of the occupational structure of the labor force would have highly important consequences. Suffice it to reflect that the attainment of this objective, by means of a more rapid rate of capital formation and the fulfillment of other requirements, would mean that the annual growth rate of the aggregate product would have risen to 7 percent by the end of the current decade, instead of the average of 5.2 percent recorded in 1950-1969. The average annual growth rate of the per capita product would thus increase from 2.5 percent to 3.9 percent. Even so, it would take a very long time and a still more rapid rate of growth of the aggregate product for the lack of dynamism to be remedied completely.

---

*For the sake of simplicity, this group of activities will henceforth be referred to as "the industry group."

Exceptional significance attaches to this projection. It must be borne in mind that for demonstration purposes the calculation was based on the assumption—afterward discarded—that neither in agriculture nor in the industry group would the growth rate of the product per worker be more rapid than in the past. To achieve these remarkable results, productive occupation of the redundant manpower migrating from the rural areas would be enough.

The explanation of this vital fact is well-known. In agriculture, the average product per active person is very low, or purely nominal; and the employment of former agricultural workers in the industry group, where the average product per active person is much higher, suffices in itself to bring about an appreciable rise in the product of the whole economy.

The problem of the enormous loss of income sustained by the Latin American countries on this account derives not only from that proportion of the active population which leaves the agricultural sector and is not productively absorbed elsewhere, but also from the redundant manpower remaining in agriculture. The reduction of the agricultural labor force will have to continue as the product per worker increases through more efficient use of the land and through technical progress. Hence it will become even more imperatively necessary to give powerful impetus to the development of the industry group.

The idea of placing the emphasis on agriculture and paying little attention to industry is dying hard; but is is indefensible in the light of the foregoing considerations. The industry group needs to develop much more intensively than before in order to fulfill one of its principal dynamic functions, as well as to provide the manufactured goods required for speeding up development.

Incidentally, the exodus of agricultural workers is inevitable if the level of living of the rural masses is to be raised. What is not inevitable is the appalling congestion in the big towns, due mainly to this population shift. In this as in other respects, the Latin American countries are suffering some of the drawbacks of the development process in advance, long before they have reaped its benefits. In the present instance, the disadvantage they have to combat is that of overconcentration in the larger towns. This again is not an ill that can be left to remedy itself. Quite the contrary. It will have to be tackled with a determination of which no categorical evidence has yet been given by the Latin American countries—not even by those in which this social evil is most flagrant.

### Social Integration and the Domestic Market

The social integration of the lower income groups in the course of development must now be understood in its true significance, as a highly important element in a process of structural change which would considerably improve the income levels of the groups in question. As has already been stated, these lower strata comprise about 60 percent of the population of Latin America. Victimized as they are by the social inequity with which the economic system operates, the consumption of the members of these groups is meager in relation to their rapidly multiplying numbers. According to conjectural estimates, not even as much as 20 percent of the total supply of manufactured goods reaches their hands.

The integration of these lower strata is a pressing social necessity. It is also an economic need, for it will extend the frontiers of Latin America's industrial development process. This is the only alternative that the dynamics of development affords. The growth of industry can no longer depend, as it did before, on import substitution alone. The fruit has been squeezed too hard by now for the flow of juice to be as plentiful as at first. New solutions, new markets must now be sought. There is a potential market of which scarcely any advantage is taken: that of the underprivileged masses. But their social integration is the only means of opening it up.

The frontiers of industrial expansion will be extended, inasmuch as the absorption of redundant manpower in industry—together with the improvement of the income levels of the rural population—will generate a considerable and continuing demand for manufactured goods, and will also give a vigorous fillip to demand for agricultural products, at present largely pent up by the poverty of the lower income groups. Thus agriculture and industry will derive a more powerful stimulus from their reciprocal demand and will give each other mutual support, propagating their growth throughout the rest of the economy.

Such is the significance of the social integration of the underprivileged masses. The task is one that cannot be postponed, but this does not mean that it can be accomplished independently of others. It is frequently argued that this internal social integration must first be achieved, and then industrial integration at the Latin American level. A great mistake. Internal integration calls for the acceleration of development. And for that a sine qua non is the integration of the dynamic industries at the Latin American level, in default of which it will be impossible to ease the external constraint that is slowing up economic expansion. This in no way belittles the importance of other measures designed to assist in correcting regional disequilibria within individual countries themselves.

### The Progress of Science and Technology, and Its Contradictions

Clearly, then, development must be speeded up. The task is much more difficult than that with which the advanced countries were faced in their own development process. For although the spectacular progress achieved by science and technology in the developed countries opens up broader prospects of human betterment for the Latin American countries—of which full advantage must be taken to further our development—it is in fact attended by grave contradictions which did not arise in former times, or at any rate not to such a marked degree. The population explosion, of course, is one of the striking consequences of the progress in question. In order to cope with it, capital formation on a very large scale is required, both because of the increasing numbers for whom work must be provided, and because the technology originating in the great industrial centers entails a steadily rising capital/worker ratio.

This difficulty is aggravated by another of the effects of scientific and technical progress, which unremittingly militates against capital formation. The higher income strata in the Latin American societies are prone to imitate the living patterns of their counterparts in the developed countries; and thanks to the ever-increasing might of mass communication media, these living patterns are forcing their way into the lower income groups, whose members are incessantly confronted with the alluring image of a consumer society to which their strained means deny them access.

Thus, the advance of science and technology has conflicting implications which are likely to widen the disparity between population growth and capital formation. Moreover, it adversely affects Latin America's export trade and helps to generate the persistent tendency toward an external bottleneck.

## THE ACCELERATION OF DEVELOPMENT AND THE OBSTACLES IN ITS WAY

### The March of Ideas in the International Field

The conflicting implications of scientific and technological progress partly explain why the dynamic impetus of the Latin American economy falls short of what is required. They are reflected in a number of internal and external factors which, within the context of the existing economic and social structure, have done much to hold back the development process. In the present report, however, the accent is placed on the internal factors of development, whose fundamental importance we do not always explicitly acknowledge when these problems are discussed at the international level. It is essential to restore the balance, although what is said of them here will certainly help—praise be!—to rekindle the flames of controversy.

With regard to the external factors that cramp development and the action that can be taken to influence them, controversy is already bearing fruit. Ideas which were considered inadmissible until only a short time ago are now infiltrating into circles where they used to be labeled unrealistic, if not flagrantly irresponsible. Such ideas, which had been evolving and establishing themselves in the developing countries, and particularly in Latin America, were crystallized in the United Nations Conference on Trade and Development (UNCTAD), and are now among the many important concepts and recommendations embodied in the Pearson Report.[1] Thus they are endorsed by the moral authority and intellectual prestige of the Report's authors, who deserve great credit for their sponsorship. The only trouble is that in the meantime some of these ideas have been left behind by the demands of an increasingly complicated set of circumstances. This, however, does not detract from the great significance of the document. Highly important, likewise, is the recent report on the Second Development Decade prepared by the United

Nations committee of experts under the chairmanship of Professor Jan Tinbergen.[2] He is one of the few eminent economists in the northern hemisphere who long ago grasped the nature of these problems and the need to tackle them on the basis of a carefully concerted strategy. A man of deep convictions, Professor Tinbergen will beyond all doubt continue his unflagging work of persuasion. Another noteworthy report is that prepared by Professor Isaiah Frank,[3] who had already adopted a highly constructive approach to these questions. A report still more recently submitted to the United States Government[4] also vigorously defends some of the primary aspirations of the developing countries, although unfortunately it does not set up a target for financial cooperation.

Thus, more and more outstanding figures in the advanced countries are espousing the cause of effective international cooperation in the development of the Third World. As far as they are concerned, we have no need to preach to the converted. But the progress achieved on the intellectual plane does not warrant complacency. Considerable energy will still have to be expended if the conviction felt by men like these is to be communicated to the policy-makers who have to take the major decisions which international cooperation entails. The path is beset with formidable obstacles, and in my view it will be difficult, if not impossible, to forge ahead unless the efforts made in this direction are given definite support.

This does not mean mere praise and appreciation. The Latin American countries must give manifest proof of their unhesitating determination to effect basic structural changes and adopt new attitudes, and to apply a rigorous and socially meaningful discipline of development; and this determination must be reflected in a strategy with clearly defined objectives. Such is the firm foundation on which international cooperation should rest.

The time has come to shake off the all too common habit of attributing the inadequacy of Latin America's rate of development to external factors alone, as though there were no major internal stumbling blocks in the way. We must fully recognize our own responsibility. While development strategy is undeniably our countries' own internal business, it is equally true that international cooperation policy is an internal affair of the advanced countries; "at the international level" is only an abstract term. In reality, development calls for a number of convergent measures which must be adopted by both groups of countries if it is universally acknowledged that the problem is common to all.

There can be no more convincing proof of the need for such convergent action than the testimony of past experience. In reviewing it here, the aim has been to draw lessons from it rather than to demarcate areas of responsibility. The matter is of such importance that it is worth while to insert a few remarks here, in anticipation of its fuller treatment in a later chapter.

### Financial Cooperation and Internal Development Policy

International financial cooperation has failed to play as dynamic a role as might have been expected, not only because its volume has been insufficient and its terms unsatisfactory, but also because of basic flaws in the development policy of the Latin American countries themselves.

Owing to this combination of external and internal factors, the funds received from abroad have not served to promote more intensive mobilization of the region's own resources. The direct effects of investment of these funds are not denied; but in none of the countries on which data were available for the purposes of the present study*—and which account for nearly 90 percent of Latin America's total product—has the coefficient of investment with domestic resources increased to any marked extent. On the contrary, it has tended to decrease in the region as a whole, and in some of the individual countries the decline is striking. But part of the explanation lies in the neglect of internal measures which might effectively have counteracted the unfavorable influence of this and other external factors.

The burden of amortization and reimbursement of foreign capital has been very heavy, and so has that of interest, although to a lesser degree. It is estimated that total annual service payments on public international funds alone are equivalent to 19 percent of the debt outstanding. There is no economy in existence—however great its potential—that could withstand such pressure with impunity. And it addition, account must be taken of the adverse effects of the deterioration in the terms of trade which has taken place during the greater part of the last two decades. These outflows have represented a heavy drain on internal investment resources. All these issues are discussed in due course in the present report, together with the question of private foreign investment.

Suffice it to point out here that private foreign investment, along with its favorable aspects, involves a number of problems which, in order to work out ways and means of living in economic and political harmony with the developed countries, must be examined from a completely objective viewpoint. In the context of these problems, it is impossible to disregard the concern aroused in Latin America by certain forms of foreign investment which in some cases have an adverse effect on the balance of payments; in others, instead of helping Latin American enterprise to make up its financial and technological leeway, they are more liable to keep it indefinitely at a disadvantage; and in others again, they introduce new patterns of dependence which are at variance with the fundamental concept of autonomy in development.

It is only fair to recognize that the unfavorable impact of such situations on the coefficient of investment with domestic resources might have been less if the persistently expansionist trend of consumption—especially in the higher and middle income groups—had been restrained.

In short, for international financing to have played the dynamic role expected of it, it would have had to be granted on a much larger scale and on reasonable terms; and internal measures would have had to be adopted to ensure the progressive growth of investment with domestic resources.

The decisive importance of this latter requisite must be stressed from the outset. Latin America has not succeeded in dealing satisfactorily with its capital

---

*These countries are Argentina, Brazil, Chile, Colombia, Guatemala, Mexico, Peru, Uruguay and Venezuela.

formation problem. If the next few years are to witness a transition to a satisfactory rate of development, investment with domestic resources will have to increase faster than consumption. To allow a considerable external debt to pile up, without energetically promoting the mobilization of the region's own resources until the point was reached at which they could fully meet capital formation requirements, would be to invite deplorable consequences.

Unless Latin America makes a strenuous investment effort, it will be unable to remedy the economy's lack of dynamism and the social ills inherent in it. External cooperation is important, but only as a means of supplementing and stimulating internal action, not as a substitute for it. Any other formula is inconceivable and, moreover, would be self-defeating from the economic standpoint and politically inadmissible.

Of great importance also is the role that financial resources from abroad are called upon to play in the gradual elimination of the external bottleneck. Here again they have failed to do their part. On the contrary, the burden of interest and amortization payments makes matters worse, since it has shown a disquieting increase in proportion to the purchasing power of exports and the saving of foreign exchange achieved through import substitution.

For this and other reasons, resolute action in respect to foreign trade is essential. The great industrial centers have left the countries of Latin America, like the other developing countries, to drift along as best they can. They have made no basic moves to offset the adverse influence exerted by their technical progress, directly or indirectly, on Latin America's export trade. Rather, they have erected what in some instances are formidable barriers. But this is yet another case in which the blame must not be laid solely on external factors, for Latin America could have done much more that it has to relieve the external bottleneck. Export opportunities have often been missed because of the negative effects of certain measures, or for want of a policy of steady encouragement.

Still more serious is the waste of Latin America's considerable intraregional trade potential. It is true that the expansion revealed by the relevant figures is by no means negligible; but at the same time, little has been done in the field of industrial integration agreements relating to the intermediate and capital goods for which demand tends to boom as development advances.*

The Latin American countries have left undone many of those things which they ought to have done in the past 20 years. And the developed countries—in particular the United States—have failed to do what might have been expected of them. There has been a want of concerted action reflecting—without the slightest suggestion of pressure from above or of paternalism—a definite consensus with respect to the attainment of certain development objectives and the nature, scale, and scope of the measures required for attaining them. This is the unequivocal lesson of the past. The inadequate and incompatible measures that have been adopted at the international level cannot be called strategy. To transfer far less resources than

---

*It is a very encouraging circumstance that in the Cartagena Agreement signed by the members of the Andean Group, special importance is attached to measures of this kind.

are needed and yet be in a hurry to recover them is manifestly inconsistent; and so is hampering the export trade which must provide the means of making interest and amortization payments and meeting the large-scale import requirements attendant upon the development process.

Nowadays all this can be clearly seen. Formerly, perhaps, it was not so plain. Hence the value of past experience. To fail to take advantage of it in facing the future would be inexcusable today. The present report, I hope, will help to guard against such neglect. It is motivated not only by a hankering for elucidation—a worthwhile end in itself—but, above all, by the conviction that the Latin American countries can no longer put off deciding in favor of deliberate and farsighted action to influence the forces of development. They must draw up their own strategy and define their common denominators and their patterns of concerted action, both in the sphere of their relations with the developed countries and in that of their relations with one another, where much of great importance can and must be done.

### Time Is No Panacea

The acceleration of development demands sweeping changes in structures and in mental attitudes. They are essential if technical progress is to be assimilated, its advantages turned to account, its contradictions resolved, and its adverse effects counteracted; and essential also for the promotion of social mobility, both for its own sake and because it too is one of the indispensable requirements of technological progress. Social mobility is not merely a matter of general education and technical training; it is a basic question of structures.

I think it my duty to speak very frankly in this report. Latin America stands in need of the changes to which I refer—with all due acknowledgment of the reforms already introduced—and it likewise needs a development discipline which has rarely existed, and when it has been applied has seldom lasted long.

Such a discipline is indispensable in order that the region may enter upon a new stage of development, since the dynamic impetus of the present phase has gradually slackened. Powerful expansionist forces exist, but they are being obstructed; a determined effort must be made to clear the way for them. What has been achieved by virtue of these forces is no good reason for going on as hitherto. There is no room for complacency in Latin America. It is often displayed in face of striking evidence of progress. The impressive growth of the region's cities, their remarkable degree of modernization, the development and diversification of their industries are sometimes taken as irrefutable proof of an encouraging process of development. It is forgotten, however, that the urban activities have shown themselves incapable of fully and productively absorbing the manpower increment, and that this and other circumstances are generating increasingly acute social tensions. It is forgotten, likewise, that the progress made in urban areas has not spread to the countryside and that, on the contrary, it is the countryside that is invading the towns. The emissaries of this movement are people who have broken loose from their own economic and social constellations without becoming properly incorporated into the urban setting. All they do is to transfer their poverty-stricken way of life to the wretched shanty towns in which the marginal population of the cities takes refuge.

The progress of the urban areas should promise a steady improvement in conditions of well-being which have been attained only in part, and their extension to those broad strata of the population to which they have not yet spread in any appreciable measure.

If all these ills are to be remedied, it is essential to accelerate development. This report will have served its purpose if it carries conviction of the necessity and possibility of doing so: a conviction which must be implanted both inside and outside Latin America.

The developed countries do not always understand this need to speed up the rate of development. It has averaged 5.2 percent yearly over the past two decades, with wide intercountry disparities. This figure cannot be described as modest in itself, since it is similar to that recorded in recent times by the developed countries in the private-enterprise group. What is more, their rates of development in the past were usually lower than those of Latin America.

Why such impatience, then? Why try to force the pace of events? If the countries now at advanced stages of development took a long time to get where they are, why should not the Latin American countries keep to the same rhythm? Cannot time perhaps solve their problems too?

Questions such as these are frequently asked at international meetings and in academic discussions, although less often than used to be the case. I hope the answer may be found in the present report. For it is highly important that in international circles—and particularly in the United States—full awareness of Latin America's problem should exist. It is a problem that we shall have to solve ourselves, in one way or another; but it so happens that the way matters a great deal, and may be considerably influenced by the international cooperation policy pursued in the coming decades. The economy's lack of the required dynamism cannot be made good by the mere passage of time. And the longer the time that is allowed to go by, the harder this weakness will be to cure, and the greater will be the social and political cost, or, in a word, the cost in human terms.

## DEVELOPMENT OPTIONS AND INTERNATIONAL COOPERATION

### Immediatism at the International Level

The times we live in do not seem particularly favorable to a policy of international cooperation. Immediatism—that is, the desire (very understandable from the political standpoint) to show quick results—generally prevails over long-term policy in the Latin American countries, and has also predominated in the attitude of the developed countries toward international cooperation. There is something more in this than short-term pressures exerted by narrow economic or political interests. It is an increasingly striking fact that countries which have made giant strides in technology have not managed to forestall the attendant evils. Too much trust has been placed in the spontaneous forces of the economy, and there has been a want of farsighted policies capable of overriding the interaction of those forces where they could not operate effectively. They can do much, but not everything. This is being recognized nowadays; and the idea of consciously looking ahead, which used to be entertained very little or not at all, is progressively gaining ground. But it has not yet extended to relationships with the developing countries; it is not being crystallized in a policy of genuine international cooperation.

It was not foresight that motivated certain attitudes which favored the developing countries during the iciest spell of the cold war. They found expression mainly in temporary expedients, seldom dictated by a broad strategy in which economic and social development played a basic and continuing part.

It is certainly true that the cold war has had its repercussions in Latin America. But it would be a grave mistake to ascribe to them the role that events themselves have been playing, and will continue to play to an ever-increasing extent if the rate of development remains the same as in the past. I have no belief whatever in the incoercible determinism of events, for the simple reason that there is great development potential in this part of the world: a potential that consists of human as well as natural resources. Creativeness abounds, and finds expression in a wide variety of ways. Latin America has great vitality. But its creative impulses are held in check, and their power to stimulate economic expansion is fettered.

Herein lie the great problem and the great open question with which Latin America is faced. The problem is that of releasing these expansionist forces by means of changes in structures and mental attitudes, and taking conscious and deliberate steps to influence them. And the open question is whether this will be done in time, and whether it will be possible to rely upon an equally timely, as well as energetic and enlightened, policy of international cooperation.

### Two Forms of Development

The transition from a relatively low rate of development with little social significance to one which will give the economy the requisite dynamic impetus and will be socially meaningful entails a considerable effort: an effort to bring about structural changes and to adopt an authentic development discipline, especially in respect of capital formation and the promotion of foreign trade. This is inevitable. If strong opposition to a conscious and deliberate discipline is put up, development by coercion in one form or another will be the ultimate outcome. For frustration is no alternative, whether it be the frustration of a policy of laissez-aller or the frustration of populism. One good point about the latter is that it has uncovered major social ills and has aroused legitimate aspirations for the social integration of the masses. In the absence of strong convictions, however, and in default of a well-knit system of ideas, populism resorts to the unfailing device of using emotion in order to exalt charismatic figures. It sidesteps difficult problems and puts immediatism in respect of income redistribution before the need for overall changes, before the basic solutions demanded by development.

Populism, therefore, is not an acceptable alternative to a development discipline. Such a discipline is an essential requisite for the considerable capital formation effort required in order to give the economy the additional dynamism it needs. It is not conceivable—must less desirable—that this should be done mainly with foreign capital. A great internal effort will be an imperative and inescapable necessity. Will it be possible without recourse to compulsion?

The reply depends not only upon the political art of development, the ability to tackle basic problems and combine immediate expedients with long-term measures, but also upon international cooperation. In a strategy for the acceleration of development there is a difficult but decisive initial phase: that of preparing the economy for the capital formation process to be put into effect without undue tensions. What is needed is a large-scale contribution of financial resources from abroad, to stimulate the rapid expansion of the economy through the utilization of idle or inefficiently used resources and other internal measures converging toward the same goal. Obviously, when the economy expands in this way, it becomes less difficult to promote capital formation without sacrificing consumption beyond certain limits.

This is the initial dynamic role of international financial cooperation: to act as a spur to domestic capital formation. With that end in view, the terms on which it is extended would have to be very different from those offered in the past.

I have no wish to put forward arguments in this report which might appear to detract from its sobriety. But I cannot attempt to hide the growing concern felt in Latin America, and among the enlightened men of the northern hemisphere to whom I have referred, with respect to the turn taken by this cooperation. I have reflected a great deal on this matter and have discussed it with people who view the facts with objective impartiality. In these discussions one question invariably arises: will the Latin American countries be able to avoid coercive methods of capital formation if external financing does not make a much bigger contribution on appropriate terms?

The experience of the socialist countries has always been followed with great interest in Latin America, although in recent times this interest has also extended to private-enterprise countries which have attained very high rates of development, in particular Japan. Perhaps the most important feature of the experience in question has been the method of capital formation. Needless to say, Marx had envisaged a different process of radical transformation of the system, one which would be ineluctably brought about by the determinism inherent in the evolution of capitalism, once a large amount of capital had been accumulated and the whole machinery of production had been concentrated in a few hands. In the specific experience of the socialist countries it was precisely this substantial accumulation of capital which did not exist, and the want had to be supplied at considerable social and political cost. In reality, socialism has been a method of development rather than a method of transforming an advanced economy.

The gradual aggravation of the ills besetting the Latin American economy is, of course, creating a propitious atmosphere for ideologies which advocate transforming the system, root and branch. But irrespective of such ideologies, the course of events might lead to the socialist method of development even if that had not been the original intention of those who set themselves to strengthen the dynamic impetus of the economic system.

## The Underlying Political Assumptions

If external financing were not obtained on a large enough scale and at the right time, consumption—or its expansion—would inevitably have to be more tightly restricted in order to speed up the rate of development.* There would seem to be a possibility of doing this. The Latin American countries are not making the savings effort which their average per capita income would allow. And the distribution of this income is such that the restriction of consumption in the upper strata might enable the investment coefficient to be appreciably increased. The problem is quite simple from the statistical standpoint, but very difficult in actual fact. The power structure is undoubtedly a major obstacle, although not an insuperable one, since it might conceivably be changed through the political process. Even so, there would be room for doubt as to the possibility of too drastically restricting the consumption of the higher income groups without arousing strong opposition, cloaked or overt, weakening investment incentives, and precipitating the flight of capital abroad on a far greater scale than at present.

If this were to happen, if the operation of the economy were thus distorted, events themselves might impel the State to take over the very sources of income of the upper strata by a process of socialization—of the major enterprises, at least—even if no ideological considerations were involved. Ideologies would come later to justify faits accomplis and strengthen their significance.

This brings us to the heart of the matter. I do not wish to reiterate the time-honored arguments with respect to State enterprise. It is a different aspect of the question that I want to stress. The fact that those who had gained political power realized the need to consolidate their authority by managing public enterprises efficiently would not necessarily mean that they could do so within the ordinary system of party politics. The pressure of electoral interests has always been a factor militating against the satisfactory operation of the State machinery in Latin America. What is more, in some countries where public enterprises used to operate at a reasonable level of efficiency, the economy's lack of the required degree of dynamism has induced the State to overstaff them, to the detriment of the efficiency previously achieved.

Hence a question of decisive importance arises: whether the determination to ensure the success of this experiment is compatible with periodic party

---

*This point will be discussed later. Suffice it here to draw attention to the necessity of ensuring that the restriction of consumption does not adversely affect productive activities.

strife, with each party's constant restless anxiety—by no means inevitable—to buttress its position by granting immediate benefits which generally conflict with basic solutions. Unless this and other defects are corrected in time, nobody would have cause for wonder—however much for regret—whether the sheer force of economic circumstances succeeded in imposing patterns of political organization which, while tending to give continuity to the groups in power, would at the same time permit them a freedom of action which they would not otherwise enjoy.

These considerations do not apply solely to issues of economic management. Any system which fails to imbue the economy with the required degree of dynamism, and to promote more equitable income distribution, will have irrevocably forfeited the right to survive. The requisite remedial measures entail substantial economic and social outlays and investment. It would be hazardous to conjecture whether the savings capacity which the higher income groups are at present wasting would or would not be sufficient to meet all these requirements. It might well prove necessary to tap the resources of lower income strata, where the new ruling groups, however great their power and their moral justification, might encounter a serious obstacle: the very understandable need to put the satisfaction of pressing consumption aspirations before capital formation.

It would be unthinkable, of course, to inflict further hardship on the rural population that ekes out so precarious a livelihood, or on the underprivileged masses that have not been incorporated into the urban development process. Consequently, it would have to be the middle strata of society that were drawn into the savings effort. Given their propensity to adopt new consumption patterns, it would be very hard to curb their aspirations, and still more difficult, in case of need, to lower their present standards of consumption.

Thus the same question arises as before: can the consumption of the middle strata conceivably be affected without recourse to compulsion? Could the restrictions be persistently maintained under the system of ordinary party politics?

The objective study of these problems calls for a very explicit definition of the underlying political assumptions, especially when supreme importance is attached to the progressive strengthening of certain values and objectives which, despite setbacks and compromises in the course of the political development process, continue to hold up an ideal image as the goal of the long journey that still lies ahead of Latin America.

This is where international cooperation could play a very significant part by helping to make the initial phase of transition to a higher rate of development less hard and to prevent it from entailing the sacrifice of political convictions formerly regarded as sacrosanct. This phase of transition is inevitable whether the economic and social system merely undergoes changes or is transformed altogether, and whether the process is carried out by design or dictated by the force of circumstances themselves.

### Inescapable Necessities

In any event, no system will have sufficient intrinsic virtue to evade certain necessities imposed by hard fact. A case in point is that of foreign trade. The tendency toward disequilibrium might perhaps be mitigated, but could not be corrected altogether unless the structure that hampers the export trade were progressively modified. Even socialist economies of enormous size, like the Soviet Union, have not found it possible to dispense with foreign trade; on the contrary, they are making strenuous endeavors to expand it.

Still more intensive is the effort that must be made by smaller socialist countries, such as those of Eastern Europe, with respect to trade not only with the Soviet Union, but also with the rest of the world, and particularly with the developed capitalist countries.

Where Latin America is concerned, the cost of import substitution must count for much in economic calculations, in the requirements of a rational approach, irrespective of the economic and social system in force. And the need to expand industrial as well as primary exports must arise in any event, and so must the necessity of promoting the integration of basic industries within the framework of regional or subregional agreements.

Competition, too, is an essential requisite in any case. It would not be indispensable for a country that was content to continue using its resources inefficiently, as is the general rule in Latin America at present. How, then, could productivity be rapidly increased and the levels of living of the masses improved? There is a stage at the start when enthusiasm for the construction of a new order might serve as a powerful spur to more efficient production. But later comes the need to introduce competition, with the stimulus it provides and the economic incentives attendant upon it. This is what is happening in the socialist countries at present: socialist competition in a market system which, despite its limitations, is called upon to play an important role from the standpoint both of the consumer and of the efficiency of enterprises. As I see it, socialist competition does not represent a swing back in the direction of capitalism but, rather, a quest for new modus operandi compatible with the collective ownership of the means of production.*

## Development and "Developmentism"

All the above are issues which cannot be shirked at the present time. For Latin America must blaze new trails, must shake off the burden of the past, must shun ideological preconceptions. The lack of the required degree of dynamism is not an episodic phenomenon, but the outward and visible sign of the critical state of the phase of development which began with the great world

---

*I make no claim that this view of the role of incentives is universally shared by technical experts in this field. Perhaps I may be permitted a personal reminiscence here. When Comandante Ernesto "Che" Guevara was the head of the Cuban delegation to the General Assembly of the United Nations, he was good enough to come to see me in my office in New York, a few months before he left Cuba forever. We had met in 1961 at the Punta del Este conference, and had established cordial relations in Geneva at the first session of UNCTAD in 1964. At the time of the interview to which I refer, there was a great deal of talk about Liebermann in the Soviet Union and about the system of market prices and

depression of the 1930's. This phase has long since served its turn, and is now generating another crisis—and a notable one at that—especially among those of the rising generation who are beginning to concern themselves with economics and the social sciences: the crisis of "developmentism." As with all the terms that spring up in the course of ideological discussion, there is some confusion about the meaning of "developmentism." Perhaps it may be interpreted as the refusal to believe that major changes are necessary in order to accelerate the present pace of development, and the trust that social disparities will gradually be smoothed out by the dynamics of development itself. The essential thing is to develop; then we shall see! Such attitudes as these jar on the social conscience of the younger generation and of others who have long left youth behind.

Nor is this all. While those who mistrust "developmentism" do not deny the value of technology as a means of freeing mankind from the agelong burden of heavy labor, the subordination of the human factor to technology causes them extreme concern. Prevalent among them, too, is the idea of a genuinely national effort incompatible with old or new forms of dependence, in economic affairs as in intellectual life and cultural patterns. They would like to tackle the problems of man and society as a whole; and without underrating the importance of a healthy economy, they do not see it as an end in itself, but as a means—one of the means—of attaining the fullness of living, of drawing nearer to the inaccessible goal of human excellence.

It is a salutary crisis, which leads to the restatement of the problem, to a reexamination of its terms, to discussion of where the Latin American societies are going and where they ought to go: all essential prerequisites for conscious and deliberate action to influence the manifold forces of the economic and social complex. This is no light task. The easy way out afforded by privilege and makeshift expedients is no longer conceivable. Can it be that the new generations are seeking that of clinging to makeshift methods, despite the increasing intricacy of the problems they have to solve? Or do they fully recognize the imperative need for calculation and rationality in face of the constant advances of science and technology: the need to take advantage of this progress to improve the lot of the Latin American population and to fulfill designs extending beyond the economic system? Emotional impulses often override calculation. Emotion has generated great collective movements and has led men to perform memorable feats. But it would not have been possible to get very far without rationality as well. Whether the aim is to introduce such changes in the system as will give it dynamic force, or to replace it with another, rationality is in any case indispensable in man's great adventure of development.

---

incentives which he advocated. Since I asked him for his opinion, Comandante Guevara, who was given to reasoning dispassionately and weighing his words with care, strongly emphasized the sacrifice which the revolution in Cuba had represented, and for that very reason rebutted Liebermann's theory, which he regarded as contrary to the essence of socialism and its design of bringing about a radical change in the motives of human action.

## NOTES

[1] See *Partners in Development: Report by the Commission on International Development* (New York: Praeger Publishers, 1969).

[2] See *Committee for Development Planning: Report on the Sixth Session (5-15 January 1970)*, United Nations document E/4776, Economic and Social Council, 49th session, supplement No. 7.

[3] See Committee for Economic Development, *Assisting Development in Low-Income Countries: Priorities for U.S. Government Policy* (September, 1969).

[4] *US Foreign Assistance in the 1970's* (Washington, March 1970), a report which a group headed by the distinguished banker Rudolf Peterson has submitted to President Nixon. (Mimeographed.)

PART **II** **THE LACK OF THE
REQUIRED DYNAMISM
AND HOW TO SUPPLY IT**

# 2

## POPULATION GROWTH AND
## THE OCCUPATIONAL STRUCTURE
## OF THE LABOR FORCE

## A BRIEF LOOK AT THE POPULATION GROWTH RATE

The extraordinary rise in the population growth rate is a relatively recent phenomenon in Latin America and—except in the lengthy period of mass immigration into the United States—is something that did not occur to the same extent during the development of what are now the industrialized countries. The rate began to rise at the end of the 1930's and gathered appreciable momentum as scientific and technological progress gradually lowered the death rate without there being a parallel decline in the birth rate. During the last five years of the 1930's, the demographic growth rate was a 1.9 percent, i.e., the population doubled every 37 years. Now, at the beginning of the 1970's, the rate has risen to 2.9 percent, which means that the population doubles every 25 years.

It has taken some time for the serious consequences of this phenomenon to be recognized and debated. And yet the population explosion made itself felt early on (1935-1940), for it affected both household and public spending, inasmuch as an ever-increasing amount of social investment was required to cover housing, health, and education needs that have still been only partly met. However, it was only later that its effects on the labor force and the difficulty of absorbing labor into productive employment were steadily aggravated, until they now have come to constitute a basic obstacle to Latin American development.

The average figures given above mask the upper and lower extremes of the scale. Some countries, such as Mexico, for example, have annual demographic growth rates of more than 3.4 percent; while Argentina and Uruguay .are at the other end of the scale, with rates of 1.5 and 1.2 percent, respectively.

We can divide the Latin American countries into three groups on the basis of the population growth rate: those with the lowest rates, i.e., Argentina and Uruguay; those with intermediate rates, i.e., Chile and Cuba; and those with high rates, comprising the remainder of Latin America. These are the divisions used in Table 1 which also shows the rate of increase of the economically active population. This naturally lags behind the growth rate of the total population.*

It is of some significance that, contrary to the general trend, population growth rates in Argentina and Uruguay were relatively high at the beginning of the century, although not as high as those now current in the rest of Latin America. This was due to a sharp reduction in the death rate—long before the same thing happened in the other countries—and to immigration. A declining trend then set in, which was interrupted at the end of the 1930's but continued thereafter. In contrast with this is the steep rise after the 1930's in the population growth rate of the rest of Latin America. Over the past two decades it has tended to level off at a high point, with marked differences between countries.

In the period 1950-1968, the contrast between Argentina and Uruguay, on the one hand, and Mexico and Brazil, on the other, is decidedly significant. The first two countries—which have relatively low population growth rates—were characterized by rates of development that barely raised the per capita product by an average of 1.3 percent in Argentina and reduced it by 0.2 percent in Uruguay. In Mexico, however, where the population grew at a rate of 3.4 percent, the per capita product rose by 2.9 percent; and in Brazil, where the population grew at a rate of 2.8 percent, the per capita product rose by 2.6 percent, albeit with considerable fluctuations. These figures alone suffice to show that a birth control policy should not be regarded as the solution to the problems of development, but merely as one of the components of development strategy, as is made clear in Chapter 7.

It is necessary here to avoid coming to superficial conclusions. The mere fact of a country's managing to bring its population growth rate down to a reasonable level does not mean that its rate of economic development will automatically rise. But if it pursues a vigorous policy of stepping up economic growth, and at the same time reduces its birth rate, the effects of the policy in question will be considerably reinforced.

It is common knowledge that the farther one goes down the income scale, the higher the birth rate rises. No systematic set of data is available on this phenomenon, but a recent survey does shed some light on it. Estimates have been made of the number of live births per married woman at the end of the child-bearing age, by level of education (see Table 2). Generally speaking, the level of education reflects income level: the lower the income level, the less the education received, and the higher the birth rate.

It is also worthwhile looking at the great difference in fertility between the urban and rural population (see Table 3). Owing to statistical shortcomings, it is not possible to say to what extent these figures indicate the rate of natural increase is higher in rural areas.

Besides posing the problem of absorbing the labor force, Latin America's high rate of population growth also means that the dependent population

---

*Unfortunately, the figures for the economically active population cover a shorter period.

## TABLE 1

### Latin America: Population Growth Rates Since 1900
(average annual percentage rates in each five-year period)

| Period | Argentina | Uruguay | Chile | Cuba | Rest of Latin America | Latin America |
|---|---|---|---|---|---|---|
| *Crude Birth Rate* | | | | | | |
| 1900-1904 | 4.4 | 3.9 | — | — | 5.0[a] | — |
| 1930-1934 | 3.1 | 2.6 | 3.8 | 3.6 | — | — |
| 1935-1939 | 2.7 | 2.2 | 3.7 | 3.6 | — | — |
| 1940-1944 | 2.6 | 2.2 | 3.7 | 3.5 | — | — |
| 1945-1949 | 2.6 | 2.1 | 3.6 | 3.4 | — | — |
| 1950-1954 | 2.6 | 2.1 | 3.5 | 3.1 | — | — |
| 1955-1959 | 2.5 | 2.2 | 3.7 | 3.0 | — | — |
| 1960-1964 | ·2.3 | 2.2 | 3.6 | 2.9 | 4.2 | 4.0 |
| 1965-1969 | 2.3 | 2.1 | 3.3 | 2.7 | 4.1 | 3.9 |
| *Crude Death Rate* | | | | | | |
| 1900-1904 | 2.0 | 1.4 | — | — | 3.8[a] | — |
| 1930-1934 | 1.2 | 1.2 | 2.3 | 2.0 | — | — |
| 1935-1939 | 1.2 | 1.1 | 2.3 | 1.8 | — | — |
| 1940-1944 | 1.1 | 1.0 | 1.9 | 1.5 | — | — |
| 1945-1949 | 1.0 | 0.9 | 1.7 | 1.2 | — | — |
| 1950-1954 | 0.9 | 0.9 | 1.3 | 1.0 | — | — |
| 1955-1959 | 0.9 | 0.9 | 1.2 | 1.0 | — | — |
| 1960-1964 | 0.9 | 0.9 | 1.1 | 0.8 | 1.2 | 1.1 |
| 1965-1969 | 0.9 | 0.9 | 1.0 | 0.8 | 1.0 | 1.0 |
| *Growth Rate of Total Population*[b] | | | | | | |
| 1900-1904 | 3.4 | 2.6 | — | — | 1.2[a] | — |
| 1930-1934 | 1.8 | 1.4 | 1.5 | 1.9 | 1.9 | 1.9 |
| 1935-1939 | 1.7 | 1.2 | 1.5 | 1.6 | 2.0 | 1.9 |
| 1940-1944 | 1.7 | 1.1 | 1.5 | 1.5 | 2.4 | 2.2 |
| 1945-1949 | 2.1 | 1.3 | 1.7 | 2.3 | 2.6 | 2.5 |
| 1950-1954 | 2.0 | 1.5 | 2.4 | 2.1 | 2.8 | 2.7 |
| 1955-1959 | 2.0 | 1.4 | 2.4 | 2.1 | 3.0 | 2.8 |
| 1960-1964 | 1.6 | 1.3 | 2.5 | 2.0 | 3.0 | 2.8 |
| 1965-1969 | 1.5 | 1.2 | 2.3 | 2.0 | 3.1 | 2.9 |
| *Growth Rate of Economically Active Population*[c] | | | | | | |
| 1950-1954 | 1.3 | 1.4 | 1.2 | 2.1 | 2.5 | 2.3 |
| 1955-1959 | 1.3 | 1.5 | 1.1 | 2.2 | 2.8 | 2.5 |
| 1960-1964 | 1.5 | 1.4 | 2.3 | 2.2 | 2.9 | 2.7 |
| 1965-1969 | 1.5 | 1.0 | 2.6 | 2.1 | 3.1 | 2.8 |

[a]Tentative data.

[b]Including migration.

[c]According to estimates, in 1900-1904 the growth rate of the economically active population of the rest of Latin America was 1.2 percent, i.e., the same as that of the total population.

*Source:* Latin American Demographic Center (LADECE).

TABLE 2

Latin America, Selected Countries: Average Number of Live Births per Married Woman
at the End of Child-Bearing Age, by Level of Education, 1963-1964

| Level of Education | Argentina (Buenos Aires) | Brazil (Rio de Janeiro) | Colombia (Bogotá) | Costa Rica (San José) | Mexico (Mexico City) | Venezuela (Caracas) |
|---|---|---|---|---|---|---|
| No Education | 3.3 | 5.4 | 7.9 | 6.0* | 6.3 | 5.6 |
| Primary Education | 2.3 | 3.8 | 5.1 | 6.3 | 5.4 | 5.0 |
| Secondary Education | 1.9 | 2.4 | 4.2 | 3.9 | 3.3 | 3.2 |
| University Education | — | 2.0 | 3.8* | 3.7 | 3.9 | 1.0 |
| Total | 2.1 | 3.2 | 4.9 | 5.2 | 5.0 | 4.4 |

Note: The end of child-bearing age is 45-49, unless otherwise stated.

*Age 35-39.

Source: The figures in this table were taken from Angel Fucaraccio, "El control de la natalidad y el subdesarrollo: América Latina," LADECE, Program of Comparative Surveys of Latin America, Urban Areas, group of tabulations No. 4 (135 x 14 x 28). (Unpublished.)

## TABLE 3

**Latin America, Selected Countries: Average Number of Live Births per Married Woman at the End of Child-Bearing Age in Urban and Rural Areas**

| Country | Year | Total | Urban | Rural |
|---------|------|-------|-------|-------|
| Brazil | 1950 | 6.2 | 4.9 | 7.3 |
| Cuba | 1953 | 3.9 | 3.1 | 5.8 |
| Mexico | 1960 | 5.0 | 4.4 | 5.7 |
| Panama | 1950 | 5.0 | 3.6 | 6.1 |
| Argentina | 1960 | 2.7 | 2.1 | 3.1 |

*Note:* The age group is 45-49, except in the case of Mexico, where it is 40-49.

*Sources: Elementos para la elaboración de una política de desarrollo con integración para América Latina,* Chapter 2, Table 15; data for Argentina taken from Ana María Rothman, "Evolution of Fertility in Argentina and Uruguay," p. 12. (Mimeographed.)

(those under 15 and over 64) is large. In this respect, too, there are sharp contrasts in the region, between Mexico and Argentina, for example (see Table 4).

The scientific and technological advances that have brought about a decline in death rates have naturally affected the expectation of life at birth, which has improved markedly throughout the region (see Table 4). While this is certainly of great significance in human terms, it must also be viewed against the background of economic and social development. It is not enough simply to prolong life; it is also necessary to improve living conditions so as to do away with privations that are morally inadmissible.

We have to discover how far the welfare of the vast mass of the population whose life expectancy is rising is compatible with the extraordinarily rapid increase in the number of births in Latin America.

## THE DISTORTION IN THE STRUCTURE OF THE LABOR FORCE

(The series for the sectoral distribution of the labor force in Latin America, both in the aggregate and by countries, were prepared by the Latin

# TABLE 4

## Latin America: Selected Demographic Indexes, 1965-1970

| | Cumulative Annual Growth Rate of the Population (percentage) | Number of Dependants per 100 Persons of Working Age[a] | Expectation of Life at Birth | | Currently |
| | | | Formerly | | |
| Country | | | Approximate Date | Expectation of Life | (1965-1970) |
| | | | (Number of years) | | |
|---|---|---|---|---|---|
| Latin America | 2.9 | 85.6 | 1900 | 25-30[b] | 60.6 |
| Argentina | 1.5 | 57.3 | 1947 | 60.8 | 67.4 |
| Bolivia | 2.4 | 82.7 | 1952 | 40.8 | 45.3 |
| Brazil | 2.8 | 84.3 | 1945 | 42.3 | 60.6 |
| Chile | 2.3 | 80.6 | 1940 | 41.8 | 60.9 |
| Colombia | 3.4 | 98.6 | 1958 | 38.4 | 58.5 |
| Ecuador | 3.4 | 97.1 | 1956 | 49.9 | 57.2 |
| Paraguay | 3.4 | 99.9 | 1955 | 54.4 | 59.3 |
| Peru | 3.1 | 93.1 | 1945 | 34.3 | 58.0 |
| Uruguay | 1.2 | 57.0 | 1957 | 67.1 | 69.2 |
| Venezuela | 3.3 | 94.0 | 1941 | 42.3 | 63.7 |
| Costa Rica | 3.8 | 104.7 | 1950 | 55.7 | 66.8 |
| El Salvador | 3.3 | 98.3 | 1956 | 46.1 | 54.9 |
| Guatemala | 2.8 | 97.9 | 1950 | 40.3 | 51.1 |
| Honduras | 3.4 | 100.0 | 1954 | 36.9 | 48.9 |
| Nicaragua | 2.9 | 102.9 | 1956 | 38.6 | 49.9 |
| Panama | 3.2 | 90.9 | 1955 | 57.3 | 63.4 |
| Mexico | 3.4 | 97.8 | 1940 | 41.5 | 62.4 |
| Cuba | 2.0 | 66.4 | 1953 | 58.9 | 66.8 |
| Haiti | 2.4 | 82.0 | 1952 | 37.5 | 44.5 |
| Dominican Rep. | 3.4 | 101.0 | 1950 | 43.0 | 52.1 |

[a]This figure was calculated by dividing the population under 15 and over 64 years of age by the population aged 15-64.

[b]Excluding Argentina and Uruguay.

*Source:* LADECE.

American Institute for Economic and Social Planning on the basis of the most recent data available, and cover the period 1950-1965.)

Let us now consider what has happened as regards the exceptional increase in the labor force in the 1950's and 1960's. As has always been the case in the course of development, irrespective of the economic and social system, agriculture lacks the capacity to retain the whole of the natural increment in the agricultural labor force. What is taking place in Latin America seems to be roughly the same sort of thing that occurred in the developed countries, although there are some major structural differences.

It is estimated that before the world depression of the 1930's approximately 63 percent of Latin America's total labor force was engaged in agriculture. At present, the corresponding figure is estimated to be 41 percent, although there are wide variations between countries. It is interesting to compare the length of time some of the developed countries took to reach the same point with the time taken in Latin America (see Table 5).

In Latin America as a whole, the decline in agriculture's share in the total labor force has been just slightly slower than in countries such as the United States and Sweden. The difference—and a very big difference it is—lies in what happened to the nonagricultural labor force, as we shall see later. Moreover, the rapidity of this process in Latin America contrasts with the slow decrease of the corresponding proportions in such countries as Italy and France.

The fact that there has been an exodus from agriculture in Latin America must on no account be taken to mean that there is no redundant labor in the agricultural sector; there still is a great deal of it in many countries, and this in itself constitutes a serious problem. Moreover, those who have left agriculture have to a large extent simply carried redundancy from the rural areas to the cities. All this signifies a considerable waste of human potential.*

If we look at this situation in terms of growth rates (see Table 6), we see that the agricultural labor force grew at an average annual rate of only 1.5 percent during the period 1950-1965, while the comparable figure for the total labor force was 2.6 percent. Thus, owing to the movement of manpower away from agriculture, the average annual rate of increase of the nonagricultural labor force—including the unemployed—was 3.5 percent in 1950-1965.

How has this increment been distributed among the various nonagricultural activities? Here we come to the inportant point, for it is here that a real distortion has occurred. Given Latin America's current stage of development, employment should increase more rapidly in the industry group than in services. But this has not happened, except in Mexico, where the proportion of the nonagricultural labor force employed in the industry group has risen; and in Argentina, where it has remained constant but at a relatively high level.

---

*This should perhaps be explained to avoid any misunderstanding. Part of the labor force leaving agriculture finds employment in the industry group. On the other hand, an equivalent part of the natural growth of the urban labor force helps to increase redundancy in the services sector. Hence, for simplicity's sake, it is said that all the labor force leaving agriculture goes into services.

## TABLE 5

### Relative Size of the Agricultural Labor Force

| Country or Region | Years in Which the Proportion of the Total Labor Force Represented by the Agricultural Labor Force Was | | Years Taken To Move from 63 Percent to 42 Percent |
|---|---|---|---|
| | 63 Percent | 42 Percent | |
| United States | 1855 | 1890 | 35 |
| Sweden | 1890 | 1924 | 34 |
| Latin America | 1930 | 1969 | 39 |
| Italy | 1860 | 1950 | 90 |
| France | 1827 | 1921 | 94 |

*Sources*: United States, Sweden, Italy, and France: Simon Kuznets, "Industrial Distribution of National Product and Labor Force," *Economic Development and Cultural Change*, supplement to V, 4 (July, 1957); Latin America: Latin American Institute for Economic and Social Planning.

Table 6 shows how the labor force in the services sector—including the unemployed—grows much more rapidly than that absorbed by the industry group. This is the reason why the proportion of the nonagricultural labor force in the industry group has fallen from 35 percent in 1950 to 31.8 percent in 1965 and slightly less than 30 percent at present, according to estimates for 1970, while at the same time the proportion in services has risen correspondingly.

The term "services" covers a wide variety of activities, which are usually labor-absorbing, and the proportion of the labor force employed in them tends to grow normally as development proceeds, to judge from what has happened in the industrialized countries. Services comprise principally energy, transport and other basic services, commerce and finance, public administration, and skilled personal services that require some degree of technical training. There is nothing strange in the fact that the proportion of people engaged in these activities has risen: the distortion lies in the scale on which this has occurred. The ranks of those employed in such labor-absorbing activities have been greatly swollen by redundant manpower that could be eliminated without any loss in efficiency. A typical example is afforded by public administration and public utilities, which generally employ more staff than

## TABLE 6

**Latin America: Growth and Distribution of the Labor Force**

*1. Cumulative Annual Growth Rates of the Labor Force,*
*1950-1965*
*(percentage)*

| Agricultural | Nonagricultural | Industry Group[a] | Services[b] | Total |
|---|---|---|---|---|
| 1.52 | 3.47 | 2.82 | 3.00 | 2.56 |

*2. Distribution of the Labor Force*

| Year | Agricultural | Nonagricultural | Industry Group[a] | Services[b] |
|---|---|---|---|---|
| | (Percentage of the total labor force) . | | (Percentage of the nonagricultural labor force) | |
| 1950 | 50.2 | 49.8 | 35.0 | 65.0 |
| 1965 | 43.1 | 56.9 | 31.8 | 68.2 |

*Note:* Table excludes Cuba, for want of data.

[a]Including industry, construction, and mining.

[b]Including overt unemployment.

*Source:* Latin American Institute for Economic and Social Planning.

they should, inasmuch as other labor-absorbing activities do not properly fulfill their dynamic role.

Redundancy, of course, is not confined to the labor-absorbing activities in the vast range of services. On the contrary, it occurs chiefly in those activities which in the normal course of development should be labor-expelling, and which comprise a variety of personal services that require little or no technical skill, together with such activities as street vending.

These activities are usually irregular, intermittent, and very poorly paid. Those engaged in them are for the most part the marginal population, in the strict sense of the term,* namely, people who have broken their links with rural life but have not yet managed to become an integral part of the ordinary life of the cities. They eke out an impoverished existence—in ever-increasing numbers, it seems—in the shanty towns which are a characteristic feature of the large urban agglomerations in Latin America.

Redundancy does not necessarily mean unemployment, for only some of the redundant manpower is actually unemployed, although this proportion is growing, especially in certain countries. Since there are no reliable data available on this point, the unemployed have been included under the catch-all head of "sercices," and it is estimated, on the basis of conjectural data, that the proportion of unemployed in the services sector has risen from 21 percent in 1950 to 24 percent at present.

It should be remembered that redundancy exists in other sectors too. Despite rural-urban migration, there is still surplus labor in agriculture, especially in some countries, and there is also redundancy in the goods-producing activities, particularly industry and construction.

The figures given are not a sufficient basis for measuring the effect of this distortion on the growth rate of the aggregate product. Suffice it to recall, for illustrative purposes—and somewhat simplifying a process which is by no means devoid of complexities—that the average product per worker in the industry group was approximately $1,750 in 1965, as against $470 in agriculture. Hence, since the industry group has absorbed only a small fraction of the labor force leaving agriculture, the product per worker has not risen as fast as it would have done had this absorption taken place on a larger scale. While it is true that average income is higher in services then in agriculture, the strongest likelihood is that the redundant labor force joining the services sector does so at a relatively low income level.

If the point when 42 percent of the labor force was engaged in agriculture is taken as a basis of comparison, there is a marked contrast between the proportion of the nonagricultural labor force employed in the industry group in Latin America and the corresponding proportion in the United States and other countries (see Table 7).

Technology has played a part here. Generally speaking, the capital goods used by Latin American industry are imported from the highly-developed countries or are similar to those now used there, and are much more labor-saving than were those used in the United States and the other industrialized countries at the end of the 19th century and the beginning of the 20th.

## STRUCTURAL CHANGES IN THE LABOR
## FORCE IN SELECTED COUNTRIES

It was noted earlier that Mexico and Argentina are the two countries in which the industry group increased and maintained, respectively, its share of

---

*This term is often used as a synonym for redundant manpower in general, but here it is used in its restricted sense.

## TABLE 7

### Proportion of the Nonagricultural Labor Force in the Industry Group When the Agricultural Labor Force Represented 42 Percent of the Total Labor Force

|  | Year | Proportion (percentage) |
|---|---|---|
| United States | 1890 | 48 |
| Sweden | 1924 | 60 |
| Latin America | 1969 | 31 |
| Italy | 1950 | 52 |
| France | 1921 | 57 |

Note: Industry group includes industry, construction, and mining.

Sources: United States, Sweden, Italy, and France: Simon Kuznets, "Industrial Distribution of National Product and Labor Force," Economic Development and Cultural Change, supplement to V, 4 (July, 1957); Latin America: Latin American Institute for Economic and Social Planning.

the nonagricultural labor force. These are two very different cases which once again point up the disadvantage of confining the analysis to general regional averages, without going into all the different situations which they encompass.

Mexico has had and still has a high proportion of manpower engaged in agriculture; but the same is not true of Argentina. To put it in brief outline—and without seeking to draw a comparison between two very different agricultural sectors, but merely looking at the factors that are relevant here—the population of Argentina has for the most part grown in step with agricultural development, and thus there has been no labor surplus on the land, at least in the pampas. In Mexico, in contrast, the pressure on the land that has existed for centuries has become more acute because of the rate of increase of the population, despite the fact that new areas have been brought under cultivation through the construction of irrigation works and roads.

Consequently, in terms of its occupational structure and the increase of its labor force, Argentina would seem to be better equipped to develop. However, for reasons mentioned elsewhere in this study, its total and per capita product has grown much more slowly than Mexico's (see Table 8).

It is interesting now to note in Table 9 how Mexico has been able to absorb labor in the industry group much more rapidly than in services, with the result that the share of the industry group in the nonagricultural labor force has

## TABLE 8

### Argentina and Mexico: Cumulative Annual Growth Rate
### of the Product, 1950-1965
### (percentages)

|           | Total | Per Capita |
|-----------|-------|------------|
| Mexico    | 6.3   | 3.0        |
| Argentina | 3.2   | 1.2        |

*Source:* Latin American Institute for Economic and Social Planning, on the basis of data supplied by the Economic Commission for Latin America (ECLA).

risen sharply. In Argentina, as early as 1950 it had attained the high level that it reached in Mexico in 1965, and this percentage remained constant throughout the period. It is approximately 40 percent in both countries. There is, however, a great difference between the two, since in Mexico the proportion of the labor force engaged in agriculture is still very large, whereas in Argentina it has fallen to a relatively low figure for Latin America. Accordingly, the share of the industry group in the total labor force* in Mexico was only 20.2 percent in 1965, while in Argentina it was 32.6 percent in the same year.

Mexico, therefore, still has a long way to go before the proportion of its labor force employed in the industry group approaches the figure for the more industrialized countries, as the redundant manpower engaged in agriculture is gradually absorbed. The scale of this redundancy is considerable at present, and will tend to increase as production techniques are improved, unless other activities expand at a faster pace than hitherto.

There are other substantial differences between the two countries that must be viewed with a great many reservations because of statistical short-comings. The share of services in total nonagricultural activities remained virtually constant throughout the period in Argentina, at the level attained by Mexico in 1965. According to other estimates, however, the annual growth rate of income per economically active person in the services sector was 2.7 percent in Mexico and only 0.8 percent in Argentina. Even if due account is taken of the differences in the internal composition of the services sector in the two countries, for a less feeble rate to have been achieved in Argentina, the tempo of economic development would have had to be much more brisk.

It would appear that the improvement of productivity in the industry group should play an increasingly important role in stepping up the overall growth rate in Argentina. Given the small proportion of the population working in agriculture, the possibility that the average product per worker in

---

*For the sake of simplicity, these figures are not included in the tables.

## TABLE 9

### Latin America, Selected Countries: Growth and Distribution of the Labor Force, 1950-1965

*1. Cumulative Annual Growth Rates of the Labor Force*
*(Percentage)*

| Country | Agricultural | Industry Group[a] | Services[b] | Subtotal | Total |
|---------|-------------|-------------------|-------------|----------|-------|
|         |             | Nonagricultural   |             |          |       |
| Argentina | −0.48 | 1.98 | 2.00 | 2.00 | 1.40 |
| Brazil | 1.72 | 2.28 | 4.73 | 4.04 | 2.90 |
| Mexico | 2.05 | 4.95 | 3.77 | 4.20 | 3.04 |

*2. Distribution of the Labor Force*

| Country | Agricultural | Nonagricultural | Industry Group[a] | Services[b] |
|---------|-------------|------------------|-------------------|-------------|
|         | (Percentage of the total labor force) | | (Percentage of the nonagricultural labor force) | |
| Argentina |  |  |  |  |
| 1950 | 27.1 | 72.9 | 41.2 | 58.8 |
| 1965 | 20.5 | 79.5 | 41.0 | 59.0 |
| Brazil |  |  |  |  |
| 1950 | 52.9 | 47.1 | 31.6 | 68.4 |
| 1965 | 44.5 | 55.5 | 24.3 | 75.7 |
| Mexico |  |  |  |  |
| 1950 | 57.5 | 42.5 | 36.2 | 63.8 |
| 1965 | 49.7 | 50.3 | 40.1 | 59.9 |

[a]Including industry, construction, and mining.

[b]Including overt unemployment.

*Source:* Latin American Institute for Economic and Social Planning.

the economy as a whole will increase simply because people are moving from rural activities into the industry group is bound to dwindle. In the rest of Latin America, on the other hand, it will still exist on an appreciable scale, although in very different degrees and with some exceptions. Furthermore, the direct effect of these population shifts is also less in Argentina, where the difference between the average product per worker in agriculture and in the industry group is smaller than in the region as a whole (see Table 10).

It should be added, moreover, that in Argentina the product per worker grew at an annual rate of 2.9 percent in agriculture, i.e., faster than in the industry group, where the corresponding figure was 2.1 percent over the period considered.

Brazil is another very interesting case, given its considerable development potential. Its labor force has grown slightly more slowly than Mexico's (see Table 9). Since Mexico has been able to retain a higher proportion of its manpower in agriculture than Brazil, the pressure on its nonagricultural activities to absorb labor has been less.* Yet Brazil has not managed to increase the share of the industry group in the labor force at anything like the same rate as Mexico.

What is the reason for this very sizable difference? Is it because the dynamic impetus of the industry group has been weaker in Brazil than in Mexico? It would not appear so, since in Brazil the gross product of the industry group increased in the period considered at an average annual rate of 6.7 percent, more rapidly than in Mexico, where the corresponding rate was 6.3 percent. This was mainly the result of the spectacular rise in the product per

## TABLE 10

### Latin America and Argentina:  Average Product per Worker in Agriculture and in the Industry Group, 1965
### (dollars, at 1960 prices)

|               | Agriculture | Industry Group |
|---------------|-------------|----------------|
| Argentina     | 1,230       | 1,800          |
| Latin America | 470         | 1,750          |

*Note:* Industry group includes industry, construction, and mining.

*Source:* Latin American Institute for Economic and Social Planning, on the basis of data supplied by ECLA.

---

*This is a very interesting point that warrants further study. Here, however, we will confine ourselves to mentioning it.

worker in the industry group by an average of 4.7 percent annually—an extraordinarily high figure for Latin America—compared with Mexico's more modest 2.5 percent.

Admittedly, the rate estimated for Brazil may be inflated by an apparent increase—greater than it actually was—in the product per worker in the import-saving industries, which did not make so much headway in Mexico. In any event, the difference in the growth of the product per worker in Brazil and Mexico may largely explain why Brazil's industry group has not had the same capacity to absorb labor as Mexico's.

While it is true that Brazil's average rate of development throughout the period (6 percent) was slightly less than Mexico's (6.3 percent), this relatively small difference is not enough to justify such a big disparity in the rates of growth of the labor force in the industry group. If the product per worker in the industry group had risen much less rapidly, perhaps Brazil might have been able to increase the productive absorption of labor in these activities on much the same scale as Mexico. But this was not the case, since the share of the industry group in the total nonagricultural labor force declined, in marked contrast with what occurred in Mexico.

Given the rapidity of the increase in the product per worker in its industry group, Brazil would have needed a higher overall growth rate than Mexico's in order to ensure that the proportion of labor in the industry group did not fall. But since this was not the case, the redundant manpower leaving agriculture in Brazil for the most part simply transferred its redundancy to the services sector.

In the other countries of the region—apart from the three mentioned (Argentina, Brazil and Mexico), which account for approximately 65 percent of the region's labor force and of the total regional product—the differences are also considerable. Unfortunately, however, no comparisons can reasonably be made unless a great deal of work is put into the screening of the available data.

## ABSORPTION OF THE LABOR FORCE
## IN AGRICULTURE

It was noted earlier that the labor force leaving agriculture has simply transferred its redundancy to the cities, owing to the inadequate rate of economic development. Could this process have been attenuated, if not prevented altogether? Could agriculture have retained more labor than the figures show, and thus have helped to relieve congestion in the cities? The answers to these questions, in addition to telling us about the past, will also help a great deal in our consideration of future development.

The level of employment in agriculture depends on the rates at which production expands and the product per worker increases. During the period considered (1950-1965), Latin America's agricultural production grew at an average annual rate of 3.8 percent, while the product per worker rose at a rate of 2.2 percent. Had production expanded at a faster pace, with the rise in the product per worker remaining the same, agriculture would have been able to retain labor at an annual rate of more than 1.5 percent.

Why did Latin America's agricultural production not expand more rapidly? A number of factors associated with supply and demand are responsible, including, in particular, the slow rate of growth of domestic and external demand, outdated marketing systems, price policies, the system of land tenure and use, and the inadequacy of technical progress.

As a general rule, the diet of the bulk of the population in Latin America, especially in the lower income strata, is very poor; thus, much more should have been produced per capita to remedy so serious a deficiency. This did not happen, however, and various reasons have been adduced to explain why—reasons which are at times of great significance in individual cases, and cannot be disregarded. Nevertheless, a more general explanation lies, in our view, in the fact that domestic demand for agricultural products, especially foodstuffs, has expanded relatively slowly. This, in turn, is a reflection of the inadequate growth of per capita income, on which the performance of agriculture itself naturally has an influence, inasmuch as all the various components of the economy are interdependent, and it is necessary to act on all of them in order to speed up the rate of economic growth.

During the period considered, average per capita income rose at an annual rate of 2.5 percent, while per capita consumption of foodstuffs expanded by 1.1 percent annually. If the increase in per capita income has been distributed more evenly than it was, to the benefit of the lower income strata, the growth of demand would have been greater, and its effects on the retention of labor in agriculture would have been marked.

There are two opposing trends here: on the one hand, if personal income rises, the proportion spent on food falls; on the other, an improvement in the income levels of the lower strata may more than cancel out any possible reduction in the coefficient of elasticity of demand for foodstuffs and may increase employment opportunities in agriculture to a greater extent than would otherwise occur. This is precisely the assumption adopted in the projections for the 1970's and 1980's, which are presented in Chapter 4.

Export-oriented agriculture affords clear evidence of the decisive importance of demand. When demand has been brisk and steady, it has frequently proved possible to overcome the internal obstacles standing in the way of agricultural expansion. Such circumstances lead, in one way or another, to the emergence of the modern farmer, capable of producing efficiently.

This has happened when land was easily accessible or the amount of cultivable land was increased as a result of State investment in infrastructure; and also when the introduction of new techniques did not require the State to play an exceptionally active role as an innovator.

Argentina provides an illustrative case in point. In past decades, the spirit of innovation has been lacking in its agricultural sector. The fertile pampas were already being used for farming by the end of the 1920's. Production, which up to that point had expanded because new areas were rapidly being brought under cultivation, could then increase only on the basis of technological progress. And yet the Great Depression, the Second World War, and a return to agricultural protectionism in the major industrial centers gave no encouragement to the introduction of improved techniques. During certain periods, overvaluation of the currency and price policies also had unfavorable effects. The consequences were very striking. Argentina, whose agricultural technology had been comparable with that of the United States in the 1920's, lagged farther and farther behind. Despite the unfavorable world market conditions, it could at least have maintained its share of world exports. But this was not to be. Once the easily accessible land had been brought under cultivation, major technological improvements were needed, and as these were introduced only to a very limited extent, production remained virtually stationary for a length period. Moreover, the steady rise in domestic consumption severely curtailed exportable surpluses and thus tightened the external bottleneck.

This state of affairs can be attributed to two main factors: first, the inadequacy of state action with regard to technological research and the dissemination of its practical results; and second, the prevailing land tenure system. The first of these defects is being corrected; but land tenure has undergone no significant change. It is true that in Argentina—at least in the Pampas—the pressure of the active population on the land is not such as to make direct redistribution of land advisable in order to facilitate the introduction of new techniques. It may be asked whether indirect expedients—including tax measures—would have sufficed to foster efficient use of the productive potential of the land and discourage underutilization. This is the great unknown quantity: whether the research on new technologies and the dissemination of its findings, in which the State is now engaged, can be successful if the obstacle of the land tenure system is not removed.*

A very significant example of how domestic demand stimulated production is what happened in the State of São Paulo in Brazil. Among other factors, the availability of land and state government efforts to promote the introduction of new techniques, combined with private initiative, gave agriculture an impetus strong enough to enable it to meet the demand of this thriving industrial state and that of neighboring states in Brazil, whose traditional methods of production could not always compete with São Paulo's more advanced techniques.

Another example worth mentioning is modern agriculture in Mexico. As a result of export possibilities, agricultural import-substitution policy, and the growth of domestic demand stemming from the steady rise in per capita income, agriculture expanded rapidly on land that was made accessible by the construction of roads and cultivable by irrigation and by official action on the technical side. This modern type of agriculture absorbs relatively little labor.

---

*In this connection, it would be interesting to look into the possibility of a relationship between changes in land tenure (tenants becoming land-owners) in the pampas over the past two decades or so, and the introduction of new techniques that have led to marked increases in output.

Thus, we have a dual situation: the new agriculture exists side by side with traditional Mexican agriculture, in which the pressure of labor on the land has been increasing as a result of the high rate of population growth. While the new agriculture is labor-saving, redundancy appears to be on the increase in traditional agriculture. One of the most significant features of the Mexican land reform, as regards the retention of labor in agriculture, is that besides having abolished an outdated social structure it has helped, with the *ejido* system, to retain more manpower on the land than would otherwise have been the case. The new agriculture is an economic solution to the problem; the *ejido* is a social and political solution, although it has not as yet proved possible to raise the living conditions of the masses above subsistence level.

Yet another interesting case is that of Venezuela, where the marked growth of both crop and livestock production is attributable to a clearly defined import substitution policy and to the extension of the frontier of agriculture, combined with the redistribution of part of the productive land.

In this latter respect, the changes now being made in Chilean agriculture warrant close study. Apparently, there are few new areas that can easily be brought under cultivation, and hence a major effort is under way to make more efficient use of the two factors in short supply—land and water. This aim has found practical expression in the land reform, which, of course, is also pursuing basic social objectives.

It would have to be accompanied by changes in methods of land use, with a view to substituting domestic production for imports of products that are needed to improve the diet of the bulk of the population, and to expanding exports of products with a high unit value. Increasing exports of this type—in addition to the expected favorable effects on the balance of payments—might also help to increase employment.

In any event, the question is whether Chile will be able to evade the dilemma described in general terms in this document: i.e., the choice between substantially raising the product per agricultural worker by the introduction of new techniques, at the expense of employment, and sacrificing this objective in favor of carrying the social integration of the rural masses beyond what might be achieved simply by redistributing land. The way out will depend on the rate of development that can be attained.

Although agricultural demand has played a primary role in production and in the retention of labor on the land, there have also been a number of adverse factors of great importance that in certain cases have prevented production from keeping up with demand, as has happened in Argentina. The land tenure system is one of them, and its negative influence will be even stronger in the future, especially if population growth is accompanied by more rapid economic development and improvements in the distribution of income.

Account must also be taken of the adverse repercussions of certain official measures. With the justifiable aim of preventing the price of foodstuffs from rising in step with inflation, price ceilings have often been fixed and have discouraged production in some countries. Overvaluation of the currency has had similar effects. These disincentives, and the lack of a policy to encourage agricultural production, explain why some countries have increased agricultural imports that could have been replaced by domestic production in order to alleviate the external bottleneck.

This substitution would not have been possible in the case of all agricultural commodities, simply for ecological reasons; but a suitable intraregional trade regime could have reduced, and even eliminated, heavy imports from outside the region.

Although agricultural imports do not have a particularly unfavorable effect on employment in Latin America as a whole, they do in some cases significantly aggravate the external bottleneck and hence tend to depress the overall rate of development. Even on the extreme assumption that all agricultural imports could have been dispensed with during the period considered, the growth rate of total agricultural production would not have increased appreciably, nor would the amount of labor employed in agriculture.

This leads to consideration of the terms in which the problem of agricultural employment presents itself. It was said earlier that demand for foodstuffs, which is far below the level needed to ensure that the lower strata have an adequate diet, has limited the growth of employment in rural areas. But this does not mean that if agricultural demand had increased faster, more labor would automatically have been retained on the land.

It is more useful in this connection to consider not what could have happened in the past, but what might happen in the future. This, however, is not the appropriate place to do so, and only a few preliminary remarks will be made here. Given rapidly rising agricultural demand, the degree to which labor is retained in agriculture depends on the amount of land available for expanding production and on the type and pace of technical progress.

As regards the first of these points, much of the increase in production—taking Latin America as a whole—has been achieved by bringing new areas under cultivation. According to estimates, some three-quarters of the increase in crop production is attributable to this factor. It is a matter for conjecture whether the agricultural area can continue to be expanded at the same rate without major investment in infrastructure, and without losses in the average product per worker. On the other hand, a substantial proportion of the land already settled is being wasted, owing to the prevailing land tenure system. If this situation were corrected, cultivation of such land would step up agricultural production in the settled areas, and either redundant labor would be better employed or more labor would be retained on the land, as the case might be.

Even if production were expanded in this way on the basis of existing techniques, the product per worker would increase, since redundant labor and idle land would be put to better use. If, on the other hand, the emphasis were placed on improving yields, with no rise in the labor/land ratio, the rate of retention of labor would decrease correlatively. And this decrease would be much more rapid if agriculture became mechanized.

In other words, an increase in agricultural demand resulting from a higher rate of development and improved income distribution would tend to retain more labor on the land because of its favorable effect on production; while raising the product per worker would tend to reduce the rate of retention, to an extent which would depend on how far labor-saving techniques were introduced.

A suitable compromise has to be found between these two aspects of the problem. Agriculture offers wide scope for the technological revolution that has taken or is taking place in the more advanced countries. In Latin America, the new technology is having hardly any impact on farming for domestic consumption, which, generally speaking, was lagging far behind the export-oriented activities in respect of techniques. Moreover, even though the process of assimilation is confined to a fairly small segment of agriculture as a whole, its effects are clearly visible in some countries, as noted earlier: little absorption of labor, and competition—at times very serious—with traditional agriculture. If technological progress had been assimilated more rapidly during the period considered, without any acceleration of the overall rate of development or any fundamental changes in income distribution, the benefit to the rural masses would have been nugatory, since the relation between agricultural prices and those of other goods and services would have deteriorated. Furthermore, either the redundant manpower in agriculture would have increased, or the shift of active population to the cities would have been stepped up, thus aggravating the redundancy problem in urban areas.

To put it briefly, had the economic growth rate been higher and income distribution more equitable in the past, it would have been possible to retain more labor in agriculture, provided the product per worker did not rise more rapidly than it actually did. The same can be said of the future. It should be borne in mind, however, that average income per worker is very low in Latin American agriculture. And although it could be raised through a more rational and equitable distribution of land—as is shown in an interesting paper which has been of great service in the drafting of the present report—it would be necessary to increase the growth rate of the product per worker, and to ensure that a fair share of it was obtained by those who work the land, through their own trade union action in concurrence with State measures to bring about the complete social integration of the rural masses.

Here we should restate the clear-cut dilemma of the choice between productivity and employment: unless the rate of economic development is stepped up, the transfer of redundant manpower from rural to urban areas will continue, to say nothing of the unfavorable effect that relatively slow-growing domestic demand may have on agricultural prices.

## ABSORPTION OF THE LABOR FORCE
## IN INDUSTRY

Industry obviously accounts for the lion's share of manpower in the nonagricultural goods-producing sectors. In 1965, it provided work for 24 percent of the whole nonagricultural labor force, while construction absorbed 6.5 percent and mining 1.4 percent.

The fact that industry has not completely fulfilled its labor-absorbing function, even with its present technical characteristics, is attributable to the relative slowness of its rate of expansion, which is closely linked to the rate of development of the economy as a whole. But it has also had internal absorption difficulties. In this connection, a distinction must be drawn between factory-type and artisan-type industry (see Table 11).

## TABLE 11

### Latin America:  Growth of the Labor Force and Employment in Industry, 1950-1965
(cumulative percentage annual growth rates)

| Country | Labor force | Employment in Industry | | | Employment in the Industry Group* |
| | | Factory-Type | Artisan-Type | Total | |
| --- | --- | --- | --- | --- | --- |
| Argentina | 1.4 | 2.3 | 1.9 | 2.2 | 2.0 |
| Bolivia | 2.2 | 4.2 | 4.8 | 4.6 | 4.2 |
| Brazil | 2.9 | 2.6 | 1.7 | 2.2 | 2.3 |
| Central America | 2.5 | 4.9 | 1.5 | 2.7 | 2.9 |
| Chile | 1.6 | 3.4 | 0.6 | 2.2 | 1.6 |
| Colombia | 2.4 | 3.7 | 1.8 | 2.4 | 3.0 |
| Dominican Rep. | 2.7 | 6.3 | 3.7 | 4.7 | 4.4 |
| Ecuador | 2.8 | 6.5 | 1.2 | 2.1 | 2.5 |
| Mexico | 3.0 | 5.9 | 3.0 | 4.7 | 5.0 |
| Panama | 2.6 | 4.9 | -1.1 | 2.2 | 2.5 |
| Paraguay | 2.7 | 3.2 | 1.6 | 1.9 | 1.8 |
| Peru | 2.4 | 5.8 | 2.2 | 3.4 | 3.7 |
| Uruguay | 1.4 | 3.0 | 1.2 | 2.4 | 2.2 |
| Venezuela | 3.1 | 6.2 | 1.9 | 4.2 | 3.0 |
| Total | 2.6 | 3.6 | 1.9 | 2.8 | 2.8 |

*Including industry, construction, and mining.

*Source:* Latin American Institute for Economic and Social Planning.

It will be noted from Table 11 that in the period considered, taking the average for all countries except Brazil, employment in factory-type industry increased at a more rapid pace than the total labor force. However, since employment in artisan-type industry grew by barely 1.9 percent, the rate at which labor was absorbed into industry as a whole was only 2.8 percent, i.e., almost the same as the rate at which the total labor force expanded.

Owing to these disparities in the growth of employment, the proportion of the industrial labor force engaged in artisan-type activities fell from 51 percent in 1950 to 45 percent in 1965. This did much to raise the average product per worker in industry, which is estimated to be 10 times higher in factory-type than in artisan-type industry. Hence, a substantial part of the average annual rise of 3.1 percent in the industrial product per worker is the result of the transfer in question.

The first column in Table 12 shows the share of the industrial product in the gross product of the economy as a whole, which is a rough indication of the level of industrial development in the various countries. The next three columns show the growth rates of the industrial product, industrial employment, and the product per worker.

The rate at which industry absorbed labor could have been higher than the growth rate of the total labor force if the growth of the industrial product, and therefore the overall rate of development, had been much more rapid, or if the average product per worker had risen more slowly. As seen earlier, employment in the industry group in Mexico increased much more rapidly than the total labor force. This is clearly apparent if industry alone in the group is considered: it was possible for employment to expand rapidly, at an annual rate of 4.7 percent, not only because the rate of economic development was high, but also because the product per worker in industry rose by only 1.9 percent. The situation was very different in Venezuela: despite an exceptional upswing of 6.1 percent in the average product per worker, the labor force in industry increased at an annual rate of 4.2 percent. This was due to the fact that industry developed more rapidly in Venezuela than in Mexico—despite the similarity in their overall growth rates—owing to a very active import-substitution policy, and also to the fact that Venezuela was at a relatively low level of industrial development at the beginning of the period considered.

Manufacturing industry in Latin America could have appreciably improved its productivity if it had been able to overcome all the obstacles in its way, and the average annual increase of 3.1 percent might have been much bigger. In reality, while there are great possibilities of raising productivity, certain structural changes are needed in order to give powerful and sustained impetus to industrial development.

Two factors stand in the way of increasing productivity in industry: the small size of the market and the weakness of competition. The significance of the concept of a small market varies with each country. In the countries which have achieved most in terms of industrial development, the market is of adequate size for a large number of industries producing consumer goods, but not for those manufacturing certain other products, for example, a great many of the intermediate and capital goods. The smaller the country, the more

## TABLE 12

Latin America: Share of the Gross Industrial Product in the Total
Product, 1968, and Growth of the Industrial Product and Industrial
Productivity, 1950-1968

| Country | Percentage Share of the Industrial Product in the Total Product | Cumulative Annual Growth Rate (percentage) | | |
| --- | --- | --- | --- | --- |
| | | Industrial Product | Industrial Employment | Product per Worker |
| Argentina | 35.1 | 4.5 | 2.2 | 2.3 |
| Bolivia | 13.2 | 2.3 | 4.6 | -2.2 |
| Brazil | 22.0 | 7.3 | 2.2 | 5.0 |
| Central America | 13.6 | 6.8 | 2.7 | 4.0 |
| Chile | 25.7 | 4.6 | 2.2 | 2.5 |
| Colombia | 18.0 | 6.2 | 2.4 | 3.7 |
| Dominican Republic | 12.2 | 4.3 | 4.7 | -0.4 |
| Ecuador | 16.9 | 5.1 | 2.1 | 3.0 |
| Mexico | 20.1 | 6.7 | 4.7 | 1.9 |
| Panama | 15.6 | 10.1 | 2.2 | 5.0 |
| Paraguay | 17.4 | 2.3 | 1.9 | 0.4 |
| Peru | 20.2 | 7.8 | 3.4 | 4.2 |
| Uruguay | 20.9 | 2.8 | 2.4 | 0.4 |
| Venezuela | 12.7 | 10.6 | 4.2 | 6.1 |
| Total | 22.0 | 6.0 | 2.8 | 3.1 |

*Source:* Latin American Institute for Economic and Social Planning, on
the basis of its own data and data supplied by ECLA.

severely will the size of its market affect its industries, including those producing consumer goods.

Even in cases where the domestic market might possibly be large enough, the lack of external competition discourages efforts to increase productivity, just as the prevailing land tenure system discourages improvements in land use. Capital is not turned to good account in industry: generally there is a great deal of idle capacity, and not enough is done to promote efficiency on the workers' side. Nor are there any strong incentives to improve technical skills at all levels.

It is recognized that protection is usually carried to excess in the Latin American countries. Nonetheless, despite its adverse influence in efficiency, it has helped to build up a measure of managerial skill and to develop industries which would hardly have been likely to spring up on their own. This initial phase has already been virtually completed in many countries.

A gradual decrease in the protection afforded to industry, in order to introduce the stimulus of competition, is something which only the experts are calling for. In actual fact, no powerful forces are supporting measures of this kind. Entrepreneurs, salaried employees, and wage-earners all seem to have tacitly agreed to maintain an excessively high level of protection, to the detriment of economic and social development. This is a very serious matter, since industrial costs are much too high, and if the position remains unchanged it will be difficult to export manufactures—a point which will be dealt with in more detail later in this report.

Another interesting aspect of the problem needs emphasizing. Despite the fact that its costs are much too high—we must be frank here—the import-substitution process has generally led to a net increase in real income. As noted above, this has been possible because redundant labor in agriculture and other activities where productivity is much lower than in the industrial sector has been transferred to the import-substitution industries. The result has generally been a sizable increase in the real income generated by industrial development.

However, as the import substitution process gradually moves into capital-intensive industries which entail highly complex techniques and absorb less labor, or which come up against the barrier of a small market, the favorable effects of industrial development decrease, and the rate of absorption of manpower slackens. And if this goes hand in hand with excessively high costs in import-saving industries, it is easy to understand why the net increment in real income drops appreciably or even turns into a negative figure.

It is precisely in the capital-intensive industries with highly complex techniques that productivity can be raised substantially, provided production is distributed in a rational manner by means of integration agreements. This is an aspect of industrial development in the more advanced countries of the region that has not yet been given all the attention it deserves. It will be essential to make up for such neglect in the future.

Thus, there are great possibilities for raising productivity. If they had been rationally exploited, the industrial product per worker would have risen faster than it actually did. If this had happened as an isolated phenomenon, however, industry's capacity to absorb labor would have been less than it was and redundancy in services would have increased. Neither in industry, nor in agriculture, nor in any other sector, can these possibilities be considered separately, out of the context of speeding up the overall rate of economic growth.

# CHAPTER 3

## EXTERNAL FACTORS HAMPERING DEVELOPMENT

## ANALYSIS OF GROWTH RATES

### The Region and Two Significant Groups of Countries

The preceding chapter discussed the distortion in the employment structure resulting from the inadequate tempo of development. Attention will now be turned to the major external factors that are involved. The figure for the average growth rate of the gross product—which is the indicator of the overall rate of development—covers a wide variety of very dissimilar situations. Why have some countries developed more rapidly than others? Why have some definitely lagged behind?

The intention in this chapter is not, of course, to make an exhaustive analysis of what has happened within each individual country, but rather to examine the interplay of external factors in each particular case, with a view to drawing lessons which will equip us to tackle a new type of development in Latin America. In the writer's view, this new type of development cannot be based solely on import substitution, but must entail a major effort to promote exports to the rest of the world and, in particular, intraregional exports.

Clearly, there are a number of factors common to the whole region which are of great importance. In all countries—albeit in very different degrees—balance-of-payments trends and, more particularly, the slow growth of exports have constituted an obstruction to more rapid development. The barrier has not been insuperable, since it has been overcome by curbing the growth of imports. It should be noted, however, that this barrier is really just a boundary, and that reaching it—or crossing it—depends on the domestic development effort and, more specifically, on the rate of capital formation. In this respect, the situation varies widely from one Latin American country to another, and each has availed itself of its opportunities to develop and to reduce the import coefficient in a different way.

Moreover, while it is true that exports have grown relatively slowly, it is equally undeniable that some countries have managed to take better advantage of their export possibilities than others. Thus, the picture is very complex: Latin America has been able to exert an influence on some of the factors involved, using the means available to it; but it has not been able to influence others, which depend for the most part on decisions beyond its control.

The same can be said with respect to capital formation. Overcoming the external barrier to development depends not only on reducing the import coefficient but also on the rate of capital formation, which reflects a country's internal capacity to generate investment resources at the expense of consumption, as well as the scale and the terms on which it receives international financial cooperation.

This is the point which the present chapter will endeavor to elucidate. To do so has not been an easy task, given the wide diversity of data that have had to be brought together; and for this reason the data have been presented in synthetic and easily accessible form, although strict precision has had to be sacrificed a little—but not much—for the sake of simplicity.

It has been repeatedly said that, because of their diversity, it is not advisable to look at the Latin American countries simply in the aggregate; it is admissible to do so only by way of an initial approach to the facts. This is what the present chapter will attempt in very general terms, subsequently going on to consider two large groups of countries and then making a more careful analysis of some representative cases.

Again aiming at synthesis, we shall begin by referring to a few data—few but extremely significant—concerning the growth of the product, exports, and other external resources, and the effect of changes in the import coefficient (see Table 13).

For Latin America as a whole, the purchasing power of exports rose at an average annual rate of only 2.7 percent over the period 1950-1968, although this figure rises to 3.2 percent if the net inflow of external financial resources is taken into account.* However, over this period the gross product grew at an average annual rate of 5.2 percent. This is evidence of how national efforts to reduce the import coefficient made it possible to cross the boundary set by the moderate growth rate of exports and other external resources: the product increased by 2 percent more than the external resources available for imports.**

This disparity shows up very clearly in Figure 1, where the lower curve represents the difference between the rate of growth that the expansion of exports would have permitted and the rate actually achieved by overcoming the export barrier through the reduction of the import coefficient, from 1950 onward: it was the upward trend of the bottom curve that enabled the top curve—which represents the growth of the gross product—to rise more rapidly than the middle curve, which shows the purchasing power of exports and the net inflow of external resources.

As the overall figures mask very different situations, the countries have been divided into two major groups, according to the movement of their

---

*Includes gross capital inflows less amortization, debt repayment, and remittances of interest and profits; also the movement of national funds abroad, which could not be eliminated from the figures.

**The growth rates mentioned in this chapter were calculated using a parabolic function fitted to the annual data by means of the least squares method.

# TABLE 13

## Latin America: Cumulative Average Annual Growth Rates of the Gross Domestic Product, and External Factors Hampering its Growth, 1950-1968
### (percentage)

| | Gross Domestic Product A | Exports Volume B | Exports Purchasing Power C | External Resources[a] D | Effect of the Import Coefficient A−D |
|---|---|---|---|---|---|
| *Latin America* | 5.2 | 4.5 | 2.7 | 3.2 | 2.0 |
| *Countries in Which the Import Coefficient Decreased* | 5.4 | 4.1 | 1.8 | 2.0 | 3.3 |
| Argentina | 3.1 | 3.8 | 2.9 | 2.0 | 1.2 |
| Brazil | 6.1 | 3.2 | 0.9 | 1.1 | 5.0 |
| Colombia | 4.7 | 3.5 | 1.3 | 2.4 | 2.3 |
| Mexico | 6.3 | 4.4 | 3.3 | 4.2 | 2.2 |
| Uruguay | 1.2 | − b | -0.8 | -1.3 | 2.5 |
| Venezuela | 6.3 | 5.6 | 1.5 | 1.5 | 4.8 |
| *Countries in Which the Import Coefficient Did Not Decrease* | 4.6 | 5.7 | 5.4 | 6.7 | -2.1 |
| Bolivia | 2.0 | 0.3 | 3.7 | 5.2 | -3.1 |
| Chile | 4.2 | 3.5 | 4.8 | 6.0 | -1.8 |
| Costa Rica | 6.7 | 6.5 | 4.5 | 7.5 | -0.8 |
| Dominican Republic | 4.5 | 3.4 | 2.7 | 6.0 | -1.5 |
| Ecuador | 4.7 | 6.1 | 4.1 | 6.3 | -1.7 |
| El Salvador | 5.6 | 7.4 | 5.5 | 7.6 | -2.0 |
| Guatemala | 4.5 | 8.2 | 5.2 | 6.2 | -1.7 |
| Honduras | 4.1 | 5.0 | 4.5 | 6.7 | -2.6 |
| Nicaragua | 6.0 | 8.7 | 8.5 | 10.6 | -4.7 |
| Panama | 6.4 | 6.9 | 6.3 | 7.1 | -0.7 |
| Paraguay | 3.5 | 3.9 | 2.2 | 4.9 | -1.4 |
| Peru | 5.6 | 8.1 | 8.0 | 7.6 | -1.9 |

[a]Equivalent to actual imports.

[b]Negligible.

*Source:* ECLA, on the basis of official statistics.

**FIGURE 1**

**Effect of Import Coefficient: Latin America**
**(indexes : 1950 = 100)**

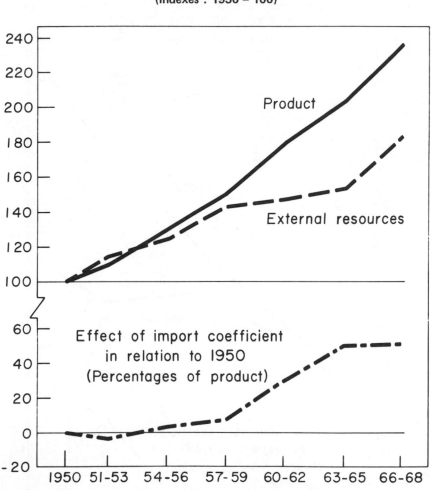

*Source:* ECLA, on the basis of official data; see Appendix Table 1.

import coefficient, which has such an important bearing on the tempo of development. The first group—which accounts for 83.5 percent of the region's product and 78.2 percent of its population—includes those countries in which the import coefficient decreased, namely, Argentina, Brazil, Colombia, Mexico, Uruguay, and Venezuela. The second group comprises the remainder of the Latin American countries. In most of the countries in this group, the import coefficient increased; the few countries in which the coefficient showed no clearly defined trend were included for the sake of simplicity. The evolution of

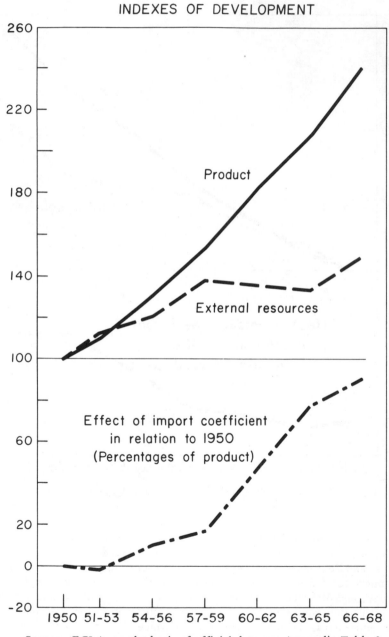

**FIGURE 2**

**Countries in Which the Import
Coefficient Decreased
(indexes: 1950 = 100)**

INDEXES OF DEVELOPMENT

Product

External resources

Effect of import coefficient
in relation to 1950
(Percentages of product)

1950  51-53  54-56  57-59  60-62  63-65  66-68

*Source:* ECLA, on the basis of official data; see Appendix Table 2.

52

# FIGURE 3

**Countries in Which the Import Coefficient Increased
(indexes: 1950 = 100)**

INDEXES OF EXPORTS

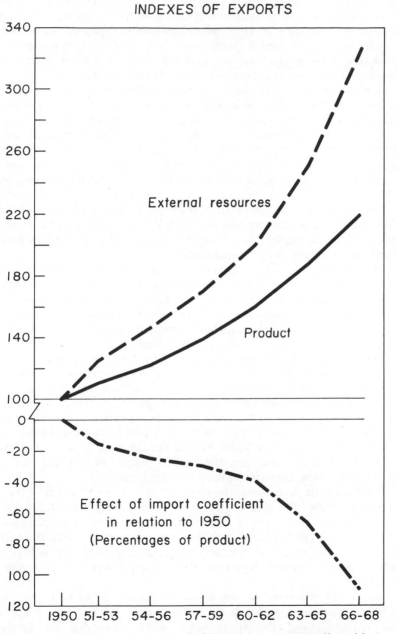

*Source:* ECLA, on the basis of official data; see Appendix Table 3.

the variables under consideration in the two groups of countries can be seen in Figures 2 and 3.

There are striking differences between the two groups. In the first, although the growth rate of external resources was very much lower, the gross product expanded much more rapidly because national efforts to reduce the import coefficient were to some extent able to overcome the barrier set up by the relatively slow pace at which external resources expanded. In the second group, in contrast, despite the relative abundance of external resources, the growth rate of the product did not reach the level that these resources would have allowed, and the import coefficient rose proportionally.

Before looking at these disparities more closely, it may be appropriate to make some brief comments on imports and the import coefficient. As a general rule, imports in Latin America tend to grow more rapidly than the product, i.e., the import coefficient tends to rise. Hence, if external resources are not sufficient to permit imports to expand at such a pace, one of two things happens: either the product increases more slowly than imports and the external resources used to pay for them, or the import coefficient is reduced so that the product can grow at the same rate, or faster.

The latter was what happened in the first group of countries, while in the second group, either nothing was done or it did not prove possible to reduce the import coefficient, with the result that it did not decrease and the product expanded more slowly than external resources.

One further digression. We have been speaking of reducing the import coefficient. In actual fact, much of the reduction in the first group of countries was effected through the replacement of imports by domestic production of the same goods; in other cases, however, certain imports were restricted or banned and demand was diverted toward other domestic goods and services. This is also substitution, but of a different kind. It is important to bear this distinction in mind when the two concepts are used interchangeably.

Let us now revert to the study of the two groups of countries. The disparities observable between them are really significant. The curves in Figures 2 and 3 move quite differently. In the first group, the curve for the gross product rises farther and farther above the curve for external resources. For the second group the reverse is true; the product falls farther and farther below external resources. The key factor here is the effect of reducing the import coefficient on the barrier imposed by the supply of external resources, excluding, of course, domestic capital formation capacity.

Analyzing the rates shown in Figures 2 and 3, we find that in the first group of countries the product increased at an annual rate of 5.4 percent (slightly lower if Venezuela is excluded), while external resources grew by barely 2 percent (slightly more with the inclusion of Venezuela). In contrast, the external resources of the second group expanded by 6.7 percent yearly—clearly a relatively high rate—while their product rose by barely 4.6 percent.

Again, the reduction of the import coefficient helps to explain these disparities. It can be seen that in the first group the product grew 3.3 percent more rapidly than external resources—which expanded by barely 2 percent—because the drop in the import coefficient made it possible to overcome the external resources barrier. In the second group of countries, on the other hand, the dynamic effects of the increase in external resources failed to strengthen the growth of the product because the import coefficient had not been reduced, and consequently the growth rate of the product was 2.1 percent less than that of external resources.

As is always the case in Latin America, the purchasing power of exports was greatly affected by the terms of trade. The terms-of-trade effect fluctuated continually throughout the period considered, but on balance it was unfavorable. Thus, while the volume of exports expanded annually by 4.5 percent, their purchasing power grew at a rate of only 2.7 percent (see Table 13).

The position is clearly observable in Figure 4, in which the rising trend of the volume of exports is offset to a steadily increasing extent by the deterioration in the terms of trade. The resulting index shows how unsatisfactory the expansion of the purchasing power of exports was.

A point worth noting is that among the principal determinants of the downward trend of the terms of trade is the rise in average import prices, especially for consumer durables and capital goods. This also explains why the relation between the prices of such goods and average export prices declined more sharply than the overall terms of trade. (For more detailed data, see Appendix Figure 1.)

The evolution of the components of external resources is another respect in which there is a contrast between the two groups of countries. Not only was the growth of external resources much greater in one case than in the other, but the variation in their components was also significant.

In the first group the deterioration in the terms of trade had a very serious effect: while the volume of exports rose at an annual rate of 4.1 percent, their purchasing power increased at a rate of only 1.8 percent (see Table 13). In the second group of countries too the terms-of-trade effect was unfavorable, but to a far lesser extent: the volume of exports grew at an annual rate of 5.7 percent and their purchasing power at a rate of 5.4 percent. On the basis of these data, Figures 5 and 6 were prepared, showing the relevant trends over the period considered.

The trends of financial resources were also more favorable in the second group. In the first group, if the net inflow of external financial resources is added to the purchasing power of exports—which rose by 1.8 percent—total external resources will be seen to have expanded at a rate of barely 2 percent. In the second group, on the other hand, total external resources increased at a rate of 6.7 percent, i.e., more rapidly than the purchasing power of exports, which rose at a rate of 5.4 percent.

This brings us to a very important point. The contrast between the two groups of countries is highly significant. In the first group the volume of exports grew more slowly, the decline in the purchasing power of exports was more marked, and the net inflow of external financial resources was much smaller. And yet the overall growth rate was higher in this group. To say that in the one case the import coefficient decreased while in the other it was not reduced or actually increased is too facile an explanation, for it does not show why the coefficient moved as it did.

FIGURE 4

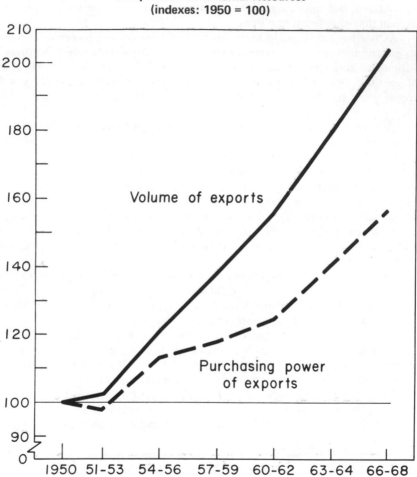

Composition of External Resources
(indexes: 1950 = 100)

*Source:* ECLA, on the basis of official data; see Appendix Table 4.

It is worthwhile to probe into this question more deeply in order to gain a better understanding of what happened and to improve our approach to development in the future. Several different explanations are possible, and can be combined in various ways. Generally speaking, reductions of the import coefficient have not stemmed from a long-term policy designed to push economic development beyond the limits set by the growth of exports and external financial resources. Rather, they have been due to measures adopted at the dictates of circumstance to counteract external disequilibria. In other words, the import coefficient is not normally reduced as a farsighted measure

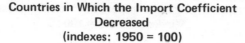

# FIGURE 5

Countries in Which the Import Coefficient
Decreased
(indexes: 1950 = 100)

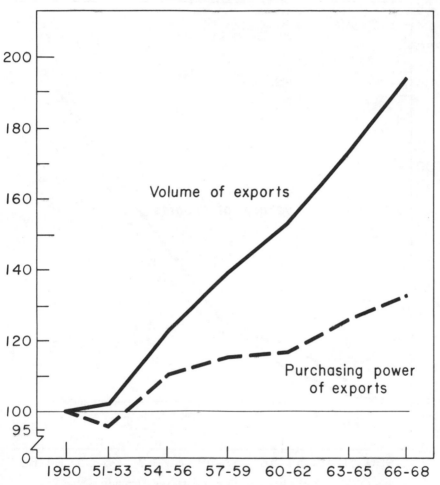

*Source:* ECLA, on the basis of official data; see Appendix Table 5.

when exports are booming—that is, when more resources are available for investment—but during slumps, when exports drop or falter, and countries find themselves constrained to take steps to restrict imports in order to correct external imbalances.

It is hardly surprising, then, that the relatively satisfactory growth rate of export earnings and other external resources in the second group of countries has in a sense weakened the incentive to import substitution.

**FIGURE 6**

**Countries in Which the Import Coefficient Increased**
**(indexes: 1950 = 100 )**

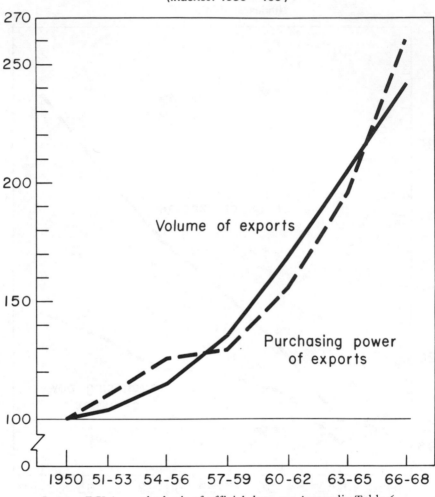

*Source:* ECLA, on the basis of official data; see Appendix Table 6.

Moreover, a question to be asked is how far import substitution can be carried in countries such as those in the second group, which have relatively small markets and where consumption of manufactures—as in most of the Latin American countries—is confined largely to the upper and middle income strata.

Lastly, import substitution, and the growth rate in general, also depend to a large extent on the supply of natural resources and the rate of capital formation. Here again, despite the greater inflow of external financial resources, the rate of capital formation has been somewhat lower in the second group of countries. This is a point to which we shall return later.

The foregoing considerations raise a problem which is of the greatest importance for development strategy, but which it is not relevant to consider at the moment. We shall now see how the factors described above affect the growth of the product in various Latin American countries. For this purpose, we shall return to Table 13 and also refer to Figures 7-18, which present separate data on the nine countries considered individually.

### Countries in Which the Import Coefficient Decreased

Let us begin with the countries in which the import coefficient was reduced. They exhibit a wide variety of situations. At one extreme are the countries where the annual growth rate of the product was higher than 6 percent over the period 1950-1968, namely, Brazil, Mexico, and Venezuela; at the other extreme comes Uruguay, whose product grew more slowly than its population; and Argentina and Colombia fall roughly halfway between the two.

Particularly striking is the case of Brazil (see Figure 7). Its product grew at an average annual rate of 6.1 percent, despite very unfavorable external conditions. The deterioration of its terms of trade held down the average annual growth rate of its exports' purchasing power to 0.9 percent, even though their volume expanded at a rate of 3.3 percent. Furthermore, the growth of external financial resources was rarely if ever sufficient to offset the slow rate at which the purchasing power of exports increased. Hence, Brazil's total supply of external resources to cover its import needs grew at an average annual rate of barely 1.1 percent.

In order to combat such adverse external conditions, Brazil pursued a very active import-substitution policy which, by giving a vigorous boost to domestic production, helped to overcome the barrier of the capacity to import and added 5 percent to the overall rate of development. Despite its intensity, however, as explained above, the import-substitution process did not suffice to provide employment in the industry group for the manpower moving away from agriculture.

Brazil's terms of trade have improved recently, owing to the rise in coffee prices. Hence, in this respect its future prospects appear to be favorable, although its sustained effort to expand its exports of manufactures is understandable in any event. The import coefficient has now fallen to a very low level—5.5 percent in 1966-1968—and whether Brazil can continue to reduce it as in the past is very doubtful. Moreover, reducing the import coefficient would not suffice to raise the growth rate of the product to levels such that the economy could gradually gain the additional dynamism still required.

Mexico's gross product (see Figure 8) grew at an average annual rate of 6.3 percent during the period 1950-1968—slightly faster than Brazil's. But there are significant differences between the two countries. Most important, Mexico's terms of trade deteriorated much less: the volume of its exports of goods and

# FIGURE 7

## Development of Brazil
### (indexes: 1950 = 100)

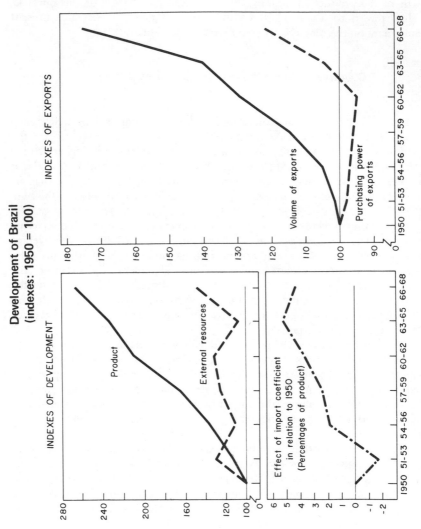

*Source:* ECLA, on the basis of official data; see Appendix Table 7.

60

**FIGURE 8**

**Development of Mexico**
**(indexes: 1950 = 100)**

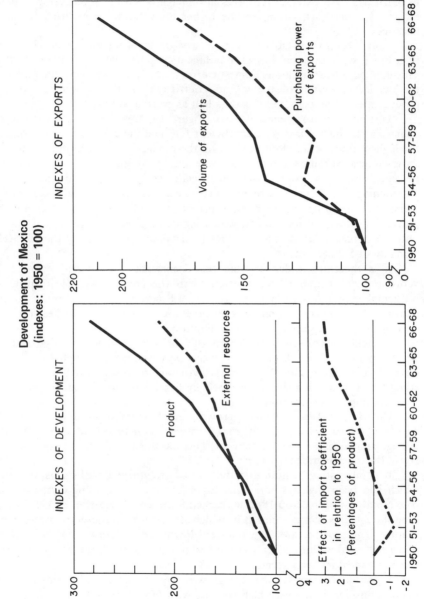

INDEXES OF EXPORTS

Volume of exports

Purchasing power
of exports

INDEXES OF DEVELOPMENT

Product

External resources

Effect of import coefficient
in relation to 1950
(Percentages of product)

*Source:* ECLA, on the basis of official data; see Appendix Table 8.

services expanded at an average annual rate of 4.4 percent, while their purchasing power rose at a rate of 3.3 percent, that is, much more rapidly than in Brazil. Its total external resources also increased faster (at an average annual rate of 4.2 percent), owing to the higher growth rate of external financial resources.

Thus, Mexico was able to achieve a slightly higher rate of development than Brazil without being forced to reduce its import coefficient so drastically. This implied a less strenuous domestic effort, which explains why the effect of the smaller reduction of the import coefficient on the growth rate of the product was 2.5 percent, i.e., less than half as great as in Brazil.

Turning now to Venezuela (see Figure 9), the third in this group of countries in which the import coefficient fell, and the country which achieved the highest rates of development during the period considered, we find that its gross domestic product grew at the same average annual rate as Mexico's (6.3 percent). But the course of Venezuela's development and the factors determining it are very different. Venezuela's terms of trade deteriorated, owing to the drop in petroleum prices, and this seriously affected the purchasing power of its exports, which increased at an average annual rate of only 1.5 percent, despite the fact that their volume expanded at the relatively high rate of 5.6 percent.

It is therefore understandable that Venezuela, like Brazil, pursued an active policy of import substitution, with the growth rate of its product outstripping that of external resources by 4.8 percent. This and other factors explain why Venezuela is one of the three countries with the highest rates of development in the group under consideration.

As will have been noted from this brief review, the average rate of development of these three countries has been similar, although trends have differed (see Figure 10). While the growth rate of the product has shown a rising trend in Mexico, it has declined in Brazil and Venezuela, despite their intensive import-substitution efforts.

Up to 1960-1962, Mexico's growth rate fluctuated around 5.5 percent, subsequently soaring so rapidly that between 1960-1962 and 1966-1968 the average annual figure was 7.5 percent. This was due mainly to the considerable rise in the investment coefficient.

It is interesting to note that the rate of growth of Brazil's gross product, which had been slightly more than 6 percent at the beginning of the period, rose rapidly until in 1960-1962 it reached 8 percent, in relation to 1957-1959, even though this was the period in which its terms of trade deteriorated most sharply. The growth rate then plunged downward in 1963-1965, when there was a net outflow instead of a net inflow of external financial resources. After that it resumed its rising trend.

It should be stressed that the growth rate of Venezuela's product in the period considered was very high to start with (approximately 9 percent), but subsequently dwindled until by 1960-1962 it was less than 4 percent in relation to 1957-1959. Later it recovered somewhat, and leveled off at about 5 percent. These trends were due mainly to the deterioration of the terms of trade and the decrease in the growth rate of the volume of exports.

# FIGURE 9

## Development of Venezuela
### (indexes: 1950 = 100)

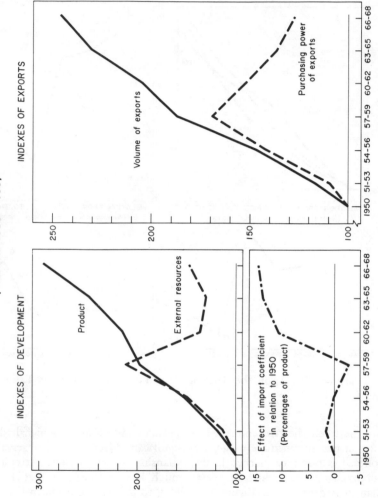

INDEXES OF DEVELOPMENT

INDEXES OF EXPORTS

Product

External resources

Volume of exports

Purchasing power
of exports

Effect of import coefficient
in relation to 1950
(Percentages of product)

*Source:* ECLA, on the basis of official data; see Appendix Table 9.

FIGURE 10

**Brazil, Mexico, and Venezuela: Growth
Rates of Product**

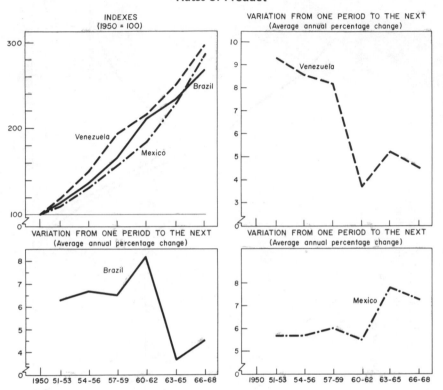

*Source*: ECLA, on the basis of official data; see Appendix Tables 7, 8, 9, and 10.

Between the two countries—Argentina and Colombia—which had growth rates in the intermediate range, very significant differences are observable. The contrast is not very marked in the expansion of exports, but extremely so in purchasing power, which increased much less in Colombia (see Figure 11) than in Argentina (see Figure 12), owing to the deterioration in the terms of trade. Nevertheless, Colombia's product grew more rapidly than Argentina's. Its external resources expanded faster than those of Argentina, owing to the inflow of funds from abroad; and in addition, Argentina reduced its import coefficient less, perhaps because it had done so to a greater extent in earlier periods.

The figures tell the story: the average annual growth rate of Colombia's product was 4.7 percent, while that of Argentina's product was 3.1 percent. The purchasing power of the two countries' exports grew at rates of 1.3 and 2.9 percent, respectively, and the volume of their exports at rates of 3.5 and

**FIGURE 11**

**Development of Colombia**
**(indexes: 1950 = 100)**

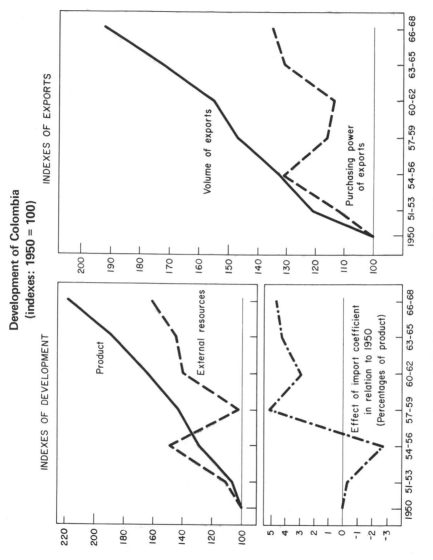

*Source:* ECLA, on the basis of official data; see Appendix Table 11.

65

**FIGURE 12**

**Development of Argentina**
**(indexes: 1950 = 100)**

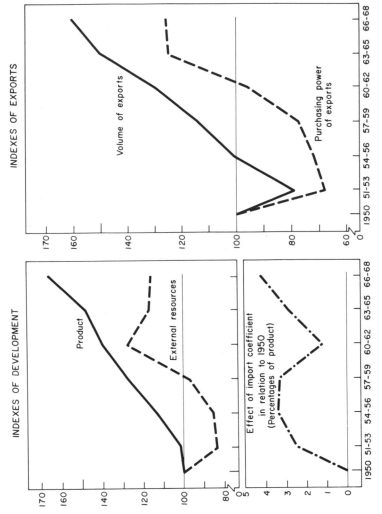

*Source:* ECLA, on the basis of official data; see Appendix Table 12.

3.8 percent. These figures bear witness to the appreciable effect of the deterioration in the terms of trade.

If we look at the factors that enabled Colombia's product to grow more rapidly, we find that its external resources increased at an average annual rate of 2.4 percent, much faster than the purchasing power of its exports (1.3 percent), while the growth rate of Argentina's external resources was barely 2 percent—slower than that of the purchasing power of its exports (2.9 percent).

As a result of the reduction in the import coefficient—attributable to the internal import-substitution effort—Colombia's product grew 2.3 percent faster than its external resources, the corresponding figure for Argentina being only 1.2 percent.

Uruguay (see Figure 13) is a unique case among all the countries considered. External resources, although fluctuating markedly, showed a clearly declining trend, falling on average by 1.3 percent annually. That this sustained decline did not pull the gross domestic product down with it is due to the reduction of the import coefficient. It would seem that this resulted from the expansion of existing import-saving industries rather than from the establishment of new ones.

In any event, it is remarkable that in a country with such a small market the reduction of the import coefficient meant that the growth rate of the product outstripped that of external resources by 2.5 percent, when in Argentina's case the corresponding difference was barely 1.2 percent. Probably—as in the other instances—the way this process has taken place in the two countries would need to be studied in greater depth.

Thus, by reducing its import coefficient, Uruguay was able to offset the adverse effect of the declining rate of increase of external resources on the growth of its product. Even so, the growth in question was very weak (an average annual rate of 1.3 percent). Moreover, this was only in the early part of the period considered, as is clear from Figure 14. The growth rate subsequently fell sharply, owing mainly to the marked contraction in the volume of exports and the still more marked decline in their purchasing power. From 1957-1959 onward, the rate of growth of the product was negligible, and between 1957-1959 and 1966-1968 the per capita product decreased by an average of 1.1 percent annually. Added to this is the fact that up to 1966-1968, exports had not managed to recover their initial level—the level attained before the growth rate plunged—in terms of volume, 'much less of purchasing power. The volume of exports remained stationary throughout the period, and their purchasing power fell at an average annual rate of 0.8 percent, owing to the deterioration in the terms of trade. As noted above, the average decline in external resources was even greater.

### Countries in Which the Import Coefficient Did Not Decrease

Let us now consider the countries in the second group. In seven out of the ten, the purchasing power of exports grew more slowly than their volume. Only in Bolivia and Chile did it rise faster, owing to the improvement in the terms of

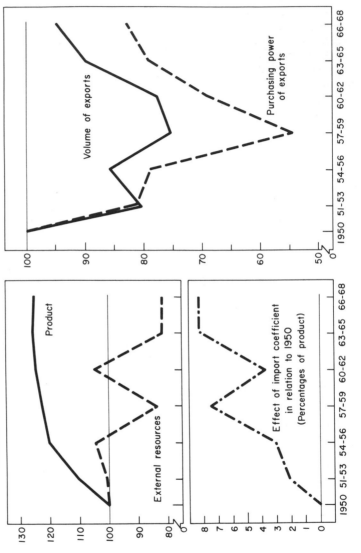

**FIGURE 13**

**Development of Uruguay**
**(indexes: 1950 = 100)**

INDEXES OF DEVELOPMENT

Product

External resources

Effect of import coefficient
in relation to 1950
(Percentages of product)

INDEXES OF EXPORTS

Volume of exports

Purchasing power
of exports

*Source:* ECLA, on the basis of official data; see Appendix Table 13.

# FIGURE 14

## Argentina, Colombia, and Uruguay: Growth Rates of Product

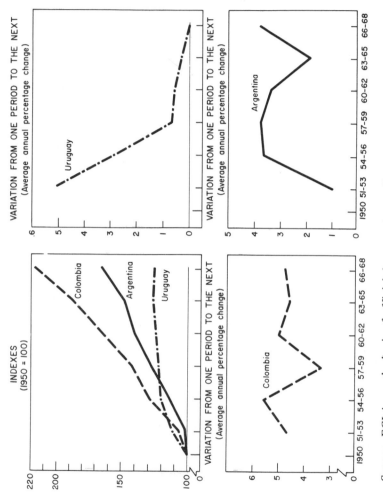

*Source:* ECLA, on the basis of official data; see Appendix Tables 11, 12, 13, and 14.

69

trade. In Peru, the purchasing power of exports increased almost as fast as the volume of exports, and both grew with exceptional rapidity.

Let us take Chile and Peru first. In Chile (see Figure 15), exports expanded at an average annual rate of 3.5 percent in volume and 4.8 percent in terms of purchasing power, owing to the rise in the price of copper. Furthermore, as a result of the inflow of external financial resources, the average annual growth rate of total external resources reached 6 percent, a much higher level than in any of the countries in the first group. However, Chile's product expanded at a rate of only 4.3 percent. The relatively high rate of expansion of external resources made it possible for imports to grow faster than the product, and hence the import coefficient rose rather than fell, with the result that the annual growth rate of the product was 1.8 percent less than that of the capacity to import.

In Peru (see Figure 16) the average rate of development was more vigorous than in Chile. The product grew at an average annual rate of 5.6 percent, which was appreciably lower than the average annual increase of 8 percent in the purchasing power of exports. Total external resources, however, grew at a somewhat slower pace: an average annual rate of 7.6 percent, which is quite satisfactory if compared with the figure for the region as a whole. As in Chile's case, Peru's imports increased faster than its product, and the average annual growth rate of the product was approximately 2 percent lower than that of external resources.

Owing to shortage of time, it unfortunately was not possible to consider all the countries of the second group in this brief analysis. Guatemala's is the only other case we can pause to examine in any detail (see Figure 17). The average annual growth rate of Guatemala's exports was very high (8.2 percent), but owing to the deterioration in the terms of trade the increase in the purchasing power of exports was only 5.2 percent per annum. And although total external resources expanded at an annual rate of 6.2 percent, as a result of the inflow of external financial resources, the product grew at a rate of only 4.5 percent, with imports rising at a faster pace. The increase in this import coefficient is reflected in the average difference of 1.7 percent annually between the growth rates of external resources and of the product.

Some brief comments are now in order on the trends of the growth rates of these three countries, which are shown in Figure 18. It will be seen that in Chile and Peru the average annual growth rates of the product, in any given three-year period in relation to the preceding one, fluctuate around a horizontal line, and that the fluctuations appear to be linked with the movement of external resources. In Guatemala, in contrast, the rate shows a rising trend, with a temporary fall which is also linked with the movement of external resources.

Another look at Table 13 will show that the average rates of development of Guatemala and Honduras are lower than those of the other Central American countries. Costa Rica and Panama, with 6.7 and 6.4 percent, respectively, had the highest rates not only in Central America but in the whole region. The rapid expansion of external resources enabled the product to increase at these relatively high rates, which were, however, lower than the growth rates of the resources in question.

**FIGURE 15**

**Development of Chile**
**(indexes: 1950 = 100)**

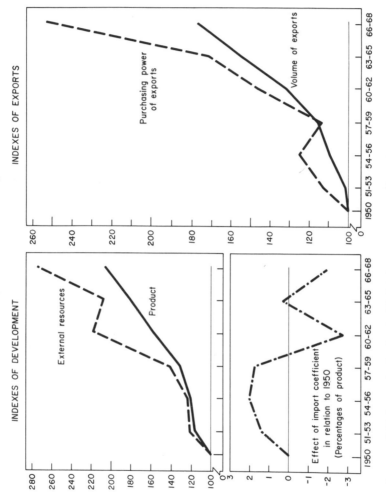

*Source:* ECLA, on the basis of official data; see Appendix Table 15.

## FIGURE 16

### Development of Peru
### (indexes: 1950 = 100)

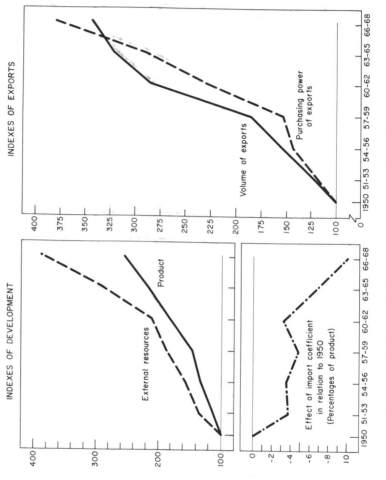

*Source:* ECLA, on the basis of official data; see Appendix Table 16.

72

**FIGURE 17**

**Development of Guatemala**
**(indexes: 1950 = 100)**

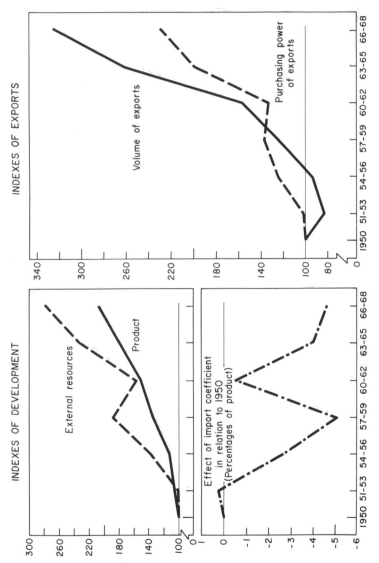

*Source:* ECLA, on the basis of official data; see Appendix Table 17.

73

## FIGURE 18

### Chile, Guatemala, and Peru: Growth
### Rates of Product

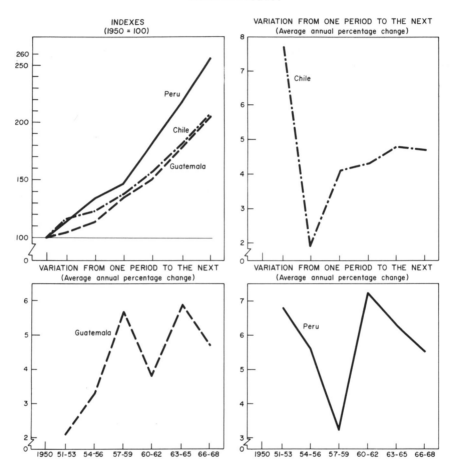

*Source*: ECLA, on the basis of official data; see Appendix Tables 15, 16, 17, and 18.

Nicaragua is the country in which external resources expanded most rapidly, because its average rate of export growth was also very high—the highest in the region. Its exports increased by 8.7 percent, and its external resources by 10.6 percent. And yet its product rose more slowly, although still at a relatively fast pace (6 percent annually). El Salvador's growth rate was somewhat lower (5.6 percent), and its external resources also grew less rapidly.

It would be very interesting to examine the influence the Central American Common Market has had on the pace of export expansion and also on the import coefficient. The figures given in Table 13 show the overall coefficient for each country; if all the members of the Central American Common Market had been taken as a group, however, the coefficient would probably have risen less rapidly or might even have fallen as a result of the development of intra-area trade.

The growth rates of the remaining countries shown in Table 13 differ a great deal. The average annual increases were 4.7 percent in Ecuador, 4.5 percent in the Dominican Republic, 3.5 percent in Paraguay, and 2 percent in Bolivia. In all these countries, external resources grew more rapidly than the product and the import coefficient increased. This poses a question which merits some study: how far can countries of this size benefit from expanding their exports without being satisfactorily incorporated in a larger economic space? The same question may be raised with respect to the Central American countries, since, although they have joined forces, the group thus formed is still not large enough for them to be able to develop as effectively as they might in a broader setting.

## EXTERNAL FINANCIAL RESOURCES AND THE
## MOBILIZATION OF DOMESTIC RESOURCES

### An Unfulfilled Role

The time has now come to discuss a very controversial issue: exactly what the inflow of external financial resources has meant to Latin America. Precisely because of its debatable character, an attempt has been made here to analyze this question with completely dispassionate objectivity, in order to draw conclusions of positive value for development strategy.

It may be useful at the outset to recall what role external financial resources should play in development: a role which is two-sided, as noted in Chapter 1 of this study. On the one hand, the inflow of such resources should help to raise the coefficient of investment with domestic resources by gradual degrees, until such time as domestic resources suffice to cover all the investment required to sustain a satisfactory rate of growth. On the other hand, investment with external resources should help to relieve the external bottleneck, so that remittances abroad in respect of such investment, as well as the imports made necessary by growth itself, can be covered comfortably through export expansion and the reduction of the import coefficient.

The analysis made in this chapter clearly shows that external financial resources are not fulfilling their role in either of these two respects in Latin America. As can be seen from Figure 19, the coefficient of investment with domestic resources has not risen; on the contrary, it has fallen in the region as a whole, with only two out of the nine countries analyzed escaping this general trend. (See Appendix Figures 2-10 and Appendix Tables 20-28.) Nor have the right conditions been created to enable service payments to be covered with ease; instead, the burden of servicing has been increasing strikingly fast, except in one country in which it was already very heavy at the beginning of the period considered, and still is.

**FIGURE 19**

**Group of Countries Considered:
Investment with Domestic Resources, and Gross
Inflow of Foreign Capital
(percentages of product)**

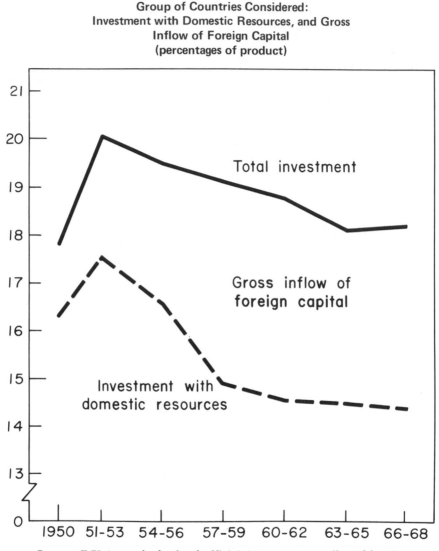

*Source:* ECLA, on the basis of official data; see Appendix Table 19.

This is all very serious, and affords clear evidence that the policy
pursued—if what has been done can be called a policy—has been ineffectual and
contradictory, at both the national and the international level. What has been
lacking on both sides is a combination of interrelated measures which would
have ensured that external financial resources had the positive effects described
above. This is not to say, however, that good use has not been made of these
resources, since they have been invested in infrastructure, in energy, in

agricultural improvements, and industrial plants, and also in health and education.

At the international level the contradictions are manifest. On the one hand, the burden of service payments, amortization, and transfers has grown considerably, now representing each year about 19 percent of the cumulative public debt. On the other hand, international trade policy has not been such as to stimulate export expansion in Latin America as a means of covering these costs. Furthermore, throughout the period under review the purchasing power of exports—except in two countries already mentioned—was seriously affected by the deterioration in the terms of trade.

It would be a want of impartiality to confine ourselves here to considering the contradictions at the international level. At the internal level, generally speaking, a greater effort could have been made to raise the domestic investment coefficient. It is true that the burden of remittances abroad, together with the effects of the deterioration in the terms of trade, has seriously limited the capacity to mobilize domestic resources. But it is equally undeniable that consumption has frequently overstepped the bounds within which it should have been contained in order to ensure that such outflows of resources did not preponderantly affect investment.

Moreover, few countries have taken positive steps to promote exports; on the contrary, on more than one occasion some of the measures adopted have had unfavorable effects. Equally serious is the fact that very little headway has been made in concerting the necessary industrial integration agreements with respect to goods which tend to be imported in greatly increasing volume as the rate of development climbs. This adds a further factor to those which have deprived the region of the financial elbow room which would have enabled the heavy burden of remittances abroad to be more easily borne.

What is needed, then, in order to step up the rate of development, is a fundamental change of policy and attitude, at both the national and the international level, and a series of convergent and properly interrelated measures.

In the context of this review of overall trends in Latin America as a whole, Figure 20 was prepared for the countries in the aggregate, while the appendix includes tables and figures relating to the two broad groups into which the countries have been divided, and to each of the nine republics studied individually (see Appendix Tables 30-40 and Appendix Figures 2-12).

The first point to note in Figure 20 is the steady decline in the ratio of domestic resources available for investment to the total product, which fell from 17.5 percent in 1950 to 14.5 percent in the period 1965-1968. The ratio of consumption to the product also decreased, although less rapidly.

As a general rule, when the proportion of investment resources falls, consumption rises, and vice versa. Why is it, then, that both these proportions declined during the period considered? The reason can be found in the top curve of Figure 20, representing the combined influence of two different components, both of which reduce the proportion of the gross product available for domestic consumption and investment: financial remittances abroad, and the effect of the terms of trade on the product.

As regards the first component, the share of financial remittances abroad rose steadily, until in the period 1965-1968 it represented 4.2 percent of the

FIGURE 20

## Group of Countries Considered:
### Financial Resources, Consumption and Investment
### (percentages of product)

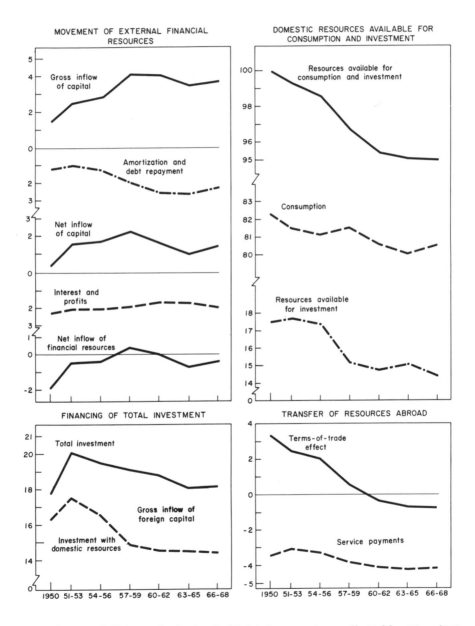

*Source:* ECLA, on the basis of official data; see Appendix Tables 19 and 29.

product. In the case of the terms of trade, the downward trend is clear in the early years of the period, is arrested in 1960-1962, and then turns slightly upward.

The combined influence of these two components accounts for the movement of the top curve, which represents the proportion of the gross product that they cause to be transferred abroad. In 1950 the gross product showed a slight improvement, since the positive terms-of-trade effect more than offset the outflow of financial remittances. Subsequently, however, the outflow of resources steadily increased, reaching a proportion of 5 percent of the total product in 1966-1968.*

It should now be noted how during this process the proportion of both consumption and domestic investment resources in the gross domestic product falls, the decline being more rapid in the case of investment resources. Evidence of this can be found in the per capita data presented in Table 14. Throughout the period considered, the regional product grew at an average annual rate of 2.2 percent; but the proportion available for consumption and investment increased at a lower rate (2 percent), owing to the outflow of resources. This increase was distributed very unevenly: while the growth rate of per capita consumption was 2.1 percent, domestic investment resources expanded at a rate of only 1.2 percent, i.e., much more slowly than the average per capita product.

This bears out what was said earlier. The steady decline in the coefficient of domestic investment resources cannot be attributed solely to the effect of external factors; it is also the result of what happens at the internal level. Given the region's relatively low per capita income, it is very easy to understand the difficulty of pursuing a policy designed to reduce the rate of growth of consumption—which is certainly not astronomical—in order to raise the growth rate of domestic investment resources.

Clearly, this is all the more difficult if the growth rate of the product is low. Were it stepped up, the possibilities of accelerating the growth of investment resources would increase in proportion, although suitable measures would have to be taken to turn these possibilities to good account.

This is precisely where external financial resources have an important role to play. If the inflow of such resources had been much greater and service payments much smaller—which would have helped to offset the unfavorable terms-of-trade effect—it would have been possible to speed up the growth rate of the product and thus raise the rate of increase of domestic investment resources.

It was noted earlier that the aggregate figures provide an initial idea of overall trends. We shall now look at the trends in the individual countries we have been able to consider, as shown in a series of very illustrative graphs (see

---

*In considering this and other graphs, it must be borne in mind that the notion of gains or losses on the terms of trade is purely relative; it depends on which year is chosen as the base year. What is important is the direction of the trend. The terms of trade deteriorated throughout most of the period considered in Latin America as a whole, although with substantial differences between countries. And whatever the base year chosen, the fact is that in countries where the terms of trade deteriorate, the amount of external resources available also declines.

## TABLE 14

### Latin America: Cumulative Annual Growth Rates of Resources for Consumption and Investment, 1950-1968
(percentage)

| | Gross Domestic Product | | Consumption | | Investment Resources* | | Resources for Investment and Consumption | |
|---|---|---|---|---|---|---|---|---|
| | Total | Per Capita | Total | Per Capita | Total | Per Capita | Total | Per Capita |
| *Latin America* | | | | | | | | |
| Including Venezuela | 5.2 | 2.2 | 5.1 | 2.1 | 4.1 | 1.2 | 4.9 | 2.0 |
| Excluding Venezuela | 5.2 | 2.2 | 5.1 | 2.1 | 5.0 | 2.0 | 5.0 | 2.0 |
| Argentina | 3.1 | 1.3 | 2.7 | 0.9 | 3.3 | 1.5 | 2.8 | 1.0 |
| Brazil | 6.1 | 3.0 | 6.1 | 3.0 | 5.1 | 2.0 | 5.9 | 2.8 |
| Chile | 4.2 | 1.7 | 4.6 | 2.1 | 1.0 | -1.4 | 4.1 | 1.6 |
| Colombia | 4.7 | 1.5 | 4.7 | 1.5 | 0.8 | -2.4 | 4.1 | 0.8 |
| Guatemala | 4.5 | 1.4 | 4.1 | 1.0 | 0.8 | -2.3 | 3.9 | 0.7 |
| Mexico | 6.3 | 2.9 | 6.0 | 2.6 | 6.2 | 2.8 | 6.1 | 2.7 |
| Peru | 5.6 | 2.9 | 5.7 | 3.0 | 4.0 | 1.4 | 5.4 | 2.7 |
| Uruguay | 1.2 | -0.2 | 1.8 | 0.4 | -4.7 | -6.0 | 0.7 | -0.7 |
| Venezuela | 6.3 | 2.4 | 6.5 | 2.6 | 2.7 | -1.1 | 5.5 | 1.6 |
| *Other countries* | 4.9 | 2.0 | 4.9 | 2.0 | 2.3 | -0.6 | 4.6 | 1.7 |

*Saving net of external payments and available for investment.

*Source:* ECLA, on the basis of official statistics.

Appendix Figures 2-10). Obviously, more thorough study would be required to determine the part played by domestic factors, in addition to the incidence of the outflow of financial resources; but such an analysis would have taken us outside the scope of the present report.

Suffice it to say here that only Mexico and Argentina were unaffected by the general downward trend of the coefficient of domestic investment resources. In these two countries, it was consumption that took the impact of the outflow of funds, and its ratio to the product declined, although more sharply in Mexico than in Argentina.

As Table 14 shows, in Mexico the annual growth rate of per capita consumption during the period considered was 2.6 percent, while investment resources expanded at an annual rate of 2.8 percent. The corresponding figures for Argentina are 0.9 and 1.5 percent, respectively.

In all the other countries examined, the decrease in the coefficient of domestic investment resources was very marked, in contrast with the rise in the consumption coefficient. Moreover, except in Brazil and Peru, per capita consumption increased while per capita investment declined.

### Financial Movements in the
### External Sector

This brings us to the earlier graphs describing financial movements. It should first be noted (see Figure 20) that the ratio of the gross inflow of foreign capital to the gross domestic product rose rapidly during the initial years of the period, up to 1957-1959; it then began to decline gradually, although later it recovered some of the ground lost.

In addition, as the gross inflow of capital rose, outflows in respect of amortization and transfers increased much more rapidly in relation to the gross product. Hence the net inflow of capital was substantially reduced, amounting throughout the period to an average of 1.6 percent of the gross domestic product.

What is more, the volume of remittances of profits and interest abroad remained at a high level. And if these sums—plus amortization and transfers—are deducted, the net inflow of external financial resources shrinks to a very small proportion of the product. Most serious of all is the fact that this proportion, after rising up to 1957-1959, then fell sharply to a minus figure. On average, the net inflow of resources was a minus figure throughout the period, representing -0.4 of the product (see Figure 20).

In order to avoid any misinterpretation, it is worthwhile to note that payments in respect of interest and profits were taken into account in considering the total outflow of resources and its adverse effects on domestic investment resources. Hence it would not be right to count them twice. The purpose of calculating the net inflow of financial resources is to show the small contribution such resources have made toward overcoming the external barrier to the growth of the product, to which reference was made at the beginning of this chapter.

Looking at the matter from a different standpoint, it is of interest to note that the deterioration in the terms of trade was to some extent offset by a relative improvement in the net inflow of financial resources. This would seem to indicate that the need for external credit increases when the terms of trade deteriorate and decreases when they improve. It is clear from the graphs, however, that throughout the period the percentage represented by the net inflow of financial resources was much less than the effect of the deterioration in the terms of trade since 1950.

The significance of the net inflow of external financial resources was outlined above. It is, of course, an important component in a country's balance of payments; but its variations do not provide a satisfactory basis for measuring its incidence on the balance of payments, since external financial resources may have exerted a favorable influence on exports and on import-saving industries. And this influence cannot be measured, both because investment with domestic resources in such activities has also been important, and because there are other forms of investment with similar although indirect effects, such as investment in infrastructure.

Since it is usually argued that total service and amortization payments should be compared with the purchasing power of exports and the effect of a reduction of the import coefficient, we have made the foregoing calculation despite the fact that there is no strict relationship between these variables, as has just been shown. However, the value of the operation lies in demonstrating that the region is not in a position to cover its remittances abroad with ease—quite the reverse, as can be seen in Figure 21. The relation between total external resources and the value of exports is also presented in Appendix Figure 13.

It is evident that the relative weight of such remittances increased substantially in the period under review. Whereas in 1950 they represented 17.7 percent of the purchasing power of exports plus the effect of the net reduction of the import coefficient,* by 1966-1968 this proportion had risen to 22.1 percent.

All this supports what was said at the beginning of the present chapter and, moreover, justifies the concern that has been aroused by this problem and the decision to seek satisfactory ways and means of solving it. The question of foreign capital should be viewed from the standpoint of the balance of payments in a broader context. It would be easy to cite a number of cases in which foreign capital has had a favorable impact in this respect; but there are also others in which its influence has clearly been negative. Among these latter, the most important consist in take-overs by foreign interests of enterprises which, besides being in national hands, use technologies that are already well-known or easily accessible. What happens in such cases is that the profits

---

*The net reduction in the import coefficient is more intensive than the gross reduction, since the net figure is obtained by deducting from imports that portion which corresponds to gross capital inflows. Thus, the decrease is greater in the net than in the gross coefficient, and its effects are even more marked than those discussed elsewhere. Apart from being the correct procedure, this method has the merit of providing a basis of comparison which gives less relative weight to the burden of remittances.

# FIGURE 21

### Relative Burden of Financial Service Payments
### (financial service payments as a percentage
### of purchasing power of exports plus effect
### of net decrease in import coefficient)

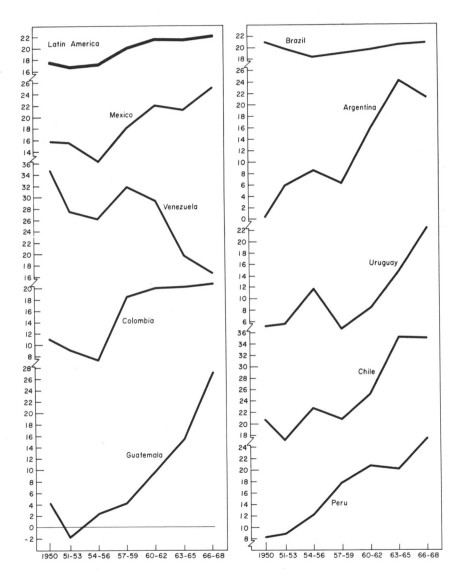

*Source:* ECLA, on the basis of official data.

which formerly remained in the country are transferred abroad, and the burden of remittances is increased. Furthermore, as the take-over usually brings with it an increase in efficiency, profits are bigger. Obviously, it is essential to increase efficiency, but there are other ways of doing so, in particular the gradual stepping-up of competition to which we have referred elsewhere.

It could be argued that the resources the national enterprise receives in respect of the take-over could be invested in export-producing or import-saving activities. But if there are national enterprises capable of such activities and lacking some of the necessary capital, it is preferable to give them the support of international loans with lengthy amortization periods and at rates of interest lower than the likely profits, if enough domestic resources are not available.

It may perhaps be justifiable for profits to be bigger if they represent not only a return on the capital used but also payment for a technology which a country does not yet have at its disposal and which it needs for development purposes. And I use the word "technology" here in its broadest sense, covering not only production techniques but also the organization of the enterprise and knowledge of external markets. From this standpoint, private foreign investment in certain export activities may be very useful, as regards both extraregional and intraregional exports, especially of those goods for which demand grows rapidly with development and for which complex technologies are required that for the moment are not accessible. In such cases, the best course would be association with Latin American enterprise. But let us not anticipate what is to be said in a later chapter.

## THE DISTORTION OF THE OCCUPATIONAL STRUCTURE
## AND THE RATE OF DEVELOPMENT

In the preceding section of this study it has been argued that Latin America's rate of economic development has not been high enough to allow the outflow of redundant manpower from agriculture to be absorbed at a satisfactory level of productivity, and at the same time to ensure a rapid rise in average per capita income throughout the economy. In addition, some account has been given of the principal internal and external factors by which this lack of the required degree of dynamism is determined.

This done, an attempt will now be made to ascertain the nature and intensity of the effort that will have to be put forth over a given period in order to cure the Latin American economy of so serious a weakness.

A word of warning at the outset: the purpose of this analysis is not to formulate a Latin American strategy. Development strategy and whatever plans may give it concrete expression are the business of each nation, although this does not preclude their coordination with a view to the attainment of objectives common to all the Latin American countries. The aim pursued here is to form some idea of the problem and of the dimensions of the components of strategy, as well as of the part played in the whole process by the various sectors of the economy.

The components of strategy referred to are relevant for all the Latin American countries, notwithstanding the great intercountry diversity of conditions and differences of kind and degree in the structural obstacles to the acceleration of development. Hence the pains that have been taken in preparing and analyzing the relevant background material. It has not been an easy task, owing partly to the familiar statistical deficiences and partly to the methodological complications implicit in such an exposition. But it was worth undertaking, especially just at this time of grave uncertainties as to the development of the Latin American countries in the coming years.

The point of departure of the present chapter is the distortion in the structure of the labor force imputable to the economy's lack of the required degree of dynamism. The correction of this anomaly alone would have very significant effects. In order to highlight these, the assumption first adopted was that during the corrective process the rate of increase of the product per

85

worker, both in agriculture and in the industry group,* would remain the same as in the past. In the space of 10 years, merely by getting rid of the distortion in the structure of employment, the rate of economic growth could be raised to 7 percent. The analysis of this first hypothesis will be followed by consideration of a second objective, consisting not only in correcting the occupational distortion but also in speeding up the rate of increase of the average product per worker. This would enable a growth rate of 8 percent to be reached by the end of the 1970's.

It must be stated at the outset that these postulates are not in the nature of forecasts, but are dictated by the need to analyze the problem under discussion methodically and in depth. The end pursued is not scientific investigation—although this is by no means to be disparaged—but is essentially pragmatic, as will be seen in the later sections of this chapter.

In order to examine the first objective—i.e., the correction of the distortion in the structure of employment—a point of reference must be taken. It will be recalled that according to estimates, the proportion of manpower absorbed by the industry group has declined from 35 percent of the total nonagricultural labor force in 1950 to 31.8 percent in 1965 and a little under 30 percent today. The point of reference, therefore, would be the industry group's recovery—through absorption of the assumed outflow of redundant manpower from the agricultural sector—of its 1950 share (35 percent), which could subsequently be increased.

No special significance should be attached to this proportion. It would merely be one of the milestones on the road of development, and this should be made clear from the start. At the stages when this milestone is reached and then passed, a pause will be made to review the effects on the economy as a whole. There is no question of retracing the same course as in the past, for a different significance would attach to the percentage of the nonagricultural labor force working in the industry group. Although it would be the same as in 1950, it would represent a much bigger proportion of the total labor force than it did then, and average per capita income would have increased considerably, with favorable effects on genuine employment in the services sector. Thus, it is not a mechanical exercise that has been undertaken, but a method of analysis which will allow us to consider the different components of our problem one by one.

The time factor is, of course, very important. This process of remedying the lack of the required dynamism is envisaged as extending over the decade just beginning and the next, or, in other words, taking the same length of time as is covered by the analysis of the distortion in the structure of employment. By the end of the 1970's there would be substantial improvements, which would be consolidated in the 1980's. The effort required would be great, in respect of both capital formation and foreign trade, especially in the first of the two decades. Other hypotheses might be formulated on the basis of different time limits, or introducing different assumptions. This would undoubtedly have

---

*A reminder may be useful here. This term is applied to the group of activities which includes industry proper, construction, and mining.

to be done if the object in view was the designing of a national strategy, so that various options could be put before the decision-makers. In the present report, for reasons of simplicity, it would be unwarranted.

It was stated earlier that the industry group's recovery of its 1950 share in the nonagricultural labor force would be the point in the development process at which we should pause to review the results. As capital formation proceeded and permitted the progressive absorption of the redundant labor force, the average annual growth rate of the aggregate product of the economy would gradually increase, until by the end of the 1970's it had reached 7 percent. In 1950-1965, as already stated, it was 5.2 percent.

This fact is highly significant, since the foregoing hypothesis is based on the assumption that the growth rate of the product per worker in agriculture and in the industry group would be no higher than before.

How would it be possible to attain an average rate of 7 percent, signifying an average annual increase of 3.9 percent in per capita product for the economy as a whole? This is a vital point, for in the past, with the same growth rates of the product per worker in agriculture and the industry group, the corresponding average rate was only 2.5 percent. How could much higher rates for the economy in the aggregate be reached? In brief outline, the explanation is as follows. This substantial increase in the growth rate is attributable precisely to the gradual correction of the distortion in the structure of employment. The overflow of redundant manpower from agricultural activities, instead of simply pouring into the services sector, would be drawn into the industry group, where the average product per worker is much higher than in agriculture. Moreover, as the considerable volume of redundant manpower at present existing in the services sector was reduced, here too the product per worker would increase. Hence it is that by the end of the 1970's the product per active person in all these nonagricultural activities works out to be 3.2 times as high as in agriculture. The switch-over of manpower from activities in which the product per worker is low to others in which it is much higher suffices, therefore, to bring about an appreciable improvement in the average growth rate of the economy as a whole, even in the absence of any change in the rates formerly recorded for agriculture and the industry group.

The foregoing assumptions, on which the hypothesis of a growth rate of 7 percent is based, were formulated solely in order to show the remarkable effects of the productive absorption of manpower. In actual fact, however, they would be unlikely to materialize, for as production of goods and services increased in response to the expansion of demand, the product per worker would tend to rise faster than in the past.

It is worth reflecting upon the income that has been lost to the Latin American economy through the enormous waste of human potential and the time that has been irrecoverably thrown away in the course of a development process marked by insufficient dynamism: as long a time—in the life of a generation—as will be required to remedy this serious defect.

The importance of all this is great, inasmuch as it involves one of the keys to the acceleration of development. In the long run, the growth of the product per worker generally depends upon increasing capital formation and upon the technical training of the labor force in the broadest sense of the term. As the capital/worker ratio rises, labor is saved and new labor-absorbing investment has to be effected. Accordingly, investment requirements are twofold: investment to economize on manpower and investment to reemploy it.

This does not apply to the case under consideration, which is typical of the stage of development through which Latin America is passing. The outflow of redundant manpower from the agricultural sector is not necessarily a consequence of labor-saving investment, but results from population growth, changes in the composition of demand, and more efficient land use. Capital is not a major requisite for the generation of this redundant manpower, except when mechanized farming is introduced. But capital is needed in order to absorb it. The same is true of the other activities: more efficient utilization of the production resources available means that with little—or relatively little—additional capital the product per worker can be increased. But if no overall expansion of demand were to take place, still more redundant manpower would be generated, and its absorption would call for more intensive investment of capital. In other words, in Latin America there is a considerable productivity potential which is frustrated, so to speak, and which must be turned to account in order to speed up the rate of development.

Let us now take a look at other aspects of this question. If a 7 percent growth rate of the product were reached by the end of the first decade and maintained during the second, it would represent a considerable increase in demand in the various sectors of the economy. Agriculture, thanks to the expansion of production to satisfy this greater demand, would need to retain a larger labor force than in the past. In 1950-1965, the agricultural labor force seems to have increased at an average annual rate of 1.5 percent. By the end of the first decade this rate would have climbed to 2.7 percent; but later, toward the end of the second decade, it would fall to 2.1 percent, inasmuch as with the rise in income levels the income elasticity of demand for agricultural products would presumably decrease.

This calculation is of the greatest interest, since it shows that if the growth rate of the product were raised to 7 percent by the mere correction of the occupational distortion and the ensuing effects on the various sectors, the rate of retention of workers in agriculture would be higher than before. This fact is socially meaningful, since it is assumed that the product per worker in the agricultural sector would continue to increase at the same rate as in the past. Would this be a desirable assumption, from the standpoint of the social integration of the rural masses?

The average annual rate of increase of the product per worker in agriculture was not negligible in the past (2.2 percent). But except in a few cases it does not seem to have brought about a correlative improvement in the income of the rural population. To that end, an indispensable requisite—apart from other measures—would be the reform of the land tenure system. This would be important enough in itself. But if the aim was to accelerate the social integration process, the former growth rate of the agricultural product per worker would have to be outstripped.

In reality, it would seem that agriculture could hardly make the vigorous production effort required for the satisfaction of demand unless such an acceleration of the growth rate of the product per worker were achieved by means of more rational land use and improved techniques. It is therefore assumed, in this new approach, that the rate in question will gradually rise from 2.2 percent to 4 percent by the end of the first decade, and will remain at that level during the 1980's.

The more effort is made to step up the product per worker in this way, however, the less will be the labor-retaining capacity of agriculture. And the exodus from the agricultural sector will increase. The dilemma is obvious. Given the expansion of demand which the first hypothesis postulates, if the object is to retain more manpower in agriculture, it will not be practicable to improve upon the former growth rate of the product per worker. And if such an improvement is the aim pursued, more intensive retention of manpower will not be feasible. The two objectives cannot be attained together.

Clearly, a smaller exodus of agricultural workers simplifies the problem of absorption of manpower in the industry group, with very significant but far from fully satisfactory results. Agriculture will lag behind again, just as hitherto. Apart from income redistribution measures, the only way of accelerating its development is to raise the rate of increase of its product per worker.

If this were achieved, a much more intensive effort would have to be made to absorb manpower outside the agricultural sector than would be implied in reaching an average annual growth rate of 7 percent by the end of the first decade. Demand and employment in all the other sectors would have to expand considerably. And with respect to the industry group too, it is questionable whether such an expansion would be compatible with the assumption that there would be no change in the 3 percent rate of increase recorded for the product in these sectors in the past.

This again is an unlikely eventuality, for the upswing in demand—much sharper than before—and possibly brisker competition would encourage greater efforts to improve the average product per worker, which is accordingly assumed to increase by 4 percent per annum in the industry group as well. This is a somewhat arbitrary assumption, but it gives a clearer idea of the nature of the problem, and calls attention to the fact that the higher the growth rate of the product rises, the more energetic the absorption effort will have to be, since the outflow of redundant manpower from agriculture will be augmented by that resulting from higher productivity in the industry group.

Thus we arrive at a second angle of approach. If in agriculture and in the industry group the average annual growth rate of the product per worker gradually rose above its past level until by the end of the 1970's it reached 4 percent, the question is what rate of development would be attained when the greater absorption effort necessitated by this increase had been made.

If the new hypothesis were worked out on these bases—and, as in the previous approach, on the assumption that the distortion in the structure of employment would be corrected—the rate of development would gradually increase until by the end of the first decade it had risen to 8 percent, at which level it would remain during the second decade.

The next step is to compare the results of the two approaches. Both hypotheses would imply significant changes in the composition of demand. In the light of past experience in Latin America as a whole—which does not differ greatly from that of the developed countries at a similar stage in their growth process—demand for the goods produced by the industry group is liable to expand much faster than demand for agricultural products; and the position of services is midway between the two. These changes in demand, and the assumptions adopted with respect to the product per worker, account for the differing degrees of intensity with which manpower is absorbed outside agriculture.

Let us first examine the case of agriculture (see Table 15). In the 7 percent hypothesis—as it may be called for simplicity's sake—the rate at which employment increases is higher than in the past. In contrast, it is lower in the 8 percent hypothesis, for although the expansion of production is greater than when the rate of development is assumed to be 7 percent, its effects on employment are more offset by those of the rise in the product per worker.

What happens outside the agricultural sector will next be considered. In the past, the annual growth rate of the nonagricultural labor force was 3.5 percent. In the case of the 7 percent hypothesis, the retention of more workers in agriculture would keep that rate virtually the same during the 1970's and 1980's; whereas in the 8 percent hypothesis the average annual rate of increase of the nonagricultural labor force would be higher than before, reaching 3.9 percent in the two coming decades.

It is now worthwhile to ascertain how this nonagricultural labor force is distributed. It should be recalled that in the past the annual rate of absorption

## TABLE 15

### Latin America: Cumulative Annual Growth Rates of Aggregate Product, Product per Worker, and Labor Force in Agriculture
(percentage)

| | Hypotheses of Growth of Product* | | | | | |
|---|---|---|---|---|---|---|
| | Product | | | | Labor Force | |
| | Aggregate | | Per Worker | | | |
| Period | 7 Percent | 8 Percent | 7 Percent | 8 Percent | 7 Percent | 8 Percent |
| 1950-1965 | 3.8 | | 2.2 | | 1.5 | |
| 1979-1980 | 5.0 | 5.4 | 2.2 | 4.0 | 2.7 | 1.3 |
| 1989-1990 | 4.4 | 4.7 | 2.2 | 4.0 | 2.1 | 0.7 |

*Relating only to the periods 1979-1980 and 1989-1990.

Source: Latin American Institute for Economic and Social Planning.

in the industry group was barely 2.8 percent, hardly exceeding the total increase in the labor force. In the next two decades this rate would have to be substantially accelerated in order to correct the distortion in the structure of employment. This would happen in both the hypothetical cases considered, although naturally to a more marked extent on the 8 percent hypothesis. On this latter assumption, the rate in question would rise to 5.5 percent, while it would reach a slightly lower level (5.2 percent) if the rate of development were 7 percent.

At first glance the difference in the rates of absorption is much less than might have been supposed. The explanation can be inferred from Table 16. The product in the industry group, as might be expected, increases faster on the 8 percent than on the 7 percent hypothesis. But this is only partly reflected in employment, owing to the bigger increase in the product per worker.

Of no less interest is the evolution of services. It was pointed out earlier that a major proportion of the redundant manpower that could not be absorbed in the industry group ended up in the services sector. As was explained in that context, its absorption here was largely spurious rather than genuine, and overt unemployment was included under this head. Thus the labor force in services—taking into account its unemployed members—expanded at an annual rate of 3.8 percent in 1950-1965, when the total labor force increased

### TABLE 16

Latin America: Cumulative Annual Growth Rates of Aggregate Product,
Product per Worker, and Labor Force in the Industry Group
(Percentage)

| | Hypotheses of Growth of Product* | | | | Labor Force | |
|---|---|---|---|---|---|---|
| | Product | | | | | |
| | Aggregate | | Per Worker | | | |
| Period | 7 Percent | 8 Percent | 7 Percent | 8 Percent | 7 Percent | 8 Percent |
| 1950-1965 | 5.9 | | 3.0 | | 2.8 | |
| 1979-1980 | 8.3 | 9.7 | 3.0 | 4.0 | 5.2 | 5.5 |
| 1989-1990 | 8.3 | 9.7 | 3.0 | 4.0 | 5.2 | 5.5 |

*Note:* Industry group includes industry, construction, and mining.

*Relates only to the periods 1979-1980 and 1989-1990.

*Source:* Latin American Institute for Economic and Social Planning.

by only 2.6 percent. It is estimated that in the next two decades the average annual growth rate of the total labor force will be 3 percent,* owing to the rate of increase of the population.

In the case of the 7 percent hypothesis, the labor force in the services sector would expand more slowly than the total labor force, at rates of 2.3 and 2.4 percent in the 1970's and 1980's, respectively. Given the 8 percent hypothesis, on the other hand, it would increase faster than the total, at rates of 3.2 percent in the 1970's and 3.1 percent in the 1980's.

What does this estimate signify? Does it mean that the higher rate of development would aggravate the redundancy of manpower in the services sector? On no account. What would happen is that instead of this redundancy increasing as before, the more rapid growth of per capita income implied by the 8 percent rate would also speed up the expansion of those services in which employment tends to increase as development proceeds.

Nevertheless, as is shown in Table 17, the services sector would increase its labor force much less than its aggregate product, since it would gradually reabsorb its own redundant manpower, including the unemployed. Thus, the situation would be so far from resembling the position in the past that the average annual growth rate of the sectoral product per active person, which used to be very low (1.4 percent), would exceed 4 percent in the 1970's and 1980's.

The time has now come to look at our two hypotheses side by side, with the help of Table 18 and Figure 22, in which the evolution of the labor force in the next two decades, according to the projections formulated here, is compared with the trends recorded in the 1950's and 1960's.

As is always the case with projections of this type, the results depend upon the length of the time-span adopted. Some surprise may perhaps be occasioned by the fact that the period they cover here is as long as that considered in the analysis of past developments; but this—with due allowance for inevitable elements of arbitrary judgment—highlights the gravity of a situation which, because it was not dealt with in time, now makes a prolonged and strenuous effort essential.

Part A of Figure 22 shows the distribution of the economically active population among agricultural and nonagricultural activities. There are two curves for each of these concepts, one relating to the 7 percent and the other to the 8 percent hypothesis. For the reasons set forth above, agriculture's share of the labor force declines much more sharply if the second hypothesis is adopted. In 1950, agricultural workers accounted for 50.2 percent of the total labor force. By 1990 this proportion would be reduced to 28.1 percent in the case of the 8 percent hypothesis and to 34.5 percent if the rate of development is assumed to be 7 percent. It should be remembered that the estimates refer to Latin America as a whole.

---

*This projection, which is slightly higher than is usually the case, must be taken with some reservations. The rate may possibly be rather higher still if, as is likely, the proportion of female workers in the labor force increases; on the other hand, the progress of education might have the opposite effect by deferring the ingress of young people into the economically active population. But the incorporation of these factors would probably make no appreciable difference to the foregoing conclusions.

FIGURE 22

## Group of Countries Considered:
## Distribution of the Labor Force
## (percentages)

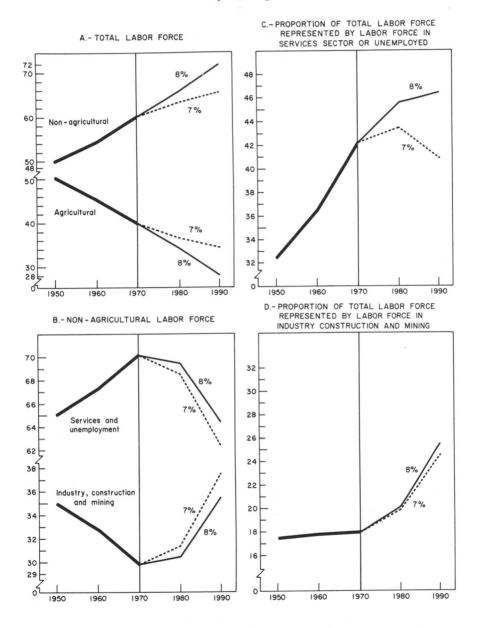

*Source:* ECLA, on the basis of official data.

## TABLE 17

### Latin America: Cumulative Annual Growth Rates of Aggregate Product, Product per Worker, and Labor Force in the Services Sector
(percentage)

| | Hypotheses of Growth of Product[a] | | | | | |
| | Product | | | | Labor Force[b] | |
| | Aggregate | | Per Worker | | | |
| Period | 7 Percent | 8 Percent | 7 Percent | 8 Percent | 7 Percent | 8 Percent |
|---|---|---|---|---|---|---|
| 1950-1965 | 5.3 | | 1.4 | | 3.8 | |
| 1979-1980 | 6.7 | 7.6 | 4.3 | 4.3 | 2.3 | 3.2 |
| 1989-1990 | 6.6 | 7.4 | 4.0 | 4.1 | 2.4 | 3.1 |

[a]Relating only to the periods 1979-1980 and 1989-1990.

[b]Overt unemployment is included under this head.

*Source:* Latin American Institute for Economic and Social Planning.


A glance may now be taken at the curves relating to the nonagricultural labor force in part B of Figure 22. Both hypotheses postulate a recovery in the industry group. As will be recalled, its share in the nonagricultural labor force, which was 35.0 percent in 1950, has gradually dwindled, to 31.8 percent in 1965 and, according to conjectural estimates, to about 30 percent at the present time. Given the 7 percent hypothesis, this proportion would rise again during the 1970's, until by the end of the decade it had approached the 1965 figure. The same rate of growth would have to be maintained until the end of the 1980's if the level reached in 1950 was to be slightly exceeded.

This gives a clear idea of the seriousness of what has been happening in Latin America. Raising the rate of development to 7 percent would entail exceptionally hard and unremitting effort. Yet this effort would have to be kept up for two decades—although more intensively in the 1970's than in the 1980's—in order to correct the distortion in the structure of employment.

A still more vigorous drive would have to be made to bring the rate of development up to 8 percent. In that case it would take rather longer to remedy the distortion in the occupational structure of the labor force (see Figure 22, part B). It would not be until 1990 that the industry group came to absorb a slightly larger proportion of the nonagricultural labor force than the 35 percent·that had fallen to its share in 1950.

## TABLE 18

### Latin America:  Growth and Distribution of Labor Force on Different Hypotheses of Growth of Product

| Period | Hypotheses of Growth of Product[a] | | | | | | | |
|---|---|---|---|---|---|---|---|---|
| | Agricultural | | Nonagricultural | | Industry Group | | Services[b] | |
| | 7 Percent | 8 Percent | 7 Percent | 8 Percent | 7 Percent | 8 Percent | 7 Percent | 8 Percent |
| *1. Cumulative Annual Growth Rate of Labor Force (percentage)* | | | | | | | | |
| 1950-1965 | 1.5 | | 3.5 | | 2.8 | | 3.8 | |
| 1979-1980 | 2.7 | 1.3 | 3.2 | 3.9 | 5.2 | 5.5 | 2.3 | 3.2 |
| 1989-1990 | 2.1 | 0.7 | 3.5 | 3.9 | 5.2 | 5.5 | 2.4 | 3.1 |
| *2. Distribution of Labor Force* | | | | | | | | |
| | *Percentage of Total Labor Force* | | | | *Percentage of Nonagricultural Labor Force* | | | |
| 1950 | 50.2 | | 49.8 | | 35.0 | | 65.0 | |
| 1965 | 43.1 | | 56.9 | | 31.8 | | 68.2 | |
| 1980 | 36.7 | 34.3 | 63.3 | 65.7 | 31.4 | 30.5 | 68.6 | 69.5 |
| 1990 | 34.5 | 28.1 | 65.5 | 71.9 | 37.5 | 35.5 | 62.5 | 64.5 |

[a]Relating only to the period 1979-1980 and the years 1980 and 1990. In the case of the 7 percent hypothesis, it is assumed that the cumulative annual growth rates of the product per worker in agriculture and in the industry group will remain the same as in 1950-1965, i.e., 2.24 and 2.97 percent, respectively. According to the 8 percent hypothesis, the above-mentioned rates climb upward from the figures recorded in the past, until by 1980 a cumulative annual rate of 4 percent is reached, which then remains constant between 1980 and 1990.

[b]Overt unemployment is included under this head.

*Source:* Latin American Institute for Economic and Social Planning.

It must not be inferred from the foregoing statement that a higher rate of development would retard the solution of a problem that derives from the economy's lack of the requisite dynamism. Such a conclusion would be paradoxical indeed. The explanation is that at the end of the first decade, average per capita income would be a good deal higher if the rate of development were 8 percent than if it were 7 percent, and this would imply, as has been pointed out, an increase in demand for those services which tend to expand rapidly once certain per capita income levels have been passed.

In other words, as per capita income rises, major changes in demand for services occur, and genuine employment in this sector, which is so intrinsically heterogeneous, is likely to increase. Thus, the structural distortion affects not only the proportional distribution of manpower between the industry group and services, but also the actual composition of employment within the services sector.

This is clearly reflected in parts C and D of Figure 22, which present the active population employed in services and in the industry group as a proportion not of the nonagricultural but of the total labor force. It will be seen that the 8 percent hypothesis implies a steady increase in the shares of these two sectors in the 1970's and 1980's, although it would be more rapid in the industry group than in services, both because of the difference in the growth rates of demand and because the services sector has to absorb its own redundant manpower.

These rising proportions should also be compared with the persistent decline in the share of agriculture as shown in part A of Figure 22. To judge from the experience of developed countries and of some countries in Latin America, the percentage of the active population working in the agricultural sector will continue to decrease, and the greater the technical progress made, the sharper this downward trend will be. Whether after the next two decades the 8 percent rate of development would still be adequate to meet this situation would depend upon a number of factors, regarding which various hypotheses would have to be adopted, all of them somewhat rash, and particularly that concerning the spread of technical progress to the different sectors of the economy. If this process were to result in higher rates of increase of the product per worker than are postulated in the second of the hypothetical cases presented here, and the population explosion were not brought under control, the rate of capital formation—and therefore of development—would have to be speeded up.

The sole purpose of the foregoing observations is to veiw this matter in a broader perspective, without venturing upon an area of conjecture which with every step forward becomes more hazardous. Some risk is already involved in the exploration of the next two decades, but it is a calculated and limited risk, deriving from assumptions which—however open they may and must be to searching question—do give a rough notion of the dimensions of our problem. A rough notion only, serving to clear the ground and prepare it for further exploration whose starting point will have to be the specific situation in the various countries.

## REQUIREMENTS FOR THE ACCELERATION OF DEVELOPMENT

### Projections and Their Significance

In the preceding pages of this chapter attention has been devoted to the rate of growth that could be achieved for the product in the coming decade if the objectives adopted were as follows: to correct the distortion in the occupational structure of the labor force, and to improve upon the past rates of increase of the product per worker in the broad sectors into which economic activity is divided here.

It must be repeated that the estimates presented relate to Latin America as a whole. Accordingly, they mask considerable intercountry differences. Nevertheless, they have the merit of giving a first approximate idea of the nature and dimensions of the phenomena to be dealt with. This is worthwhile in itself, but it would be unwise to carry the interpretation of these macroeconomic projections too far. They must be used with the greatest possible care, and their limitations and the premises on which they are based must be constantly borne in mind.

This first approximation, however, is not enough. It is essential for each country to formulate its own projections. Enough progress has been made in the relevant techniques for the task to be undertaken, and as results are achieved, it will be possible to arrive at new and more realistic approximations with respect to Latin America as a whole.

Such exercises as these are not, of course, prompted by mere theoretical curiosity as to the possible course of development. They are of great practical interest. Without them, it would be impossible to define the major features of the development strategy by which planning activities are to be guided. In this context, the significance of the projections in the present report calls for further clarification. They merely constitute a logical set of hypotheses quantifying the principal components of the problem. A certain amount of confusion often exists on this point, and must be dispelled. With a little imagination—seconded nowadays by computers—innumerable exercises can be devised and worked out. If the basic premise of the present chapter is a hypothetical rate of development of 8 percent per annum, it is not because this rate is considered preferable to any other, but because it would mean that the economy's lack of dynamism, measured in concrete terms, could be made good within a reasonable space of time. This objective could not be attained, however, unless exigent requirements were met. Here again no element of prediction is involved. No forecasts are offered as to whether the requisite conditions will or will not be fulfilled. A different but a very important aim is pursued: to show that their fulfillment is a sine qua non for achieving the rate of development which will bring the objectives under discussion within reach. Projections are a factor of persuasion in the formulation of a development strategy and policy, besides shedding light on the requirements implicit in a specific rate of growth.

Except in a few cases, these problems have not yet been the object of enough attention in Latin America, nor have statistics been improved sufficiently for them to be studied in depth. Macroeconomic exercises such as those presented here enable us to form a somewhat rough impression of them. But it will not do to go on in the same way. A highly desirable step toward understanding them more thoroughly would be the improvement of statistical material in each country, since this is of primary importance for national development strategy.

It must be frankly admitted that although in the last two decades great headway has been made in statistical and econometric techniques in Latin America, and those trained in them handle them with astonishing skill, statistics themselves have progressed much more slowly, and the same serious defects are still in evidence. Hence there is some risk that the very precision of the calculation process may make us lose sight of the innate flaws in the raw material.

The advances achieved at the international level also leave much to be desired. The important Indicative World Plan of the United Nations Food and Agriculture Organization (FAO) takes no account of how the possible development of agricultural production and the introduction of more advanced techniques may affect the retention of manpower in the agricultural sector. Neither does this question seem to have been considered as yet in studies on the Second Development Decade. And we may well wonder what point there is in setting up this or that rate of development as a target without relating it to the productive absorption of manpower. It was all very well 10 years ago for a figure of 5 percent to be conjured out of thin air as an expression of development aspirations. The time has now come to go deeper, and to persuade countries to look more searchingly into these questions.

The proposal of the International Labor Organization (ILO) to study the employment problem with the collaboration of other international institutions is a very timely move. Whatever means may be found of employing more manpower in this or that activity, the only way to strike at the roots of the problem is by speeding up the rate of development. So long as this were borne in mind, piecemeal solutions would not be without their subsidiary usefulness; but considered by themselves, they might lead to deplorably frustrating consequences.

Attention will now be turned to the chief requisites that will have to be met if the product is to grow at a rate of 8 percent. In the present section we will begin by noting what will need to be done as regards absorption of manpower in agriculture, industry, and services. Next we shall examine foreign trade requirements before going on to discuss those relating to capital formation. Those of a structural nature will be expounded in Chapter 6.

If the average annual rate of development recorded in the past for Latin America as a whole—5.2 percent—is to be raised to 8 percent in the course of a decade, the effort made will have to be really exceptional. Exceptional in its nature, and on an exceptional scale. It will call for an expenditure of energy that will severely test the Latin American countries' ability to shoulder their heavy development responsibilities. This does not mean that great difficulties have not had to be faced in the past. But those that will have to be overcome now are much greater. The region had to strive hard to recoup the decline in its export trade, and did so mainly through import substitution. Import substitution, however, with the support of an internal market that existed beforehand, is not the same thing as exporting manufactured goods to markets that will have to be painstakingly opened up.

Equally difficult will be the problem of capital formation. However greatly the present prospects for international financial cooperation may alter, the region will have to embark upon an intensive mobilization of internal resources such as, generally speaking, has not been satisfactorily effected hitherto.

The very conception of Latin American development has not yet properly assimilated a vital fact: the population explosion. The development problem is complex and should not be arbitrarily simplified. But there can be no doubt that the implications of demographic growth create an imperative need to seek new ways of influencing the forces of development.

Clearly, the magnitude of the effort required will depend upon the special situation of each individual country, the nature and extent of its lack of dynamism, and the length of time in which this lack is to be made good. For some countries a rate of development of 8 percent would not be high enough, while for others a lower rate would suffice, according to the gravity of the redundant manpower problem in agriculture and in urban activities, and to the position in respect of other basic factors. These differences will have to be taken duly into account in the following pages.

### Absorption of Labor in Agriculture, Industry, and Services

Let us first consider the case of agriculture. Whereas in 1950-1965 the annual average rate of increase of agricultural production was 3.8 percent, the 8 percent hypothesis would imply that the average over the 1970's and 1980's would be 4.8 percent. How could the agricultural sector meet so exigent a requirement?

This is a highly important question which has not been explored in sufficient depth in the Latin American countries. Perhaps in no other field is the development economist so liable to be involuntarily caught up in dangerous generalizations such as those relating to agrarian reform, technological changes—"the green revolution," as is now the fashionable term— the need to improve diet, and other matters of unquestionable importance. Systematic repetition of these generalizations does little to further our acquaintance with something so diverse, so multiform as agriculture in Latin America. Nor will the perfecting of econometric exercises help us much, until more progress is made toward a thorough knowledge of the agricultural situation.

These incidental comments are intended not so much to condone the shortcomings of the present report in these respects as to emphasize, first and foremost, the need for new research which will gradually fill the present wide gap between macroeconomic estimates and a number of microanalyses of specific problems. Some of the latter are undoubtedly useful contributions, but fragmentary. It is necessary—almost urgently so, I would say—for agricultural experts and development economists to join forces in pressing on from the aforesaid generalized approach to systematic factual analysis.*

---

*The Inter-American Development Bank recently took the felicitous step of convening a meeting of agricultural experts to exchange experiences. This seems to be a good start on a long and far from easy road, which in any event will have to be traveled.

For the reasons stated, it seems best to pose a series of questions as guidelines for the investigation which, in this as in other instances, will have to be undertaken in each individual country in order to meet the demands of its own national development strategy.

How far will the agricultural sector be able to satisfy the considerable increase in internal demand resulting from the acceleration of development? Will it be possible to continue doing so as in the past, by bringing new land under cultivation? It is often said that there are still vast tracts of virgin ground in Latin America, and that pushing forward the agricultural frontier presents no difficulties. Much talk is heard of tropical agriculture and its immense potentialities. But how much progress has been made in research on ecology and on methods of exploiting these potentialities? Moreover, it is common knowledge that making new land accessible involves heavy investment in infrastructure, which has to be carefully weighed in the balance against other economic and social investment requirements.

Given the diversity of the conditions prevailing in each country and in each of its widely varying regions, the specific information available—despite the experience acquired in some countries in this connection—is undeniably inadequate. Thus another question arises: how far are the possibilities of exploiting new land compatible with development requirements over the next two decades?

The stress laid on extending the frontier of agriculture is sometimes due to unwillingness to admit the need for structural changes in the land tenure system. In much of Latin America's agricultural sector a great deal of production potential is wasted because of the unsatisfactory distribution of land; there can be no question that, apart from its social significance, more efficient land use, would be economically sounder than opening up new land at the cost of substantial investment in infrastructure.

Furthermore, there is usually a high proportion of redundant manpower in agricultural activities in Latin America. More efficient land use would enable this redundant labor force to be reabsorbed; and, with the same amount of land and the same number of people, a bigger product could be obtained. In other words, an increase in the product per worker and per unit of land would thus be achieved without the introduction of changes in current farm practices.

The situation varies from one country to another. As the possibilities for more efficient utilization of the existing and easily accessible resources are gradually exhausted, two alternatives offer themselves: the opening up of new land by virtue of investment in infrastructure, or the expansion of yields by the introduction of new techniques. The latter proceeding also calls for investment in technological research and training, as well as in production of inputs.

In any event, all this would imply an increase—greater or smaller, as the case might be—in the product per worker. The 8 percent hypothesis assumes that the growth rate of the product per worker recorded in the past—2.5 percent—would rise by the end of the first decade to 4 percent, at which level it would be maintained during the 1980's. It is impossible to make a valid estimate for Latin America as a whole without information on actual conditions in the various countries; the rate named should, rather, be regarded as the highest compatible with the 8 percent hypothesis. It would involve a bigger exodus of agricultural workers than in the past; and this would lay a heavy burden of manpower absorption on the industry group, especially insofar as it might be desired to raise the product per worker above 4 percent. In that case it would be indispensable for the growth rate of the overall product to exceed 8 percent. It is not idle to repeat that the problem of the agricultural sector and the social integration of the rural masses cannot be solved out of the context of economic development.

The foregoing consideration is very important from the standpoint of mechanization. This is one of the cases in which the calculations of the agricultural entrepreneur generally come into conflict with the interests of the community as a whole. Mechanization lowers costs by reducing the volume of manpower required, and raises agricultural profits and land rents. It is economic from the standpoint of the individual entrepreneur; but if the labor force thus displaced is unable to find employment and goes to aggravate the problem of redundancy in the cities, where is the social advantage of mechanization?

The worst of it is that mechanization is sometimes artificially encouraged: tariffs and other import restrictions are reduced or eliminated, tax exemptions are offered, credit privileges are granted. All this seems laudable from the individual point of view. But is it compatible with the interest of the community? However, for the time being this line of reasoning can be shelved, as it forms part of a general problem which will be discussed elsewhere.

What should be noted here is the difference between labor-saving techniques and techniques which increase yields per unit of land. It is not always possible to draw a clear-cut dividing line, since there are cases in which mechanization also has an effect on yields, especially when it shortens the time taken over given operations and thus reduces the risk of weather contingencies.

Be this as it may, mechanization and the techniques that improve unit yields are creating a very marked duality in the agricultural sector of some Latin American countries. This duality used to exist between export activities, where techniques are generally advanced, and production for domestic consumption, which lags in the rear of technical progress; but today it is apparent within farming for domestic consumption itself. It is worth asking whether the countries that have most intensively increased their production for the home market—as well as for export and import substitution purposes—could have done so without modernizing their agriculture in this way.

If demand becomes much brisker than in the past, the modernization process is likely to gain powerful momentum. In the long run, it will not be possible to achieve or maintain a high rate of development unless agriculture is modernized. But it is no less true that the duality in question poses serious problems, as can already be seen in some of the Latin American countries, and also in such countries as India and Pakistan, where agriculture has been so far modernized that wheat production, for instance, has strikingly increased, thanks to the introduction of Mexican varieties of seed.*

---

*I was told two years ago in New Delhi by Chester Bowles, then the United States Ambassador, that the technical improvement had been achieved among a relatively small number of farmers who had substantially increased their income, and who were reminiscent of the kulaks in the Soviet Union of the already distant past.

If modernization were in fact to make steady progress, this duality would be aggravated: the large-scale agricultural entrepreneur would employ relatively little manpower, and in traditional farming redundancy would continue to increase. This is not a prophecy. It is a fait accompli in certain countries: in Mexico, for example, where underabsorption of labor in the new agriculture exists side by side with the absorption of more and more manpower in traditional farming. It is true that the land reform has liberated the agricultural worker from an outdated social system, but it has not been able to provide more land than there always was. The new techniques are also finding their way into activities of this type, but the natural result is additional redundancy. Only the attainment of a higher rate of development can gradually relieve this situation until a reasonable balance can be struck between human resources and the land. In the meantime, the *ejido* is still one of the dikes that effectively dam up the flood of social unrest. But even the strongest dikes can resist pressure only up to a certain point, which, in this case, would have to be calculated with due foresight by the engineerings of social development.

Each country has its own special problems, different from those of the rest. But as the increasing pressure of the economically active population on the land is something that is common to a large number of Latin American countries, the duality of the agricultural sector must be viewed with great concern. Herein lies another of the important aspects of the reform of the agrarian structure, apart from its favorable influence on technical progress. Giving more land to those who know how to till it and yet possess little or none would have two advantageous consequences. It would enable the product per worker to be increased in cases where land use was not satisfactory; and, in some extreme instances of demographic pressure, it would allow redundant manpower to be retained in agriculture, at the expense of the growth of the average product, until, as economic development proceeded the surplus was genuinely absorbed in other activities.

Moreover, this sweeping change in the agrarian structure transfers to the agricultural worker at least part of the rent formerly received by the landowner, and likewise enables him to keep the benefits of technical progress in his own hands, provided that demand is sufficient and the system for marketing agricultural commodities is rationalized.

These are some of the problems which the speeding up of the rate of development would imply for agriculture in Latin America. Production would have to be considerably expanded, though methods of doing this would vary according to the country concerned. To put it in a few words, it would seem that there are real possibilities of achieving such an expansion by more efficient exploitation of the land already in use, rather than by heavy investment in infrastructure so that new land could be settled. In any case, the latter would be a task for a subsequent stage of development. In view of the redundancy of manpower, the labor force already working on the land would suffice, or at least its rate of increase could be lower than in the past. But there is a limit to the expansion of production in this way which would be reached before very long, and techniques would have to be improved in order to increase yields. Accordingly, technological research should be vigorously spurred on in the areas in which it is not being undertaken on an adequate scale.

This is an aspect of the problem which must be viewed in a long-term perspective. Just as reference was made before to the need for thorough knowledge of the accessible land and its expansion potential, it should likewise be asked whether enough technological research is being conducted in the Latin American countries to enable them to meet the growing requirements that will be generated by the increase in the population and the improvement of its levels of living. A high proportion of agricultural expansion will have to be effected in the tropics: has enough research been undertaken on soils, possible crops, and suitable techniques? Notwithstanding some significant studies and experiments, there are still many unanswered questions here, and it is time to seek replies to them.

Lastly, and certainly without exhausting the list of the most urgently needed research projects, mention should be made of the analysis of import substitution possibilities, either at the national level or at that of intra-Latin American trade, not so much from the standpoint of employment, which has been touched upon elsewhere, but from the angle of agriculture's contribution to the elimination of the external bottleneck.

Let us next consider the case of industry. How far will it be able to cope with the increase in demand by improving its productivity? As in the case of agriculture, the boom in demand is likely to be accompanied by a higher growth rate of the product per worker than in the past. There are several reasons for this assumption. In any event, it is essential for industry to be able not only to absorb in its own cadres, by virtue of its own expansion, a large proportion of the manpower which becomes redundant as a result of the rise in the product per worker, but also to provide employment for the labor force migrating from agriculture into the towns. Let us now examine the reasons for the assumption that the product will increase.

In the first place, use could be made of idle capacity, of which, generally speaking, there seems to be a considerable amount. Keeping machinery permanently in operation through the system of work shifts would allow the absorption of manpower to be stepped up appreciably, especially if it proved possible to remove obstacles on the labor side which make it difficult to adopt this system at present—understandably enough, when the labor-absorbing capacity of the economy is insufficient.

Next, the enlargement of the domestic market would also permit specialization in production and more economic industrial plant sizes, with the consequent improvement in productivity.

Furthermore, as industrial output would expand much faster than in the past, the labor force in artisan-type industry could be more quickly absorbed, and the average product per worker would then be increased ipso facto.

Lastly, external competition within the framework of intra-Latin American trade might constitute an important factor in the expansion of productivity. Much emphasis has been placed on this in the present report. Of course, competition must be introduced by very gradual degrees, for two principal reasons. In the first place, industry must be given time to adapt itself to the new conditions thus created. Secondly, this process of adaptation must evolve alongside the expansion of demand; less difficulty is experienced when demand increases rapidly than when it does so at a sluggish pace.

On the other hand, the integration of key industries cannot be deferred for long, since it is a step of primary importance if a higher rate of development is to be achieved. Suffice it to bear in mind that any considerable increase in investment requirements will mean that they have to be met largely through the production of capital goods within Latin America. If, as has happened hitherto, import substitution in respect of capital and intermediate goods is attempted on the basis of the individual country markets, its cost will generally be higher—and in many cases much higher—than in the consumer industries, where the substitution process has already almost reached saturation point. The heavier the cost of substituting domestic production for imports of capital goods, the more exacting will be the task of raising the investment coefficient, by no means easy in itself. Moreover, this heavier cost will offset the favorable effects of the improvement in industrial productivity on the expansion of established industries.

In the 8 percent hypothesis, as will be recalled, it is assumed that the growth rate of the product per worker in the industry group, which was 3 percent in the past, rises to 4 percent. Here, too, as in the case of agriculture, this is a ceiling figure related to development at the rate of 8 percent. A higher rate of increase in productivity would, of course, entail accelerating still further the rate of economic development; otherwise, the labor-absorbing capacity of the industry group would diminish, and it would take longer to correct the distortion in the occupational structure of the labor force. A lower rate would have a better effect on this process, but would not offer the same possibilities of relieving social tension in the big towns, an objective which should on no account be forgotten.

Then again, what will happen in the heterogeneous group constituted by services? As has been shown, they will continue to absorb manpower, but in a decreasing proportion, and at a rate of increase much slower than that of the demand corresponding to this sector. By degrees, as less manpower is incorporated into administration and the public services, the basic services, trade, and transport will be able to absorb their own redundant labor force and increase their product per worker. These are labor-absorbing activities. In the labor-expelling activities too—especially the immense range of unskilled or semiskilled jobs—income levels will also improve as the proportion of the labor force that used to find its way into these occupations gradually declines. And in the course of this process, structural unemployment may be reduced. Its evolution will inevitably be slow, since the transfer of redundant manpower from agriculture to the services sector has been going on for two decades. A higher rate of development will be an indispensable requisite for speeding up this reabsorption of manpower.

Hence the question of productivity gives rise to the following reflection. In many countries surplus manpower is a cause of concern, especially in administration and the public services, which are fulfilling a spurious, not a genuine, labor-absorbing function, inasmuch as they are obliged to employ people for whom there is no room in the industry group. It would be oversimplifying the problem if they merely got rid of redundant staff and shut their eyes to the consequences, disregarding the economy's labor-absorbing capacity. To turn disguised unemployment into overt unemployment or into other forms of redundancy would be no solution at all.

The same might be said of the marketing of agricultural commodities and of the retail trade. They follow outdated patterns which still persist—although not to so marked an extent as before—largely because the economy's dynamic impetus is not strong enough. Accelerated development would enable this problem, too, to be tackled from a more favorable vantage point than at present.

### Foreign Trade Requirements

In order to form an initial impression of the development requirements that will next be discussed, some of the figures recorded in the past should be recalled. The preceding chapter contained an account of the main factors that went to determine a rate of development of 5.2 percent in 1950-1965. In the first place, the purchasing power of exports increased at an annual rate of 2.7 percent, and the effect of the net inflow of external financing on the growth rate of the product amounted to 0.5 percent; in other words, the incidence of total external resources was 3.2 percent. Secondly, import substitution enabled the product to increase at a rate 2 percent higher than the 3.2 percent growth rate of external resources.

What requirements would be entailed if a rate of 8 percent was to be reached by the end of the 1970's? The first and most essential relates to imports. It is common knowledge that an acceleration of the growth rate of the product brings with it significant changes in the composition of aggregate demand in the economy, which influence import requirements. According to estimates prepared jointly by ECLA and the Latin American Institute for Economic and Social Planning, if the growth rate of the product were 8 percent, by 1980 demand for goods at present imported would expand at a rate of 8.8 percent.

How could potential demand for imports possibly increase faster than the product? The explanation lies in the aforesaid changes in the composition of demand. As a result of the acceleration of development itself, there would be a more rapid expansion of demand for those goods which are obtained mainly from abroad. For example, a higher growth rate means a higher rate of investment, and capital goods still have to be imported on a substantial scale.

This poses a major problem: how would the region be able to afford an 8.8 percent growth rate of demand for imports by the end of the current decade? That is the question which will now be briefly analyzed with the help of the carefully prepared projections appearing in the ECLA/Institute study referred to above.

The task in hand is to ascertain the various possible means by which such an import growth rate could be covered. To this end, Table 19 is presented, showing as a first possibility an annual rate of increase of current exports calculated at 4.9 percent (on the basis of the exports that Latin America has been effecting and an estimate of the prospects for their expansion). Secondly, the very moderate assumption is adopted that the net inflow of external financing would cover 0.4 percent of the import growth rate. Consequently, total external resources accruing from exports of the type hitherto effected,

## TABLE 19

**Latin America: Means of Covering the Potential Demand for Imports
Corresponding to an 8 Percent Growth Rate of the Product
at the End of the Current Decade**

|                                                                                  | Percentage |
|----------------------------------------------------------------------------------|:----------:|
| Annual growth rate of the demand for imports that would have to be satisfied      | 8.8        |
| Means of covering this demand                                                     |            |
| Exports currently effected, and their expansion                                  | 4.9        |
| New industrial export lines                                                       | 0.5        |
| Import substitution                                                               | 3.0        |
| Net inflow of external financial resources                                       | 0.4        |

*Source:* Latin American Institute for Economic and Social Planning.

plus funds from abroad, would represent 5.3 percent of the rate in question. The proportion remaining to be covered would thus be 3.5 percent.

How would it be possible to make up this remaining percentage? There are no alternatives but to promote the intensive growth of industrial exports to the rest of the world and to pursue import-substitution policy much more energetically than in the past. In my own view, however, given existing conditions in Latin America, this substitution policy would have to be resolutely founded on regional and subregional integration of basic industries.

The above figures, as previously stated, in no way represent a forecast, or even targets at which a Latin American strategy should aim, inasmuch as strategy must be formulated at the national level, with due coordination in the field of inter-Latin American cooperation. Accordingly, the purpose of the figures is to give an idea of the various directions in which efforts should be made and of their order of magnitude. They also make it clear that if some of these efforts are not as vigorous as they should be, others will have to be intensified in compensation, if a rate of development that will remedy the economy's lack of the required dynamism is to be attained.

For example, if exports failed to expand as indicated above, it would be essential to step up the import substitution process; and if that proved overwhelmingly difficult or impossible, the only recourse would be to obtain a larger net inflow of external financing for a greater length of time.

In that case, a situation would arise which deserves comment, for—as suggested in the relevant section of the present report—after the 1970's Latin America as a whole might conceivably generate enough savings to cover all the investment implied by the 8 percent growth rate of the product. If this were achieved, continued recourse to external financing would be dictated by trade reasons, that is, by the necessity of counteracting the tendency to an external-sector bottleneck, because exports had not yet been expanded sufficiently or because the advance of the import-substitution process had not been rapid enough.

Attention will now be devoted to the various factors of which brief mention was made in connection with Table 19. There are several solutions which must be appropriately combined. None of them could be overemphasized without the risk of entering, so to speak, upon the stage of diminishing returns on effort. Thus, the way in which the different possibilities are combined must be such as to ensure a rational distribution of effort among all of them.

*Expansion of Exports*

The average annual growth rate of total exports is assumed to be 5.4 percent (see Table 19). Once more it must be repeated that this figure is neither a forecast nor a target, but an estimate of rates that might be attainable, as far as can be judged at the present time on the basis of the available data. Traditional primary exports are included under this head, and another assumption adopted is that in addition to the increase resulting from the growth of world demand for these commodities, trade in some of them would expand considerably by virture of certain programs that are under way. Cases in point are copper in Chile and Peru, tin and petroleum in Bolivia, and possible new agricultural export lines—comprising tropical products in particular—such as are being developed in some of the Latin American countries. Another example is the action that is being taken to promote tourism.

In recent years, exports of manufactured goods to the rest of the world have increased at a rate of 9.1 percent. This especially reflects the promising industrial export drive started some years ago by several of the Latin American countries. But an even more vigorous effort would have to be made if appreciably higher rates were to be attained.

What rates? It would be unwise to give the imagination free rein in this field, without taking into consideration what other countries have managed to do. In the ECLA/Institute document referred to, study is devoted to the cases of four countries—Australia, Finland, Spain, and Yugoslavia—which have been successful in this direction, and the composition of their industrial exports is taken into account. On the assumption that in each of the groups of goods analyzed Latin America would make an effort similar to the action taken by these four countries, it is estimated that the region could expand its industrial exports at an annual rate of about 15 percent. Any greater increase could not reasonably be projected for the coming decade. This does not mean that such a figure could not possibly be exceeded or that every endeavor should not be made to do so, but it was decided to take this percentage as a point of reference for assessing how much should be expected of the other possible means of solving the problem.

*Further Remarks on Industrial Exports*

The growth rate of 9.1 percent given above for industrial exports relates to sales to the rest of the world. With the addition of intraregional exports, which increased at an annual rate of 25.5 percent, the aggregate growth rate of industrial exports between 1961 and 1967 rises to 12.4 percent.

It is worthwhile to note in passing that even though progress in the direction of a Latin American common market is still unsatisfactory, the fact that intra-Latin American exports of manufactured goods have expanded at so exceptionally high a rate suggests how great is the potential of this type of trade.

The composition of intraregional exports of manufactures differs substantially from that of Latin America's exports to the rest of the world. As can be seen from Table 20, the products exported to countries outside Latin America are generally those characterized by simpler processing and slower growth rates; they include, for instance, food items—canned meat, fruit, and vegetables—and petroleum products. In contrast, the goods produced by industries in which more advanced techniques are used and the proportion of industrial value added is higher* are exported mainly within Latin America. On an average, more than two-thirds of the products of the metal-transforming industries are intended for the region's markets, and in some cases the corresponding proportion is virtually 100 percent.

A very high proportion of Latin America's total exports of manufactured goods, both intraregional and to the rest of the world, is constituted by only 15 products or fairly homogeneous groups of products. The 15 types of goods included in Table 20 account for more than 73 percent of the total industrial exports of the group of six countries studied, whose sales of these products of course represent a very large share of the Latin American total.

The significance of this point is worth stressing. The fact that the promising expansion which has taken place has been confined to very few goods and largely to intra-Latin American trade is suggestive of the prospects that would be opened up if the number of products were increased, and an endeavor were made to break out of the Latin American market and seek advantageous outlets in the rest of the world, especially the industrial centers.

The development of extra- and intraregional exports of manufactures would have an increasingly powerful impact not only on the structure of Latin America's foreign trade but also, of course, on its internal industrial structure. Should the assumptions presented in Table 19 be fulfilled, the share of industrial exports (excluding petroleum products) in Latin America's total external sales would rise from its present level of about 9 percent to some

---

*For example, the products of the metal-transforming industries, such as machines for office use, pumps for liquids, sewing machines, and machinery for the textile and publishing industries.

# TABLE 20

## Latin America: Exports of Manufactured Goods, by Markets of Destination, 1967

| Item | Millions of Dollars | | | Percentage of Total | |
|---|---|---|---|---|---|
| | Latin America | Rest of World | Total | Latin America | Rest of World |
| Canned Meat | 0.2 | 116.5 | 116.7 | 0.2 | 99.8 |
| Canned Fish | — | 2.4 | 2.4 | — | 100.0 |
| Canned Fruit | 2.1 | 26.8 | 28.9 | 7.3 | 92.7 |
| Canned Vegetables | 0.6 | 7.8 | 8.4 | 7.1 | 92.9 |
| Petroleum Products | 21.5 | 690.9 | 712.4 | 3.0 | 97.0 |
| Paper Products | 1.1 | 8.3 | 9.4 | 11.7 | 88.3 |
| Clothing, Including Furs | 1.2 | 4.4 | 5.6 | 21.4 | 78.6 |
| Pharmaceutical Products | 14.8 | 20.6 | 35.4 | 41.8 | 58.2 |
| Machinery Other Than Electrical | 39.7 | 18.5 | 58.2 | 68.2 | 31.8 |
| Machines for Office Use | 9.2 | 7.9 | 17.1 | 53.8 | 46.2 |
| Machinery for Specialized Uses | 19.6 | 5.3 | 24.9 | 78.7 | 21.3 |
| Electrical Machinery | 12.5 | 5.7 | 18.2 | 68.7 | 31.3 |
| Motor Vehicles | 3.7 | 1.0 | 4.7 | 78.7 | 21.3 |
| Ships | 1.5 | 2.2 | 3.7 | 40.5 | 59.5 |
| Printed Matter | 22.3 | 4.9 | 27.2 | 82.0 | 18.0 |

*Note:* This table is based on Argentina, Brazil, Chile, Colombia, Mexico, and Venezuela, which in 1967 accounted for 82 percent of Latin America's total exports of manufactured goods.

*Source:* Latin American Institute for Economic and Social Planning, "Elementes para la elaboración de una política de desarrollo con integración para América Latina." (Mimeographed.)

12 percent in 10 years' time and, if the same rate of growth were kept up, to approximately 26 percent in the space of 20 years.

This would be a process of great significance, since it would lead to the gradual metamorphosis of an outdated structure of foreign trade, which, as is all too well known, is stifling the development of Latin America. The change in the composition of exports would enable the region to gain a steadily increasing share in the more dynamic international trade flows and to shake off its dependence upon exports of primary commodities, demand for which grows slowly, while their prices are always subject to gravely prejudicial fluctuations.

As the process in question took place, new requirements would supervene. And they would no longer consist in the attainment or maintenance of very high export growth rates—fully justified in the transition period—but in the progressive assimilation of new technologies which would make it possible to increase productivity, improve the quality of the goods manufactured, and participate intensively in world trade flows on a competitive footing.

The hypotheses presented in this document—especially where the scale of the requisite effort is concerned—demonstrate the need for the Latin American countries to avail themselves of the recently created machinery to obtain a progressive relaxation of the restrictions hindering the entry of their goods into the United States, and for this machinery to be extended to other industrial centers. In pursuit of this same end, the region should continue to join forces with the other developing countries in the campaign that is being conducted at the world level.

The same might be said of general and nondiscriminatory preferential treatment for industrial exports. This would be a valuable incentive, but by no means sufficient in itself. Preferences would simply afford opportunities. It would be up to the Latin American countries to take advantage of them.

To this end, it would be essential for all the countries of the region to adopt a number of measures such as have already been very successfully applied by some of them: for example, the abrogation of a number of taxes that increase the burden of industrial costs. In addition, promotional action is needed, ranging from technical and financial assistance in the improvement of productivity to market studies and export credits. A clear awareness of all these requirements—both internal measures and international cooperation—is now growing up.

Stress must be laid here on the role of private foreign investment. Whether through the transfer of technology—to which reference is made elsewhere—or through knowledge of external markets, it may be of great importance for industrial exports, especially sales to the rest of the world. The policy to be pursued should be very flexible, in order to encourage such investment and at the same time ensure that except in very special cases it is effected in combination with domestic enterprise.

Furthermore, attention has already been drawn elsewhere to the importance of progressively encouraging industrial competition in Latin America with a view to securing increases in productivity and improvements in quality. Otherwise it will be difficult, if not impossible, to reach worthwhile industrial export targets.

The strong opposition which all this arouses in the industrial centers should always be borne in mind. It has been clearly evidenced in the case of preferences. Unquestionably, if the Latin American countries do all they should to take advantage of any preferences conceded, the initial opposition may swell to more formidable proportions. It will not be enough to obtain the preferences; persistent and well-concerted action vis-à-vis the industrial centers will be needed for the attainment of the objective in view.

In the light of my experience in UNCTAD, it seems to me that the Latin American countries could carry much greater weight in the determination of this issue if they showed themselves resolved on their own part to give vigorous impetus to their reciprocal trade. They have not done so hitherto. They have urged the need for the industrial centers to adopt a trade policy favorable to Latin America's exports, and have demanded a definite program for the elimination of tariff and other restrictions; but they are far from having displayed the same zeal in the cause of intra-Latin American trade.

## Import Substitution

In commenting on Table 19 at an earlier stage, it was noted that import substitution has a very significant role to play in covering part of the considerable increase in potential demand for imports—i.e., 3 percent out of a growth rate of 8.8 percent. The questions is, what share in this function will be incumbent, respectively, upon the continuance of the traditional substitution process at the national level and upon import substitution on a regional basis.

No precise dividing line can be drawn, inasmuch as this is an area which, notwithstanding its importance, has not been properly explored. There is room for grave doubts as to whether the substitution process can, as before, be carried out to any considerable extent on national bases, since the import items for which domestic production must be substituted in this phase—capital goods and intermediate products—are just those whose manufacture generally calls for complex technology, broad markets, and heavy investment.

As shown elsewhere, countries forming a group which carries decisive weight in Latin America's total product have rapidly reduced their import coefficient in the last two decades. The process had begun some time before, as can be seen from Figure 23, in which the three countries that have reached the most advanced stage of industrial development are dealt with separately. It will be noted that in the last few years the downward trend tends to flatten out, or is interrupted altogether. Is this the result of passing circumstances? Or is it a sign of progressive exhaustion in the substitution process?

The possibilities of quickening the recent tempo of import substitution on the basis of the national market alone depend largely upon the cost which each country would be prepared to incur. As a general rule, this cost has been very high in the past. And, broadly speaking, it may well prove much higher still when the industries involved are—as in the future they will primarily have to be—those producing intermediate and capital goods.

A policy of regional cooperation would mean that each country, instead of substituting domestic production for a wide range of goods imported from the rest of the world, would import some items from other Latin American countries, to which it would export its own manufactures in return. Private enterprise, especially in the case of industries based on foreign investment, has been beforehand with the governments of the

## FIGURE 23

### Evolution of Import Coefficients
### (percentage)
### Semi-logarithmic scale

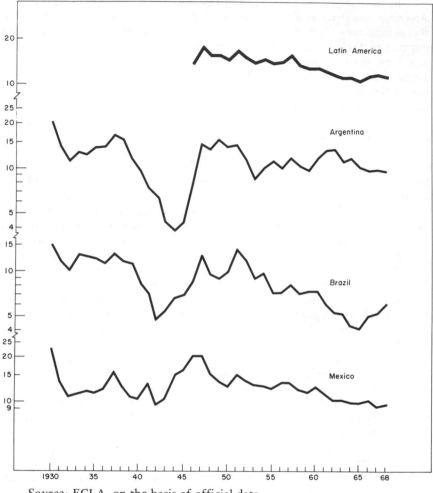

*Source:* ECLA, on the basis of official data.

region in this respect, and distributes production of certain goods among various countries.

There is a point to be clarified here. In alluding to the regional market, I have had in mind no special form of such a market, but simply a joint effort made by a number of the Latin American countries—not necessarily all of them—to relieve the external-sector bottleneck.

The ideal formula, of course, would be for the whole of Latin America to be drawn in as soon as possible, but this does not detract from the value or the merit of more limited arrangements, provided that the parties to them do not lose sight of the more ambitious objective; or, in other words, provided that they regard what they are doing as a stage on the road toward the regional common market. This applies particularly to the Andean Group. As pointed out elsewhere, it would seem that the aim of this group is to advance faster than the Latin American Free Trade Association (LAFTA) toward the common market, while at the same time linking up with the Association. It is of interest to form a first impression of what the problem discussed in these pages would mean for the Andean Group.

According to preliminary studies which are being carried out by ECLA and the Institute at the request of the heads of planning offices of the countries signatory to the Cartagena Agreement, an average annual rate of development of 6.5 percent between now and 1985 would imply a potential demand for imports expanding at a rate of 9.2 percent, whereas the relevant projection places the annual growth rate of the purchasing power of traditional exports at 3.6 percent. A first approximate evaluation of substitution possibilities within the Andean Group suggests that the aforesaid rate of 9.2 percent might be reduced to 6.5 percent.

A wide margin would thus remain to be covered by achieving a more rapid rate of increase for exports both to the rest of the world and to other Latin American countries. The higher level of industrial efficiency attained in the Andean Group would presumably be a major factor in stepping up the exports in question. It must be recalled that a specific experiment in joint action at the subregional level already exists in the shape of the Central American Common Market. The growth of intra-Central American trade has signified an intensive import-substitution process.

But let us go back to the projections relating to Latin America as a whole. It is assumed that the contribution of import-substitution efforts of a purely national character would cover 0.8 percent* of the growth rate of demand for imports, and that the remaining 2.2 percent would have to be coped with by means of regional import substitution. It would be interesting at this point to see what the latter process would mean for the import coefficient of Latin America as a whole, which is currently 11.5 percent and, if the substitution process were not carried farther in the coming decade, would rise to 14.2 percent. The value of this estimate—a purely hypothetical one, since in the writer's view it could not be fulfilled—lies in the idea it gives of the magnitude of the substitution process that would have to be undertaken. Meanwhile, if imports from the rest of the world were replaced by domestic production as envisaged in Table 19, the coefficient would be reduced from 14.2 to 10.2 percent.

If this coefficient is viewed in relation to the imports of those Latin American countries which have reached the most advanced stage in the substitution process—in particular, Brazil—it does not seem exceptionally low, but if it is compared with those of a group of industrialized countries in

---

*This estimate is based on the assumption that the import substitution process at the national level would continue at the same tempo as in the past.

TABLE 21

**Selected Countries: Import Coefficients in Relation to**
**Gross National Product, 1960 and 1968**
**(percentage)**

| Country | 1960 | 1968 |
|---|---|---|
| Federal Republic of Germany | 14.2 | 15.2 |
| France | 9.5 | 11.0 |
| Italy | 14.0 | 13.8 |
| United Kingdom | 17.7 | 18.3 |
| The Netherlands | 40.3 | 37.0 |
| Finland | 21.5 | 19.7 |
| United States | 3.0 | 3.8 |
| Canada | 15.4 | 16.7 |
| Japan | 10.3 | 9.2 |

*Source:* United Nations, *Monthly Bulletin of Statistics.*

Europe, it turns out to be lower than many of them (see Table 21). Macroeconomic comparisons of this kind do not, of course, prove very much. It would be truer to say that in the present case they are significant only insofar as they offer further evidence that this problem has not been sufficiently studied in Latin America and that in-depth research on it is urgently needed.

*External Financial Resources*

The figures mentioned with respect to the various possible means of covering the 8.8 percent growth rate of demand for imports, although conservative estimates, imply a very intensive effort in all the directions indicated. Whatever was not achieved in one of these fields, therefore, would have to be made up for in the others. The basis for postulating so arduous an effort was the idea that the net inflow of external funds should be reduced in the greatest possible measure, as (in line with our hypothesis) domestic resources were progressively generated to cover the investment required for raising the rate of development to 8 percent.

However, if by 1980 the suggested combination of trade expedients had not sufficed to cover the whole of the growth rate of imports, it would be essential to obtain a bigger net inflow of financial resources from abroad. The net contribution assumed in our hypothesis is estimated on the supposition that Latin America would receive 15 percent of the international financial resources obtained by the developing countries under the terms of the UNCTAD recommendation that the developed countries should transfer the equivalent of 1 percent of their gross product. But in the past Latin America's share of the total inflow was larger, amounting at one time to considerably more than 20 percent. Consequently, if additional funds were required, the region's former margin of participation would still not be exceeded.*

In conclusion, viewed from the standpoint of the external bottleneck, the attainment of a rate of development which will enable a clear and reasonable answer to be given to the redundant manpower problem calls for the complementary application of measures to promote intra- and extraregional exports of manufactures and, at the same time, measures providing for international financial cooperation on much more favorable terms than in the past.

Far from representing alternatives to each other, regional cooperation and the opening out of the economy toward the rest of the world are both indispensable as components of a development strategy for the Latin American countries, and both must be energetically promoted. Another inference that can clearly be drawn from the foregoing exercises is that if these two policies were jointly applied, it would not be necessary to push the corresponding measures beyond reasonable limits in order to attain an annual rate of development of 8 percent within the next 10 years and keep it up thereafter. It is worthwhile to repeat, however, that we must not let this blind us to the magnitude of the effort that would have to be put forth in each of the suggested fields, or to the changes—in the whole apparatus of production, in technology, and in access to foreign markets, inter alia—that would be implied in making these targets feasible.

## CAPITAL FORMATION AND
## INTERNATIONAL FINANCIAL COOPERATION

The contention of the present report is that owing to serious shortcomings in international cooperation, as well as in the development measures adopted by the Latin American countries in general, the foreign capital received has not

---

*It must be remembered that this decrease in Latin America's share is largely due to the fact that the heavy burden of the short-term debt led several governments to reduce the scale on which they resorted to external financing until their balance-of-payments position improved.

succeeded in fulfilling two of its primary objectives: first, to promote the mobilization of domestic investment resources until they suffice for the maintenance of a satisfactory rate of development; and second, to contribute to the progressive alleviation and ultimately the complete elimination of the external-sector bottleneck in the economy.

The exceptional intensity of the export drive which will have to be made to relieve the external bottleneck has already been indicated in earlier pages. The next question to be discussed is capital formation and the role of international financial cooperation.

The development policy of the Latin American countries, and the necessary convergent measures at the international level, should include among their aims both the above-mentioned objectives, for unless they are achieved it will be impossible to give the economy the additional dynamism required.

The fact is that the period of transition from an inadequate to an adequate rate of development is bound to be difficult. For the rate must be adequate to ensure not only the productive employment of manpower but also the attainment of the two aforesaid objectives. It is by no means essential that both should be attained at the same time. That would be mere coincidence. In the hypothetical case presented here, the point at which a net inflow of foreign capital was no longer necessary would be reached in the not too distant future, sooner than the point at which the structure of foreign trade would be such that exports could be allowed to develop normally and the exceptional effort made in the transitional period could be discontinued. Everything depends upon the assumptions adopted. If it were possible for the export drive to be even more vigorous than has been estimated, the point at which foreign trade was normalized could be reached earlier. It must always be borne in mind that this is not a forecast, but a method of analysis of requirements and possibilities.

With regard to the point at which domestic saving suffices for the maintenance of an appropriate rate of growth, the following observation will not be out of place. A country cannot continue borrowing from abroad indefinitely. Adequate domestic investment resources must be a primary objective. Accordingly, as a given country gradually approaches this goal, a time will come when the net inflow of foreign capital, after attaining a maximum, begins to diminish. Meanwhile, the amount represented by payments of interest and profits naturally continues to increase. And in the course of the process, these service payments first come to equal the net inflow of new capital and later to exceed it; thus a net outflow of funds takes place.

Such is the *logical* evolution of this process. "Logical" is the operative word, for it is this logic that has not existed in Latin America. If a country is to reach the point at which service payments exceed the inflow of capital in normal fashion, without disturbing consequences, an essential prerequisite is that it should have satisfactorily expanded its exports and reduced its import coefficient. The net outflow of financial resources can thus be afforded comfortably, without prejudice to the imports required for development. During this process the coefficient of domestic saving will have to be raised gradually so that smaller and smaller net inflows of foreign capital are needed.

This is the logical evolution which has not taken place in Latin America. The net inflow of funds from abroad has progressively diminished, and in many cases the stage of a net outflow of resources has been reached long before the essential changes have been effected in the structure of foreign trade, and also long before the capacity to generate domestic saving has become adequate.

Herein lies the basic flaw in the process. The stage of remitting funds abroad in excess of the net capital received is reached by a country too early, when it has not yet entered upon the phase of development in which the remittances can be covered without consequences that defeat the ends pursued. The stage in question is, of course, inevitable; it is bound to come sooner or later. The only trouble is that the Latin American countries have gradually approached and have actually reached it abnormally far ahead of the proper time. According to our hypothesis, which is not based on complacent assumptions with regard to domestic effort—quite the contrary—the Latin American economy as a whole would attain sufficient maturity to cope with the effects of the logical evolution described only in the 1980's where savings are concerned, and later still in respect of the external sector*—always provided that the postulated foreign trade effort is made to good effect and that a reasonable international cooperation policy is applied.

### The Requisite Adjustment of External Financial Resources and of the Terms on Which They Are Obtainable

What could be considered a reasonable financial cooperation policy? Reasonable on both sides: on the Latin American side, where it should be accompanied by stringent measures to ensure the progressive increase of the domestic saving coefficient, as well as efficacious foreign trade measures; and on the international side, where it is assumed that by 1975 the net transfer of capital would reach the target of 1 percent of the gross product of the industrialized countries recommended by the United Nations and adopted up to a point in the Pearson Report. (See Chapter 5.)

As stated above, Latin America's share in net transfers of capital has been 15 percent. If the target indicated were reached in the year suggested and approximately the same proportion were maintained thereafter, the net inflow of foreign capital would make a significant contribution to the satisfaction of the requirements implied in our hypothesis.

Let us now consider the terms of this reasonable policy. The following observation is important as a point of departure. If the burden of financial remittances—profits and interest, amortization and debt repayment—were eased in the manner about to be described, the gross inflow of foreign capital obtained in 1966-1968 would not need to be expanded to the same extent. Accordingly, as a bench mark, an amount slightly smaller than the average for that three-year period is postulated; and it is assumed that this quantity would gradually increase in accordance with the assumptions mentioned

---

*On the assumption that new loans would be issued on the terms proposed in alternative A below.

above: that by 1975 the 1 percent target for net transfers of capital would be reached, and that 15 percent of these transfers would fall to the share of Latin America.

If these assumptions are fulfilled, the proportion of Latin America's gross product represented by the gross inflow of capital will gradually decrease. From the data analyzed in Chapter 2, it can be inferred that in 1966-1968 this proportion was 3.8 percent. But since the product has continued to increase, if the gross inflow of capital remains approximately the same, the proportion will of course decline. For our present purposes, therefore, it is assumed to be initially 3 percent of the product.

If internal measures were duly taken to raise the savings coefficient, this proportion would not be maintained, but would gradually decrease. The explanation is simple. According to our hypothesis, the growth rate of the gross product in Latin America as a whole will rise from the 5.2 percent that it averaged in 1950-1968 to 8 percent in 1980, whereas the estimate of transfers of capital from the developed countries is based on the assumption that they will continue to increase their gross product as in the period 1957-1967, i.e., at an average annual rate of 4.5 percent.

To make this point clearer, Figure 24 was prepared, in which the variables we are considering are presented in relation to the gross product; in addition, in Figure 25 they are quantified in absolute terms. The relevant data are also shown in Table 22.

The upper curve in Figure 24 relates to the gross inflow of foreign capital to which allusion has just been made. Let us now look at the amortization curves. While amortization payments constituted 2.3 percent of the product in 1966-1968—and somewhat more in the two preceding three-year periods—in the initial year of our hypothesis (1970) the proportion falls to 1.2 percent. As will be seen later, this substantial reduction of amortization payments explains why the proportion that the gross inflow of foreign capital is assumed to represent need not be higher than in the recent past in order to complement and encourage domestic saving. But it is also necessary to ease the burden of remittances of interest and profits, as will be explained later. By dealing with one thing at a time, more light will be shed on the problem.

Outgoings under the head of amortization and debt repayment have been really very heavy, and an additional drain has been the flight of domestic capital abroad, totaling sums of which it has not been possible to make a reliable estimate. It is thus essential to stretch out the amortization period, adjusting it to the capacity for external payments.*

---

*This idea of a stretch-out reminds me of a personal experience in Argentina. The world depression of the 1930's and the sharp fall in agricultural prices which it involved placed the Banco Hipotecario Nacional (National Mortgage Bank) in a critical position. Mortgage service payments fell into very considerable arrears, which made it increasingly difficult for the Bank to meet its commitments on the "mortgage bonds"—as they were called—issued on the market to obtain the funds for making loans. There was constant talk of the collapse of this institution, just as there had been four decades previously in the case of other State financing agencies. The crisis was unexpectedly overcome by the rescheduling of the mortgage bonds and loans. It was an orthodox, not a forced, rescheduling, which enabled the rate of interest to be lowered from 6 percent to 5 percent; and the amortization

(continued on page 121)

# TABLE 22

## Latin America: Projection of Movements of External Financial Resources

|  | Gross Inflow of Capital | Amortization | Net Inflow of Capital | Interest, Profits | Net Inflow of Financial Resources |
|---|---|---|---|---|---|
| | *Millions of Dollars* | | | | |
| Annual Average, 1966-1968 | 3,829 | 2,274 | 1,555 | 1,952 | -397 |
| | *Hypothesis A* | | | | |
| Amortization 4 Percent Interest 2 Percent | | | | | |
| 1975 | 4,626 | 1,299 | 3,327 | 2,665 | 612 |
| 1980 | 5,782 | 1,660 | 4,122 | 3,379 | 677 |
| 1985 | 7,320 | 2,202 | 5,118 | 4,322 | 722 |
| 1990 | 9,237 | 2,823 | 6,414 | 5,519 | 813 |
| | *Hypothesis B* | | | | |
| Amortization 4 Percent Interest 6 Percent | | | | | |
| 1975 | 4,626 | 1,299 | 3,327 | 3,327 | -60 |
| 1980 | 5,782 | 1,660 | 4,122 | 4,676 | -621 |
| 1985 | 7,320 | 2,202 | 5,118 | 6,326 | -1,282 |
| 1990 | 9,237 | 2,823 | 6,414 | 8,342 | -2,010 |
| | *Percentage of Product* | | | | |
| Annual average, 1966-1968 | 3.8 | 2.3 | 1.5 | 1.9 | -0.4 |
| | *Hypothesis A* | | | | |
| Amortization 4 Percent Interest 2 Percent | | | | | |
| 1975 | 2.9 | 0.8 | 2.1 | 1.7 | 0.4 |
| 1980 | 2.5 | 0.7 | 1.8 | 1.4 | 0.3 |
| 1985 | 2.2 | 0.7 | 1.5 | 1.3 | 0.2 |
| 1990 | 1.9 | 0.6 | 1.3 | 1.1 | 0.2 |
| | *Hypothesis B* | | | | |
| Amortization 4 Percent Interest 6 Percent | | | | | |
| 1975 | 2.9 | 0.8 | 2.1 | 2.1 | -0.1 |
| 1980 | 2.5 | 0.7 | 1.8 | 2.1 | -0.3 |
| 1985 | 2.2 | 0.7 | 1.5 | 1.9 | -0.4 |
| 1990 | 1.9 | 0.6 | 1.3 | 1.7 | -0.4 |

*Note:* The inflow of capital net of amortization gradually rises to 1 percent of the gross product of the developed countries. It is assumed that Latin America's share in the total inflow remains constant at 15 percent.

*Source:* Latin American Institute for Economic and Social Planning.

# FIGURE 24

## Group of Countries Considered: Projection of Movements of External Financial Resources
### (percentage of product)

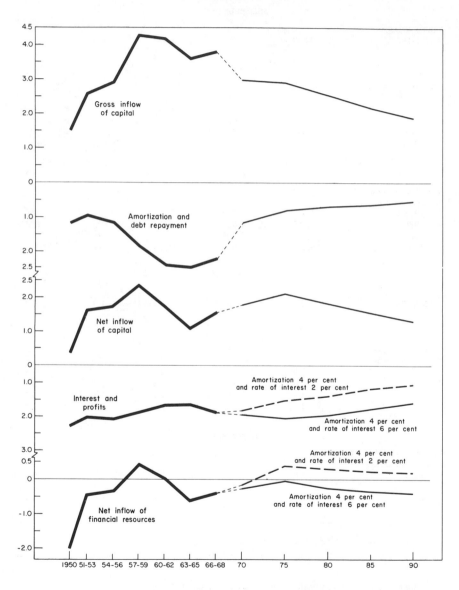

*Source:* ECLA, on the basis of official data.

120

**FIGURE 25**

**Group of Countries Considered:
Projection of Movements of External
Financial Resources
(thousands of millions of dollars at 1960 prices)**

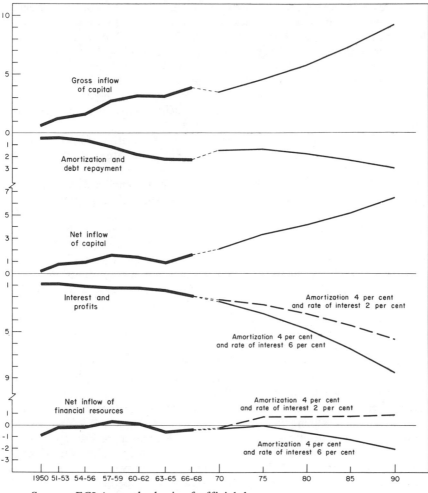

*Source:* ECLA, on the basis of official data.

(*continued from page 118*)
period, which had become very burdensome because the average duration of the loans in force had been considerably shortened by the actual mechanics of financial servicing, was once again extended to 30 years. This operation, carefully planned and executed, sufficed to reduce the arrears in loan service payments to very modest proportions and to normalize the activities of an institution which enjoyed great prestige in Argentina and abroad.

I do not think the importance of relieving Latin America's financial burdens need be urged further. A consensus has been reached in this respect, and it was not long ago that President Nixon stressed the necessity of easing the load. As a result, the Inter-American Committee on the Alliance for Progress (ICAP) has been recommended to present specific proposals such as are also under study in other international agencies. In the meantime, estimates based on two recent reports are submitted here. The Pearson Report recommends cutting down annual rates of interest on official loans to not more than 2 percent, which implies heavily subsidizing the rates of interest in question; while another report (which has not been published yet, but which the writer has had an opportunity of consulting) considers it reasonable that service payments on the external debt outstanding (excluding direct investment of private capital) should be reduced to 10 percent, of which 6 percent would correspond to interest and 4 percent to amortization payments. It should be recalled that at present the proportion of the debt outstanding represented by such remittances is approximately 18.9 percent.

The estimates given here present these two alternatives for the rates of interest—2 percent (alternative A) and 6 percent (alternative B)—and a single amortization rate of 4 percent in both cases.

To revert to Figure 24, the decline in the proportion of the product represented by amortization is due to the application of this latter rate of 4 percent. For caution's sake, however, it is not assumed that the whole of the debt outstanding would be amortized at this rate, but simply the gross capital inflows received from the initial year of the projection onward. It is further assumed that the whole of the existing short-term debt—which has caused so much trouble for years because of its unsatisfactory average duration—would be replaced at its expiration date by new inflows amortizable at the rate of 4 percent.

The time has now come to take a look at the curve representing the net inflow of capital, that is, the gross inflow minus amortization payments. There are some important points to note in this analysis. The curve indicating the proportion of the product represented by the net inflow of capital shows extremely erratic fluctuations in the past.* Our basic assumption is that the net inflow of capital would constitute 1.77 percent of the product, for the reasons already given, and would rise little by little until it reached 2.09 percent in 1975, afterward declining by gradual and regular stages as Latin America's product increased faster than that of the countries transferring the capital.

It remains to explain the movements of interest and profits in terms of their relation to the product.** Here the influence of the two alternative rates of interest is clearly in evidence. In alternative A (2 percent for new loan

---

*It rises rapidly from 0.36 percent of the product in 1950 to 2.34 percent in 1957-1959, then drops to 1.08 percent in 1963-1965 and climbs again to 1.54 percent in 1966-1968. The average for the whole period works out at 1.48 percent.

**In these projections it is assumed that private investment will represent 20 percent of the total gross inflow of capital and that remittances of profits will be equivalent to 10 percent of the total figure for cumulative direct investment.

operations) the proportion of the product represented by interest payments decreases from 1.90 percent at the start to 1.67 percent in 1975, subsequently continuing its downward trend. In the case of alternative B, the curve remains higher than that of alternative A throughout the decade.

It is worthwhile to pause here for a moment to glance at the last curve in the figure, i.e., the net inflow of financial resources, or, in other words, the gross inflow of capital minus amortization, interest, and profits. This net inflow is influenced by the trends indicated for the three items in question. In the past, as will be recalled, there was no net inflow, but a net outflow in relation to the product, except in 1957-1959 and 1960-62, when a net inflow did take place, albeit in the second of these periods it was virtually negligible. The last curve in Figure 24 shows that alternatives A and B for the terms of the external debt would both represent an improvement in the relation between the net inflow of resources and the product, largely attributable to the lightening of the burden of amortization.

Although the net outflow of financial resources implied by alternative B would represent much lower percentages than in the past, if the net inflow of external financing was to reach positive figures during the period covered by the projection, not only amortization but also interest rates would have to be lighter, as in alternative A. If this latter alternative were not adopted, the effort made to step up import substitution at the regional level and exports to the rest of the world, which would have to be considerable even on the assumption of a 2 percent interest rate, would need to be more intensive still. This difference is very important because of its internal implications.* A point to bear in mind here is the effect of an outflow of funds on the resources available for consumption and investment.

### Raising the Coefficient of Domestic Investment Resources

Let us first consider the terms in which the problem of raising the coefficient of domestic investment resources presents itself. The total

---

*Given hypothesis B, which postulates annual amortization and interest rates of 4 percent and 6 percent, respectively, as against hypothesis A, in which the rate of interest is only 2 percent, a more vigorous policy for the promotion of regional import substitution or extraregional exports of manufactured goods would have to be pursued in order to make up the difference between the two hypotheses by 1980. Thus, the coefficient of imports in relation to the gross domestic product would be reduced to 9.6 percent, instead of 10.2 percent, to meet the requirements implicit in the 8 percent growth rate of the product. If the only solution adopted was a more dynamic policy to expand exports of manufactured goods to the rest of the world, the annual rate of increase of such exports would have to be 19.6 percent during the 1970's, instead of 14.4 percent, as would be the case if the average rate of interest on the external debt were 2 percent.

These figures for the import coefficient (9.6 percent) and the growth rate of industrial exports (19.6 percent) give some idea of the scale and intensity of the additional effort that would be required in respect of each of these solutions, considered separately, in order to cover the difference between the two hypotheses for the rate of interest on the external debt.

TABLE 23

Latin America:  Total Gross Investment Coefficient and Share of
Domestic Resources and of Gross Inflow of Foreign Capital
(percentage of product)

| Period | Domestic Resources* | Gross Inflow of Foreign Capital | Total Gross Investment |
|---|---|---|---|
| 1966-1968 | 14.5 | 3.8 | 18.3 |
| 1980 | 24.0 | 2.5 | 26.5 |
| 1990 | 24.6 | 1.9 | 26.5 |

*Including the additional domestic savings effort required to meet the implications of the 8 percent growth rate, as will be shown later.

Source: Latin American Institute for Economic and Social Planning.

investment coefficient would have to be raised from 18.3 percent in 1966-1968 to 26.5 percent in 1980 in order to attain a rate of development of 8 percent by the latter year (see Table 23 and Figures 26-28). Given the foregoing assumptions as to the gross inflow of foreign capital, the coefficient of domestic investment resources* would have to be increased.

Viewed a posteriori, the problem of raising the coefficient of domestic investment resources from 14.5 percent to 24 percent looks very simple. In 1980 the per capita product for the whole of Latin America—after deduction of the above-mentioned outflows of financial resources—would be much higher than in the base year (see Table 24). Thus, the vigorous growth of the product available for consumption and investment would make it possible, if appropriate measures were adopted, for the domestic resources allocated to investment to increase as postulated above and at the same time leave a considerable margin for the expansion of per capita consumption in absolute terms. But this would be the goal reached at the end of the first decade. The real problem is how to get there. The initial effort would have to be arduous indeed. It must be borne in mind, first and foremost, that during the transition period, saving must increase faster than the product and consumption must increase less rapidly. Once the target coefficient had been attained, it *might* be

*The concept of "domestic investment resources" represents the real amount of financial resources available for this purpose, i.e., the proportion of domestic saving which can make an effective contribution to the financing of investment. It can therefore be quantified by subtracting the amortization of the external debt from domestic saving.

## TABLE 24

### Latin America:  Per Capita Product and Percentages Assigned to Consumption and to Investment

| Period | Average per Capita Product (dollars) | Percentage Assigned to | | Total Percentage Growth Rate in Relation to 1966-1968 | | |
|---|---|---|---|---|---|---|
| | | Consumption | Investment | Consumption | Investment | Total |
| 1966-1968 | 400 | 85 | 15 | – | – | – |
| 1980 | 630 | 75 | 25 | 2.6 | 7.5 | 3.6 |
| 1990 | 1,030 | 75 | 25 | 3.6 | 6.2 | 4.2 |

*Note:* The table excludes outflows of financial resources abroad.

*Source:* Latin American Institute for Economic and Social Planning.

possible for consumption and saving to grow at the same rate as the product. I underline the word "might" because, if it were decided that the amount of the external debt was to be gradually reduced, saving would have to continue to increase more rapidly than the product.

An estimate was previously presented—one among the many that might be formulated—of the gross inflow of external capital which could be obtained during the transition period. Accordingly, the problem here consists in determining how great an effort would have to be made in respect to domestic saving, given this assumption with regard to foreign capital. But we must beware of misinterpretation. In practice, the necessary saving is not of a residual nature, or, in other words, does not represent what must be done to supplement foreign capital. Just the contrary: once the domestic savings effort has been quantified—with due regard, of course, to the possibilities of obtaining funds from abroad—the amount of external capital required can then be estimated.

Foreign capital must act as a spur to domestic saving. This would be possible in the economy as a whole if the gross inflow of foreign capital—especially in the early years— stimulated the growth of the product to such an extent that in order to increase saving, current consumption would not need to be restricted, but only the additional consumption which the rise in the product would permit. This is the first assumption adopted in our hypothesis, i.e., that the growth rate of the product would climb steadily during the first decade until it reached 8 percent as the investment coefficient increased, and that in this coefficient the importance of the gross inflow of foreign capital would be considerable to begin with, and subsequently would gradually diminish in relation to the product, as the mobilization of domestic saving was stepped up. The purpose of this assumption is to assess the extent to which the

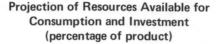

**FIGURE 26**

**Projection of Resources Available for
Consumption and Investment
(percentage of product)**

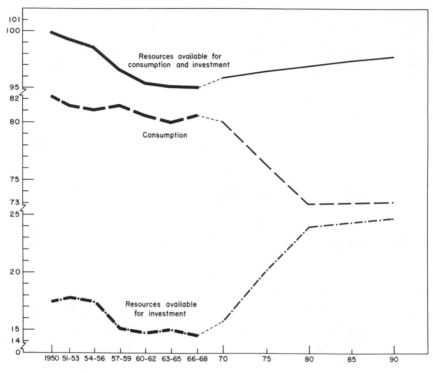

*Source:* ECLA, on the basis of official data.

consumption increment would have to be restricted and the various ways in which this might affect the broadly classified income distribution strata.

From the social standpoint, this is a vital aspect of the subject, of supreme concern to the political art of development, which cannot be effectively practiced in default of an objective presentation of the main development options for decision-making purposes.

This topic of saving is one on which only conjectural evaluations relating to Latin America as a whole can be hazarded. They must, therefore, be taken as such—very rough estimates of orders of magnitude—and the wide intercountry disparities must not be overlooked.

One of the keynotes of the present study is equitable income distribution. The social integration of the masses relegated to the lower income strata is an imperative necessity. Accordingly, the projections envisage an acceleration of the rate of increase of their personal income. The present level of consumption among the groups in question is so low that to restrict its

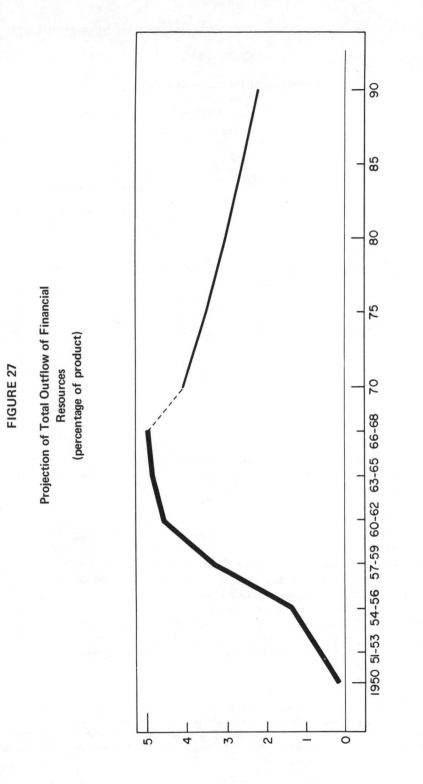

FIGURE 27

**Projection of Total Outflow of Financial Resources**

(percentage of product)

*Source:* ECLA, on the basis of official data.

127

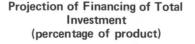

FIGURE 28

Projection of Financing of Total
Investment
(percentage of product)

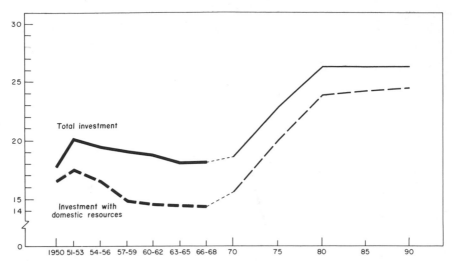

*Source:* ECLA, on the basis of official data.

expansion is unthinkable, at any rate in the early years of the period considered. The additional savings effort would therefore be incumbent upon the higher strata. To facilitate the exposition of the problem, the conjectural estimates, by strata, included in the ECLA/Institute study,* are presented in Table 25.

It will be noted in Table 25 that the highest income stratum constitutes a relatively small proportion of the Latin American population and absorbs a substantial share of total income. Understandably enough, it is the members of this group who pay the highest taxes and show the highest rate of saving. Taxes account for 25 percent of their income and 18 percent is saved; thus, the remaining 57 percent is spent on consumption.

It is worthwhile to pause for a closer look at these figures. If the whole burden of the additional savings effort postulated were to be shouldered by the highest stratum, its per capita consumption would have to be reduced—through increased saving and heavier taxation—by 0.8 percent yearly during the first of

---

*Unfortunately, no more recent data—at any rate, none systematically organized—are available for the purposes of the present commentary. However, there are indications that the situation has undergone no radical change. At all events, it should be recalled that this document is not concerned with formulating proposals, but represents an illustrative exercise.

**TABLE 25**

**Latin America: Conjectural Estimates of Income Distribution and Use, 1960**

| Stratum | Proportion of Population | Proportion of Personal Income | Average Monthly Income per Household (dollars) | Use of Personal Income (percentage) | | |
|---|---|---|---|---|---|---|
| | (percentage) | | | Consumption | Taxation | Saving |
| I | 40 | 9 | 35 | 90 | 10 | — |
| II | 20 | 10 | 82 | 80 | 20 | — |
| III | 35 | 50 | 228 | 77 | 20 | 3 |
| IV | 5 | 31 | 1,000 | 57 | 25 | 18 |

*Source*: ECLA/Latin American Institute for Economic and Social Planning, "El estrangulamiento externo y la escasez de ahorro en el desarrollo de América Latina. Análisis de los problemas y algunas de las soluciones" (Santiago, March, 1970).

the two decades covered by the projection. Thus, in view of what these two items represent today, the proportion of expenditure on consumption in this social group would be cut down to 36 percent of average income per household.

This highest stratum is far from homogeneous. Its expenditure on consumption, according to Table 25, probably averages about $570 a month per household. In a group within this stratum that constitutes not more than 2 percent of the region's population, the corresponding figure must certainly be appreciably higher, and there would seem to be no doubt that the capacity of this group to increase the present proportion exceeds that of the remainder of the stratum.

Other possibilities must now be explored. In recent years, the middle income groups have been increasing their consumption at an annual rate of 2.3 percent per household. According to our hypothesis, average consumption per household could expand faster, owing to the postulated growth of average income. For example, it might increase at an average annual rate of 2.7 percent and still leave a considerable margin for saving either directly, or indirectly through taxation. And in that case, what savings effort would the highest stratum have to make instead of that assumed above? The answer is as follows: although in the early 1970's the expansion of consumption per household in these groups would have to be restricted, over the whole decade their consumption could increase at the significant average annual rate of 1.7 percent.

In any event, the foregoing figures are conjectural, and these comments on them should on no account be interpreted as proposals, for which there would be no foundation. Nevertheless, they do indicate an appropriate course to follow in the study of the various specific situations in Latin America. One conclusion which I hold to be important can safely be drawn. If in the early years of application of a development strategy a policy of expanding economic activity is pursued, whereby the product can be increased fairly quickly, it should be possible to make the additional savings effort without insurmountable difficulties, provided it is also accepted that in order to give so powerful an impetus to the Latin American economy, a reasonable degree of discipline in the capital formation process is essential.

Table 26 shows trends in consumption, saving, and taxation in the various strata under consideration, in line with the hypotheses to which reference has been made; it is assumed that in the two lowest strata, consumption and income will grow at the same rate as the product.

In the first decade the product would increase by 47 percent. Consequently, this would represent the rise in the level of consumption of the lower strata. The middle income groups, on the other hand, would have expanded their consumption by 31 percent and the highest stratum by 18 percent, owing to the savings effort made. During this first decade, for the reasons already explained, saving would have to increase much more than the product. But if the growth rate of the product had reached 8 percent by the end of the 1970's, so exceptionally strenuous an effort would no longer be necessary in the second decade. Thus the expansion of consumption could approach the increase in the product, which would total 65 percent. This

## TABLE 26

**Latin America: Projection of Consumption, Saving, and Taxation in the Various Income Strata**
**(percentage)**

| | Annual Growth Rate of Per Capita Consumption | | | Proportions Used for Saving and Taxation | |
| | At Beginning of First Decade | | Average Rate | At End of | |
| Stratum | 1970-1971 | 1971-1972 | 1970-1980 | 1960's | 1980 |
|---|---|---|---|---|---|
| | *Hypothesis A* | | | | |
| I | 2.3 | 2.7 | 3.9 | 10 | 10 |
| II | 2.3 | 2.7 | 3.9 | 20 | 20 |
| III | 2.3 | 2.7 | 3.9 | 23 | 23 |
| IV | 2.3 | 2.3 | −0.8 | 43 | 64 |
| | *Hypothesis B* | | | | |
| I | 2.3 | 2.7 | 3.9 | 10 | 10 |
| II | 2.3 | 2.7 | 3.9 | 20 | 2- |
| III | 2.3 | 2.7 | 2.7 | 23 | 32 |
| IV | 2.3 | 2.3 | 1.7 | 43 | 54 |

*Source:* Latin American Institute for Economic and Social Planning.

would facilitate income redistribution measures designed to hasten the social integration of the lower strata.

There is room here for various alternatives, calling for very careful consideration of incentives to economic activities, on the one hand, and of the growing social investment and expenditure requirements, on the other. Exploration of this field would be inappropriate here. However interesting the speculations it might lead to, it would overload this part of the report.

It is assumed in this context that the lower strata spend the whole of their income on consumption, a state of affairs which, although consonant with existing conditions, might be altered during the process described above. And it would be a good thing if this could be brought about through measures to encourage saving, for even with the investment coefficient necessitated by our basic proposition, it would be impossible to wipe out certain social deficits, such as that of housing, from which Latin America suffers. If a modest proportion of the increase in the income of the lower strata were earmarked for saving, it might mean that a great deal more low-cost housing could be built.

## Some Aspects of Development Strategy and International Cooperation

The transition period is beset with difficulties. The significance of what was termed in Chapter 1 "development discipline"—meaning the tenacious and systematic effort which would have to be made over and above the structural changes required to clear the way for the forces of development—will now be readily understood. Discipline in overcoming external constraint; discipline in making efficient use of resources from abroad, and building up more and more capital with internal resources, in order to accelerate the pace of development; discipline in adapting, assimilating, and creating technology; discipline, in short, in implementing an economic and social development plan embracing these and other matters of vital importance.

The saving postulated in our hypothesis will gradually increase proportionally as the product grows. In the logical sequence of events, the savings effort should become less and less exacting until the requisite savings coefficient is attained, and then kept constant without any additional effort.

As regards foreign trade, the rate of expansion of new export lines will have to be much faster than the growth rate of the product. Exports of manufactures will be of decisive importance. But as the composition of aggregate exports changes and the share of the new export lines is enlarged, their growth rate will decline naturally as the goal established in our hypothesis is approached. This goal is the point beyond which no out-of-the-way effort would need to be made to increase exports much more rapidly than the product. Such a rate of expansion would˙be necessary only when the import-substitution process, in spite of being carried out on broader bases than each individual country's narrow market, had arrived at a stage at which it could no longer be continued at the same rate as before.

Attention has repeatedly been drawn to the important role of capital from abroad during this transition period. Apart from its direct effects on investment, its function could be summed up as follows: to stimulate the domestic savings effort, and to relieve the external bottleneck until the foreign trade measures listed above were yielding full results.

It is assumed in our hypothesis that the product will grow at a steady rate and that saving should increase along with it, although less rapidly. However, there are possibilities of giving a stronger initial impetus to the growth of the product. It is a well-known fact that when, in the course of the external fluctuations which characterize the Latin American economy, exports expand or the flow of external capital increases, the growth rate of the aggregate product rises by two or three points. This is due primarily to the existence of idle capacity in the economy, the utilization of which enables the product to be increased without a correlative expansion of investment. A more powerful external stimulus, with its multiplier effects on overall demand and income, suffices to ensure that the upward movement will spread throughout the economy. This is what has happened in some of the Latin American countries in recent times.

Instead of deriving spontaneously from an impetus originating in the external sector, this positive result might be deliberately brought about. It is precisely here that the initial dynamic role of external financial resources lies. They are indispensable for the purposes of making investments which will boost overall demand.

No domestic activity, however important, could step up demand on its own account by the mere expansion of its production, since only part of the income thus generated would give rise to demand for this larger output. The rest of the demand created—or to be more accurate, most of it—would be channeled toward other goods and services. The resulting surplus on the supply side would call the expansion of production to an enforced halt.

It is true that the other activities among which the increase in demand would be distributed would also have to expand in order to meet it; but this process would take too long for the imbalance in the activity originating the demand to be righted.

To put it briefly, neither industry nor the other economic activities can provide their own stimulus. What is required is an overall increase in demand which will simultaneously encourage the whole body of economic activities and speed up their expansion. The role of promoting this was formerly discharged mainly by export activities. Their expansion causes an overall increase in domestic demand, while the corresponding production increment is marketed abroad, without giving rise to internal disequilibria. When the impetus given by exports slackens, import-substitution activities come to the fore. The additional demand thus engendered is also spread throughout the economy, but without causing internal imbalances, since the new lines of production barely fill the gap created by import restrictions.

Exports no longer play the same dynamic role as before in the expansion of the economy through demand, although this does not mean that the movements of internal demand are not powerfully affected by their fluctuations. But they will continue to be the cornerstone of the capacity to import, and as such they set the limit to the growth of the economy: a limit which can still be extended by means of import substitution, above all if this process is not conducted within the narrow framework of the individual country markets. Hence, neither exports nor substitution industries have ceased to be important in the development process, but their role is no longer the same.

Some explanation must be given of the significance attaching to the more rapid expansion of demand. Briefly, it must be given sufficient impetus to permit the attainment of the highest rate of development envisaged as a target. This impetus must be deliberately promoted until the economy attains a new growth rate and adapts itself to the ensuing requirements. The problem then changes its character. It is no longer merely a question of speeding up the growth rate, but of lessening the elements of instability in the system.

During this phase of transition from one rate of development to another, State investment in economic and social infrastructure is called upon to set the machinery of reciprocal demand in motion in all the economic activities of the system. The expansion of public expenditure may produce the same effects. But perhaps investment should be assigned a higher priority because of the great unsatisfied needs that generally present themselves, because of its strategic importance, and because of its social significance. Investment of this type differs from direct investment intended to expand the economy's production apparatus. The latter tends to follow in the wake of demand, meeting its requirements as it increases, but is powerless to originate an acceleration of demand, for the reasons explained above; whereas investment in infrastructure creates new flows of demand which raise employment and income to higher levels and thus impart greater momentum to the operation of the whole system.

Consequently, the expansion of investment in economic and social infrastructure must help to give the initial "big push" to the acceleration of development. Some types of investment in this field do more than others to increase employment. If the emphasis is placed on these, the multiplier effects will make themselves felt at an early stage: an overall expansion of demand, higher employment levels and utilization of the idle capacity in the economy, additional income, and new increases in demand and employment, and so on in succession. This is the familiar multiplier pattern. But as the process is completed and idle capacity is put to use, first in some activities and then in others, new investment in the various branches of production becomes necessary to enable them to keep pace with the growth of demand. Accordingly, this new investment is added to the initial investment in infrastructure and shares in its dynamic role. And as this happens, the proportion of total investment represented by investment in infrastructure can be gradually reduced, in line with the order of priority deemed advisable for the application of investment resources.

Generally speaking, the need for new investment would not seem to be pressing in industry, except in a few specific cases. The existing idle capacity should make it possible to cope with the initial upswing of demand without much additional capital. The same would be true, within limits, of the stepping up of agricultural production by means of more efficient land use.

This possibility of expanding the product with relative ease pertains to the opening phase of the transition period. And by following this line of action it is less difficult to raise the savings coefficient, whether the increase in consumption is restricted less than in our basic hypothesis, or whether its restriction is equally stringent and thus enables the target to be attained more quickly.

All this looks very simple, but let us not be led astray by a mirage. A policy of this kind is no easy matter, and stress must be laid here on the possibility that it may be partly or wholly unsuccessful in producing its effects, and may even defeat its own ends, in default of that development discipline whoe indispensability cannot be too strongly urged.

The object of the expansionist process described is to give the initial impetus to the implementation of development strategy, not to replace it with an immediatist view of the problem. As the economy expands, however, increasingly acute tensions arise, owing to difficulties either on the entrepreneurial side or on the labor side, among others. These difficulties prevent expansion from continuing, as the idle capacity is used up, without serious inflationary problems. In any case, this policy—we repeat—must be the beginning of a development program which gradually prepares the economy for higher rates of growth. Its expansionist effects might also be largely frustrated if advantage were not taken of this phase to launch from the outset a number of measures designed to relieve the tensions previously mentioned, to tap savings, and to promote exports. In other words, the phase of expansion is the time for taking the sort of action which has generally been neglected during export booms, and thus giving lasting impetus to development.

In any event, the contribution made by external capital would seem an indispensable requisite for covering any increase in imports that the rapid growth of the product may involve. Without this contribution, the additional imports could be afforded only if exports expanded to the necessary extent, or if there were a clear margin for import substitution. But unless this were the case—as is highly unlikely, save in the event of a temporary coincidence with one of the periodic spells of external prosperity, which seldom last long—external financing would be needed to cope with the growth of import requirements. These resources might come at an early stage, in order to stimulate the expansion of demand, or, if this expansion had been achieved by means of more liberal internal credit, later on, to compensate balance-of-payments deficits.

The amount of external financial resources previously postulated in this report might or might not prove insufficient to sustain the initial economic expansion that we have been discussing. If that were the case, the inflow of such resources would have to be increased. But any surplus contribution received at the beginning would mean that so much the less was needed later, as the savings capacity of the economy expanded. In other words, the effort would have to be particularly strenuous in the early years of the decade, instead of being evenly distributed throughout the period.

Possibly, however, if additional foreign capital were needed, it might be mainly to cover the effects of product growth on imports. Imports of capital goods would not be greatly needed as long as there was still a margin for full utilization of existing installed capacity.

In the context of investment, there are a few observations to be made of importance from the standpoint of the external bottleneck. It might take longer to relieve this constraint than to reach the point at which domestic savings suffice to meet requirements. This is the inference to be drawn from our hypothesis, in which every endeavor has been made to avoid rash assumptions, however true it may be that those formulated in respect of foreign trade would entail very intensive effort. In such circumstances, the region would have to continue receiving more external capital than has been estimated as indispensable for the purpose of supplementing internal saving. This does not mean that the extra capital should be used for consumption. That would be a most unwise proceeding, for huge economic and social investment requirements still remain to be met. Much as it deserves comment, however, it is not this aspect of the problem but the following that will be dwelt on here.

The alleviation of the external bottleneck will call for clearly defined and continuing cooperation on the part of international credit institutions, in addition to the technical assistance needed. Clearly, such cooperation could be based only on the relevant government decisions, although the institutions concerned could do much in the sphere of persuasion and could draw upon their experience and their resources to contribute to preinvestment studies, with the support of the United Nations Development Program.

The International Bank for Reconstruction and Development (IBRD) and the Inter-American Development Bank (IDB) are called upon to play an important part in the financing of the projects concerned, whether they relate to the promotion of exports to the rest of the world or to regional or subregional import substitution. Close cooperation between the two institutions would be highly desirable, but the emphasis of their activities could differ in accordance with their individual experience, although this would by no means imply a strict division of functions. The IBRD group, by virtue of its wide experience and its important links with the industrialized countries, could give vigorous support to projects concerning exports to the rest of the world, with due regard to the advisability—to which attention has already been drawn—of promoting Latin American initiative in both national and multinational enterprises. On the other hand, IDB, because of its experience in the Latin American countries and its close contact with their economic and political situation and with their men of action, should play a stronger part in the promotion and financing of subregional and regional import-substitution projects. The establishment of a subsidiary or branch office to promote and support Latin American private enterprise, both technically and financially, would be a very appropriate means to this end.

Here again, no strict dividing line can be drawn between projects concerned with exports to the rest of the world and integration projects. In this case, too, it is a matter of emphasis.

If the moment were politically opportune, and the governments felt it to be so and adopted the relevant decision, one of the most important examples of this pooling of effort might be the formulation of an integration program for the iron and steel industry. Latin America has already learned to produce iron and steel. This is an industry which is almost entirely in national hands. All that is lacking is to make it economic, through the expansion of markets and the rational distribution of production. Preliminary studies have shown that integration could result in a saving of investment and a reduction of costs in an industry of such fundamental importance for the manufacture of capital goods. None of the countries currently producing iron and steel would have to cease to do so. Far from it. It would simply mean manufacturing a different range of products on much more economically sound and rational bases.

Apart from its economic significance, starting the integration process with this industry would be of unquestionable political importance, since it would provide specific evidence that the primary purpose of integration is not to open up new fields for foreign private enterprise—however justifiable it might be—but to encourage Latin American initiative and to help the region to make up its technical and financial deficiency. Moreover, it would afford a shining example of what a purely Latin American multinational enterprise could be.

It will not be superfluous to recall that concern is felt as to the imbalance which might arise if this and other integration possibilities were considered separately, instead of in the aggregate. It is true that in many cases the products of a single branch of industry could be distributed among various countries. But should there not be enough to go round, it would be necessary to resort to other projects in order to ensure the practical operation of the system of reciprocal benefits.

In import-substitution industries, both at the national and at the regional level, association with foreign private enterprise would be valuable on financial and technological grounds.

In any industries installed to export to the rest of the world—and particularly to the industrialized centers—knowledge of the market and of means of gaining access to it is of the highest importance. In this respect foreign enterprise can play a very significant role, and although the aforesaid association with domestic initiative would also be advisable, a flexible approach would be necessary in those industries in which the Latin American countries have not yet acquired sufficient experience and whose technology is highly complex. But this flexibility should not be allowed to weaken the basic considerations formulated in the present report in respect of Latin American private enterprise.

Outstanding among these considerations are those relating to the external bottleneck, especially in the transition period. Foreign enterprise must help to eliminate the bottleneck, not to aggravate the constraint, as it does when it acquires control of enterprises or invests in industries whose techniques are already familiar. This is a point worth stressing. If satisfactory rates of development are to be reached, great care will have to be taken to see that external payments—at least in the transition period—are limited to what is absolutely essential. From this and other standpoints, and as long as technological considerations permitted, the financing of Latin American enterprise by the multinational credit institutions at relatively moderate rates of interest would be preferable to foreign private investment, unless investors were willing to limit their remittances abroad and to reinvest their profits during the long transition period through which the region will inevitably have to pass.

These cautions with regard to external payments also apply to imports. Freedom to import at will, subject to the payment of reasonable duties, is often counseled from outside, with strong backing in some internal circles. How far this advice could be followed in the transition period it would be impossible to tell beforehand. The foreign trade effort would be arduous, and it would not be surprising if supplementary measures had to be adopted to restrict certain imports, although in the light of Latin America's plentiful experience it seems desirable for this to be done through general measures rather than by means of direct controls.

Conceivably, too, in consequence of import pressures the possibility of influencing the consumption patterns of the upper and middle income strata might be studied, with a view to investigating their direct or indirect incidence on imports and how it could be lessened.

To sum up, one of the conclusions to be drawn from the present report is that it is not advisable to go on being content with rough approximations, and that the time has come for a more thorough analysis of the possibilities of combating the external bottleneck through regional or subregional import substitution—especially in respect of intermediate and capital goods—and through restriction of certain nonessential imports. This would not, of course, detract from the importance of encouraging exports by every possible means.

With all the appropriate reservations, the estimates formulated here are justifiable only as preliminary pointers to possible solutions, as has already been stated. But although this method of dealing with so important a problem is inevitable for the moment, to persist in it would be a mistake.

At this point I should like to add a pertinent comment. So great is the concern aroused by the difficulties of the transition period, that some allusion must be made to the incidence of military expenditure on the balance of payments and on domestic capital formation. This is an extremely delicate subject, and I am totally unqualified to express an opinion on its technical aspects. But I do wonder whether the time has not come to think of looking into the possibility of concerting agreements on the limitation of armaments compatible with unavoidable defense measures.

### Domestic Capital Formation

One of the vital factors in the success of any national strategy for the acceleration of development in Latin America consists in raising the coefficient of domestic investment resources until, with the passage of time, they can cover the whole of the investment required. There is no need to stress this further after what has already been said in the present study. The trends recorded in the past do not set a good example. Except in two cases, as was explained earlier, the coefficient decreased in the period under consideration (1950-1968). The increasing burden of financial outflows in the shape of profits and interest, amortization and debt repayment, together with the deterioration of the terms of trade, have affected investment rather than consumption. International cooperation could help to keep these outflows from exceeding all proportion, as they have in the past. But of course that would not be enough. It is absolutely essential to adopt energetic and persevering internal measures to promote a steady rise in the coefficient of domestic investment resources.

This is unquestionably the most important and the most difficult task relating to the acceleration of development. In view of the explanations already given in the present report, it can be summed up in very few words. The Latin American economy is not saving enough to speed up its development as rapidly as is needful. Incentives could be provided to encourage saving and to improve the existing instruments for tapping the resulting resources, and the tax systems in force could be made more efficient and turned to better account as sources of capital formation through the State.

All this is important, but it falls short of the exceptional effort implied by a rapid increase in the coefficient of domestic savings, as postulated here. Why this assertion? Because we have reached the conviction that this objective cannot be attained in default of the vigorous mobilization of all the productive resources which the Latin American economy is wasting because of the vicious circle in which it is trapped.

Generally speaking, land is inefficiently used; the same is true of capital goods; and redundant manpower is still left in the rural areas, while only a minimal proportion of the labor force that has migrated to the cities in the last two decades has succeeded in finding employment at a satisfactory level of productivity, and the rest has needlessly gone to swell the ranks of the services sector. There is no need to dwell further on this problem. What is the vicious circle of which I spoke? The economy is at a deadlock. To put it succinctly, and without reference to the complex of factors mentioned above, the economy is not saving what it should because it is wasting its production potential, and that potential is being wasted because the economy is not saving more. Latin America must break out of this vicious circle. And that will be impossible without an initial "big push" to set the machinery of acceleration in motion.

A key contention of the present study is that international financial resources would make a valuable contribution to this start, provided that they were invested in conformity with a clearly defined and unswerving strategy. Such support would considerably lighten the initial capital formation effort; but even in default of it, the effort will have to be made, if the oppressive vicious circle is to be broken.

It is in the light of these considerations that the subject of the present section will be examined. First and foremost the following question must be asked: if the vicious circle were broken and the expansionist forces of the economy were able to realize their potential, so that new investment opportunities were created, how far would a rise in the savings coefficient be spontaneously brought about? In other words, if the expansionist forces were curbed, saving may have been curbed as well. Should they be released, could saving increase of its own accord?

Presumably the mere fact that the product rose rapidly during the initial phase of the transition period would suffice in itself to increase marginal savings, as usually happens in such circumstances. But the effort needed to reach the requisite coefficient would be so great that it could hardly be made unless it were powerfully and deliberately stimulated. This is the point at issue. The question is how incentives to private investment and discouragement of nonessential consumption would have to be combined with tax and other fiscal measures that would tap some proportion of the additional income generated, in order to hasten the process of capital formation.

In other words, the problem to be faced is the delicate one of balancing these various means to the end pursued. Recourse to taxation as an instrument of capital formation does not necessarily imply that the State will widen the radius of its direct economic activities. It is perfectly conceivable that the resources thus obtained might be channeled into private enterprise, through suitable institutional machinery, and in the context of an investment program under a development plan. This point will be discussed later, but in the meantime some comments may be made on the encouragement of saving and private investment. Latin America has an interesting stock of experience in this respect which must be turned to account, but the scale of the effort required is so great that the imagination naturally looks for out-of-the-ordinary ways of reaching the goal in view.

We were asking a moment ago how far it would be possible to stimulate an adequate savings effort by means of the new investment opportunities opened up. This is a vitally important matter where firms and enterprises are concerned. How can they be induced to invest a bigger proportion of their profits? Would tax measures to encourage investment and discourage the overt or disguised distribution of profits be enough?

How far could this mechanism be effective? Would it not incite to overinvestment in labor-saving equipment, as seems to have happened in some cases in Latin America? This is a matter which calls for more careful study. So does the following question. In view of the exigent demands of the transition period, might not limits conceivably be set to the distribution of profits, so that they could be used for investment, either in the same firm or enterprise or in others, or in public or private savings institutions? This measure is worth some thought, since it would allow incentives to productivity to be reconciled with the need for capital formation and the necessity of restricting the expansion of consumption during so difficult a period.

There is another observation worth making in connection with the attitude of enterprises toward capital formation. We have urged the need to lengthen amortization periods and lighten debt servicing in order to adjust them to a country's external payments capacity. But this does not mean that enterprises, whether public or private, must necessarily be subject to the same terms. In most cases they might be able to carry heavier financial burdens. Full advantage would have to be taken of such possibilities—not, however, in order to generate yet another increase in remittances abroad, but with a view to building up more domestic resources for financing purposes.

From another point of view, IDB has carried out highly interesting studies on the promotion of capital markets in Latin America. These might be useful instruments for helping to increase the savings coefficient rather than merely to change the form in which savings were effected.

Consideration should also be given to other expedients with regard to saving in the middle and even some of the lower income strata. The means which might be efficaciously employed include, of course, the creation of capital markets and the more widespread use of instruments for tapping savings—such as adjustable bonds—which have already been successfully tried out in Latin America, in cases where inflation had seriously weakened the propensity to save.

But would these methods be a sufficient spur to savings consciousness, or would new procedures also have to be resorted to? If a policy whereby income could be increased quickly were implemented, would it not be possible to interest the staffs of firms and enterprises in the idea of investing part of the increase in their real income in shares or bonds issued by their own or other firms? Here again new incentives would have to be considered. If the enterprises needed national or international public credit to expand their production systems, could they not conceivably use a reasonable proportion of medium- or long-term credit from such sources to offer their staffs facilities for buying shares or bonds issued either by the enterprises they work in or by other concerns?

Elsewhere in the present report emphasis is laid on the importance of basically Latin American multinational enterprises in the integration process, and on the role of IDB in promoting them. The idea of exploring this possibility in relation to enterprises that would mean so much for Latin American life is certainly alluring. If they were not to be exposed to the temptations associated with monopolies, however, it would be indispensable for their establishment to go hand in hand with commitments to reduce the external tariff by gradual degrees, until a point was reached that would facilitate competition from the rest of the world. It could thus be brought home to entrepreneurs and workers alike that the source of profit must be efficiency, not protection. This of course is equally applicable to enterprises operating at the national level.

Needless to say, this is not the only way in which saving could be encouraged in the middle and part of the lower strata. As pointed out elsewhere in the present chapter, even the latter could be drawn into the savings effort, mainly through low-cost housing incentives.

Increased capital formation in all the social strata should depend not only upon the encouragement of saving and investment, but also upon the discouragement of certain forms of consumption, of which mention has already been made. Taxation is an appropriate instrument for this purpose. But it is not the only one. It is somewhat paradoxical that here in Latin America, where there are so many unsatisfied investment requirements, incitements to consumption have continued to proliferate in wide variety. They are provided partly by mass communication media, and partly by the constantly increasing consumer credit facilities that enable the higher and middle income groups—which are those that benefit by them most—to use a significant proportion of the community's savings potential for expenditures of this type.

Reference has been made to the importance of taxes as an instrument of capital formation. The taxation picture in Latin America is far from uniform, not only as regards the tax base but also in respect of the progressiveness or regressiveness of the system. There are some countries in which tax pressures are unquestionably severe. In others a margin of tax potential is still available, and in others again—though these are fewer—the tax burden is moderate. And this last group includes some very interesting cases in which the State has managed to mobilize increasing resources by means of savings certificates.

The vicious circle in the Latin American economy also affects the State. Reactivation of the economy would permit a considerable increase in tax revenue, thus creating the right conditions for certain adjustments which would make for a more equitable distribution of the tax burden. The progress made in tax organization and administration in several countries during recent years is deserving of mention. But tax evasion, although less widespread than before, continues on a considerable scale; and this, apart from its intrinsic effects, is a factor making for inequity.

Consequently, the acceleration of the growth rate of the product and the aforesaid tax adjustments would enable the State's financial resources to be appreciably increased. But this is only one side of the picture; the other is expenditure and investment, to which brief reference will next be made.

The State should invest on a large scale in economic and social infrastructure, both because of the requirements implicit in the social integration of the underprivileged masses, and because of the need to lay broad foundations for the expansion of economic activity. It will also have to increase its social expenditures—especially on health and education—and, of course, to keep up with the natural growth of other current expenditure.

The State has been compelled to expand its current expenditure in order to absorb redundant manpower. And this has been prejudicial to investment in infrastructure and social expenditure. If the lack of the required degree of dynamism was gradually made good, the State would be able to regulate such current expenditure more satisfactorily, so as to rationalize the distribution of its resources. It could not, therefore, shirk the development discipline of which we have spoken. On the contrary, it would have to give this discipline expression in a clearly defined program of expenditure and investment, based on an order of priorities consonant with the national development strategy.

In several Latin American countries workers are paid less by the State than by private enterprise, and this situation—apart from what it implies from the standpoint of equity—has made for a loss of efficiency. Restoration of the level of efficiency is an indispensable requisite.

Alongside public enterprises which operate normally in Latin America, there are others which are inefficiently run. This affects capital formation and economic development; and its importance is all the greater in the case of enterprises concerned with basic services or operating at key points in the system of production.

But the deficit shown by such enterprises is not always a symptom of mismanagement. In many cases it has been impossible to increase tariff rates, however justifiable it would have been to do so, and this is often because of understandable social considerations or economic development aims. The deficit originating in this way may have a demoralizing and disturbing effect on the operation of the enterprises concerned, leading to further disequilibria whose financial implications adversely affect capital formation and the role of the enterprises in the economy.

If the State considers that it ought to subsidize the price of certain public services, it should do so explicitly, transferring the resources directly to the enterprises, in order not to distort their operation. It is true that in many instances the enterprises themselves want reorganizing, and well-defined objectives need to be established, together with management criteria.

In these brief remarks it is impossible to pass over the concern aroused in Latin America by the serious defects generally characterizing the social security system, both because of its own intrinsic flaws and because of its high administrative costs. The adverse repercussions of these deficiencies would be all the greater if the system were extended, as it should be, to the whole of the rural and urban masses. As in the preceding case, the financial deficit thus generated militates against capital formation.

Elsewhere in this study stress has been laid on the necessity of applying the spur of competition and gradually reducing excessive protection in order to induce private enterprise to improve its productivity. A great deal of productivity potential is wasted, and consequently substantial possibilities of capital formation are thrown away.

It is not only capital formation in itself that is at stake, however, but the capital goods in which it must take concrete shape. If the inevitable import-substitution policy continues to be implemented at the national level, the cost of those goods which will have to be home-produced on a very large scale will be extremely high, and this will add to the difficulties of the capital formation process.

In other words, it is essential that Latin American prices—beginning with those of intermediate and capital goods, which have so direct an incidence on production costs—should draw progressively closer to world market quotations; not merely for the foregoing internal reasons, but so that Latin American industry can enter the world market on a competitive footing.

It is often said that Latin America's internal price system needs to be made more fluid and efficacious. Perfectly true. But it is generally forgotten that a necessity for that purpose is a close linkage with the world market price system.

## THE TECHNIQUE AND POLITICAL ART OF DEVELOPMENT

The effort entailed in giving the economy the requisite additional dynamism will be very great and very complex. This has been emphasized over and over again. Now, at the end of this chapter, we must ask ourselves whether in advocating this effort we have not been guided by the tenuous thread of a visionary ideal. Can such an effort possibly be made in Latin America? And, at the same time, will it be possible to induce the industrialized centers to adopt a clear-sighted policy of international cooperation?

The world would have made very little headway if the triumph of an idea had been fought for only when the probabilities of success were great. Conviction is what matters, and it is with deep-rooted conviction that I write these pages. They are a summons to rationality and foresight. They are addressed to the holders of a whole range of opinions. To those who do not want change, in order to show them that it will come in any event—since the Latin American economy cannot go as it is, with its present seriously inadequate degree of dynamism—and to open their eyes to the supreme importance of the political and social cost of failing to bring the changes about in time. To others, who are convinced of the need for these changes, in order to discuss with them the inexorable demands of hard fact and to look calmly and objectively at the political assumptions underlying the various methods of influencing economic forces. And to those who want to destroy in order to rebuild on new and radically different lines, so that their model can be considered in relation to those inescapable terms imposed by reality itself, and to certain imperative demands of the present state of world affairs. Rationality and foresight are indispensable, it must be repeated, both in order to transform and in order to rebuild.

But there is no need to go so far. We should not allow the turmoil of politics and ideological controversy to trouble us overmuch, because in Latin America there is a substantial fund of common sense, and in this patrimony the masses too have their share. I am certain that a clear, honest, and persistent presentation of the great problem of development can clear the way for new ideas. New ideas which will enable each of the social groups to understand that the discipline asked of it will not be in vain.

I do not think it fanciful to suppose that a large measure of agreement can be reached on basic points in a development strategy, especially on those which cannot be sidestepped if the necessity of accelerating development is universally recognized. In any case, a vast field of major differences would still remain, chiefly in connection with the ways and means of distributing the burden of capital formation entailed by development. It would be well worthwhile even to reach agreement on the need for this capital formation and on the proportions it should attain. I should like to think that this will be possible if action at the national level is governed by a strong sense of continuity and a clear-sighted view of the future.

And also insight into the present and its immediate needs. A strategy which shelved these questions would not be politically viable. It is a great temptation to establish targets for 10 years hence and demonstrate their feasibility with the logic that will then be valid, not with the logic of today, and today's pressing demands. Hence the present report emphasizes the necessity of starting this strategy with an expansionist policy which, while taking into account the immediate needs that will not brook delay, will at the same time initiate the far-reaching measures which will gradually bear fruit in the course of this decade.

I should also like to see new impetus given to national strategies and to their coordination at the Latin American level. I am not blind to the great difficulties that have to be surmounted, but neither do I fail to recognize that time will not solve problems of its own accord but, on the contrary, steadily makes them worse. This is exactly what has been happening in Latin America.

If wait we must, let us not wait too long. This I say also to the decision-makers upon whom the new turn to be taken by international cooperation will depend. In default of a long-term view of trade and financial questions, the basic assumptions of our hypothesis would have to be drastically overhauled. It would no longer be a matter of slipping new equations into the computer, but of changing the political assumptions; and perhaps of taking the extreme way out represented by development through coercion. But the trouble is that in the course of formulating this new hypothesis, certain inescapable requirements, both internal and relating to international cooperation, would once again present themselves.

The object of this study is also to call for rationality and foresight at the intra-Latin American level. It is to be hoped that the more advanced countries, in their relations with those that are less developed, will increasingly be prompted by basic principles of economic, political, and human solidarity.

Let me now bring a little grist to my own mill. I believe that ECLA, together with the Latin American Institute for Economic and Social Planning, which operates under its fraternal aegis, must resolutely enter upon another stage which will extend their radius of persuasive influence to the maximum. It is not enough to conduct research and present substantive reports to governments. This is very important work, of course, and it must be done, and carried into new fields. Neither is it enough to train a select group of economists in development techniques and strategy. These boundaries must be crossed with determination. We must reach the men who are active in politics, in the economy, in the trade unions, especially those who belong to the rising generations: the men who move in other spheres of thought and action. With all of them opportunities of fruitful dialogue must be sought. Not mere Socratic dialogue—stimulating as it is in itself—but such dialogue as may culminate in the discovery of common ground, in a pragmatic consensus conducive to the action that can no longer be put off.

PART **III** INTERNATIONAL COOPERATION AND DEPENDENCE

# 5 INTERNATIONAL COOPERATION AND DEPENDENCE

## CONCEPTS OF PRIMARY IMPORTANCE

### The International Cooperation Picture

As was remarked elsewhere, considerable headway has been made in recent years in respect of international cooperation, but mainly in the intellectual field. Only to a limited extent have the developed countries adopted the major decisions which must go to shape a genuine cooperation program.

Such decisions are, of course, of a political nature; and while some countries have adopted them or are intending to do so, others, in particular the United States, find serious difficulty not only in expanding their program but even in preserving its continuity. Nevertheless, recognition must be accorded to what has been achieved in relations between the Latin American countries and the United States.

Encouraging signs of progress are already visible on the horizon. Through the Special Committee on Latin American Coordination (SCLAC), the Latin American countries are able to speak with a single united voice in the affairs of the hemisphere. With the help of sound technical advice, SCLAC has begun to strengthen the position of the developing countries vis-à-vis the developed countries. The United States in its turn seems to be reacting constructively, inasmuch as it has begun to eliminate some of the impediments to cooperation on its part and to allow its loans to be used for making purchases in Latin American markets.

Another step forward that deserves mention is the Unites States' announcement of a new policy of channeling more of its aid through multilateral than through bilateral conduits. Card should be taken, however, to see that the increase in multilateral contributions does not signify a decrease in the total inflow.

In all fairness, likewise, certain favorable events in recent years must be underlined. The Inter-American Development Bank (IDB) has opened up new channels and fulfilled highly important functions, and a very promising field of action lies ahead of it. The Inter-American Committee on the Alliance for Progress (ICAP) represents a valuable experiment in new ways of coming to an understanding and new lines of concrete action, which will have to be further developed on a liberal scale. The Agency for International Development (AID) has rendered effective services to the Latin American countries, especially in respect of the financing of programs. A substantial technical assistance effort has been made. More recently, at the last meeting of the Inter-American Economic and Social Council (IA-ECOSOC), a Special Committee for Consultation and Negotiation was set up, which may prove of great efficacy in relations between Latin America and the United States. And, above all, the basic principles of the Charter of Punta del Este still hold good. The principles themselves must not be confused with the attempts that have been made to put them into practice.

Be this as it may, further advances could perhaps be made if a clear distinction were established between the conception of an international cooperation policy and the specific measures adopted to implement it. What is essential is that the policy and its objectives should be defined, even if present circumstances are such that the measures cannot take concrete and appropriate shape in all cases until later on. Thus, it may be hoped, the progress achieved in the realm of ideas could be consolidated and the lessons of experience turned to account, both in operations and in institutional machinery.

In the light of experience, it would seem extremely important that the measures comprised in an international cooperation policy should not be of a residual character, but should be assigned a high order of priority in the developed countries.

However, temporary circumstances must not be held entirely responsible for what is happening. Certain attitudes exist which for some time past have been hindering the crystallization of an international cooperation policy. There are many who seek in such a policy instruments for negotiating with the Latin American countries and obtaining economic or political benefits as and when occasion arises. Thus, cooperation would not be prompted by the intention of genuinely helping to speed up the acceleration of the Latin American countries' development. In this connection, it is consoling to note that none of the reports mentioned in Part I contains even the remotest suggestion of views like these. But there can be no doubt that they still exist and that their roots still strike deep.

The United States and other developed countries could not possibly be expected to sacrifice their own national interest to such a cooperation policy. It would be idle to suppose that any country would do so, however strong its moral sense. Everything depends on the concept of national interest itself. It would have to be based not on short-term considerations, but on the sort of long-term outlook which is needed in all the fundamental problems of community life: an outlook farsighted enough to discern a great deal of common ground between the national interests of the countries offering cooperation and those of the countries receiving it.

One of the great merits of the Peterson Report is that it recognizes the need for adopting this long-term outlook and dismissing considerations of immediate interest. "This country," it says, referring to the United States, "should not look for gratitude or votes, or any specific short-term foreign policy gains from our participation in international development. Nor should it expect to influence others to adopt United States cultural values or institutions. Neither can it assume that development will necessarily bring political stability. Development implies change—political and social, as well as economic—and such change, for a time, may be disruptive."

And the report goes on to stress those long-term objectives with regard to which the interests of the developing countries and of the Unites States are the same: "the building of self-reliant and healthy societies in developing countries, an expanding world economy from which all will benefit, and improved prospects for world peace."[1]

### The Autonomy of Development

Where the Latin American countries are concerned, the intention to develop their economies is closely linked to a consideration whose importance is beyond question: the compatibility of international cooperation with definite autonomy in decision-making. Concern is thus aroused by the possibility that external loans may involve conditions which violate this autonomy. Naturally, a country must make its decisions in line with what its own interests counsel and taking into account its relations with other countries, in the light of that long-term outlook to which reference was made above. But it should not tailor them to the short-term demands of a commercial or financial negotiation.

In default of this autonomy in decision-making it would be impossible to work out politically sound and stable formulas, however palpable were the direct effects of international cooperation measures.

Up to a point, the image of the past is still projected into the present. In the days of outward-looking development, significant contradictions between international action and the nature of that development seldom arose. But the Latin America of today is no longer that of yesterday. The Latin American peoples have a different concept of the world they live in, and cherish different aspirations. And the world in which they live is constantly changing. From the economic standpoint, these countries used to constitute a sort of prolongation of the industrialized centers—their periphery—and here the developed countries came to purchase the primary commodities they needed; there was no such thing as a trade policy problem. Investment was affected, in one way or another, in relation to primary exports; there was no such thing as a financial cooperation problem either. Nor were there complex internal development problems. Outside the activities linked to foreign trade, the bulk of the population—save in a very few instances—stood passively aside while economic development passed them by.

The ruling groups in the Latin American countries fitted into the requirements of this phase of development. Sporadic conflicts might arise, but they did not affect the underlying coincidence of interests between the industrialized centers and the Latin American periphery. No serious contradictions emerged, nor did the alluring image of other economic and social systems beckon from the horizon.

This outline description suffices to point up the contrast between those days and the present time. Nowadays it is difficult to export, owing to the effects of technical progress and the protectionism prevailing in the industrialized centers; a strenuous and tenacious effort is needed in order to sell them manufactured goods, and it must be made without lapsing into new forms of dependence. Foreign capital is needed, but this time for internal development.

Internal development poses problems which could hardly have been glimpsed in the past. Not only economic problems, but also problems of a political, social, and cultural character. There is the population explosion to reckon with. And new forces are emerging, chiefly in the middle strata of society, which have expanded considerably. It is mainly from these middle strata that the men who are striving to transform the Latin American economy have been coming to the fore. Not in vain have long decades gone by. These men—who are not very many, but whose significance is great—are conscious of their own worth, of their ability to learn and assimilate things that others can do, and to assume their own responsibilities. They are tired of being background figures on the development stage. They want to be leading actors. They are animated by the very legitimate desire to achieve something better than peripheral status.

Unless due allowance is made for this maturation process which has been taking place principally in the middle strata of the Latin American societies, it is impossible to understand certain apprehensions increasingly aroused by foreign private investment. Nobody could question the usefulness of such investment when, in addition to bringing in financial resources on reasonable terms, it introduces technologies which are needed for the type of development aimed at, and which for the moment are inaccessible to Latin American industry. But it is essential that foreign private investment should help to overcome the technological and financial handicaps of Latin American enterprise, rather than make for their perpetuation.

What might at a superficial glance seem like hostility or antagonism to foreign private capital is at bottom an expression of the sense of economic and social upward mobility among the dynamic members of the Latin American community. Social mobility is not a question of education and technical training alone, but also of tangible opportunities of doing what the technicians from abroad can do. It signifies the definite idea that the nationals of any given country are not debarred from assuming their own responsibilities and developing their aptitudes at all technical and economic levels. This calls for energetic national promotion measures and, in addition, on the part of foreign private investment—wherever it is needed—new attitudes of willingness to offer openings for the initiative and creative ability of the people of the country concerned, by means of new formulas which were not, and had no reason to be, dreamed of in the past.

Just as real social mobility is of great importance both for the acceleration of economic development and for the political evolution of the Latin American countries, it also has a significant part to play in the devising and establishing of patterns of international coexistence different from those prevailing today.

The United States is a geographical, economic, and political reality in this continent, with which Latin America must come to a sound understanding. On both sides a clear-sighted and systematic effort is needed. I do not think that this essential objective would be attainable if foreign private enterprise, by virtue of its very financial and technological superiority, were to make its way progressively into all those fields of action which offer the most attractive prospects, whether in relation to internal development or in connection with the advance toward a Latin American common market. Left to its own resources, Latin American enterprise would be unable to stand up to the superiority in question, and would fall behind completely in the absence of a firm supporting policy. Hence the importance of finding appropriate formulas for association or combination of interests with foreign private enterprise in cases where its admittance is deemed necessary or desirable.

Precisely because the aforesaid modus vivendi must be arrived at and must cover the whole set of reciprocal relationships, this delicate matter must be discussed in the clearest terms possible. If a policy of support for Latin American enterprise were not applied, the infiltration of foreign investment would become impossible to control. And if this were to happen under a system of North-South preferences which increasingly channeled Latin American trade toward the United States, the economic results might be spectacular for the moment; but the bases of political coexistence would be very seriously undermined.

The conjunction of the trade and financial interests of the Latin American countries with those of a hegemonic center, as in the system of outward-looking growth, could not be reproduced today. Sooner or later, such constellations would be doomed to destruction, perhaps with serious attendant upheavals. For far from ensuring equality of opportunities for national enterprise, they would keep it at a disadvantage indefinitely.

This point may be further stressed by means of an analogy. A country in which education is accessible only to a few does not offer equality of opportunities in the economic development process, however loudly it may raise the cry of education for all. The same applies to foreign investment; there will be no equality of opportunities for domestic enterprise in default of an enlightened policy designed to put the region on an equal technological and financial footing.

In this connection, the primary thesis of the present chapter is that it suits the permanent interests of Latin America to discover new formulas for harmonious coexistence with the United States and the rest of the developed world. This is also in the interest of the industrialized countries, according to the same thesis. If such formulas are not discovered, and the inferiority of domestic enterprise becomes more and more marked, the resentment and frustration of those who are capable of assuming responsibilities and playing their proper part in development might be reflected in political disturbances, since they would have plenty of popular backing, which would be all the stronger, the farther the process of social integration of the underprivileged masses had advanced.

Not in vain has Latin America participated, and is continuing to participate, in a contemporary upsurge of cardinal ideas on political evolution, equality of opportunities, national responsibility, and autonomy in development. Great as may be the difficulties encountered in putting these ideas into practice, they could be disregarded only at a heavy political cost.

Nor has the experience of other economic and social systems lacked significance for Latin America. Although in the past it seemed a Utopian fantasy to think of approaching, if not attaining, the level of technology of the countries in the vanguard of progress, it has now been proved that this fantasy can become a reality. Two centuries of ever-advancing industrial revolution can be short-cut if the developing countries show a firm determination to do so. Peoples who were formerly ignorant and oppressed are now being found to possess an enormous latent potential of imagination and creative ability, which are essential ingredients of technology, development, and culture. The Latin American countries are not as far as they were from their own industrial revolution. It has already begun. All that is lacking is to define what they want it for and in what form they want it.

It must be acknowledged that ideas of the foregoing kind on the role of foreign private enterprise take time to find acceptance. This is not true of international technical assistance. Its underlying principle is precisely the idea that a country which is unfamiliar with certain techniques essential for its development should be visited by experts who can teach it the techniques in question. Nobody supposes that these experts are to remain permanently in the country to do work that its own nationals cannot. Their mission is to show the local technicians how to do it. But this objective is usually overlooked when foreign private capital is concerned. Naturally enough, such capital is attracted by the possibilities of making profits, and this must be the point of departure for any relevant formula. But is is not incompatible with arrangements for an appropriate combination with domestic enterprise whereby the latter can be guaranteed training in the requisite know-how, with the result that fruitfully cooperative relations will be ensured.

### Development as a Transitional Phase

It is not surprising that matters should stand as they are, since the influence of the past is still very strong. The peculiar nature of Latin America's development phenomena is not always understood outside or even inside the region. They are phenomena pertaining to a phase of transition. The economy is neither what it was yesterday nor what it will have to be tomorrow. To reach this future stage it needs international cooperation. The position of the developed countries is different. Even a small one has at its disposal a capacity for domestic saving which enables it to continue growing at an even pace without needing to resort to foreign capital. It may or may not wish to do so for financial or technological reasons, but its rate of development does not depend upon a regular inflow of international funds.

The same applies to foreign trade. The developed countries, thanks to their own economic structure, move on a plane of interdependence. The continuance of their development is not contingent upon a change in other countries' trade policy—as is the case in the developing countries—since they are all integral parts of a machinery which operates effectively, and which needs only to be watched and gradually adapted to the changes that take place.

Size does not enter into the question. However important a country's dimensions may be at the military and political levels, it is equally true that at the level of the world economy, there is seldom any strict correlation between differences of size and a country's degree of autonomy, that is, its ability to make decisions without outside intervention.

In all these respects, there is a marked contrast between developed and developing countries. The former have established a network of economic relationships in which the risk of arbitrary decisions is considerably reduced. In the field of foreign trade, for example, there is the contractual system of the General Agreement on Tariffs and Trade (GATT), which embodies principles worked out in the course of long experience. Among the various developed countries a certain balance of benefits exists, which none of them can disturb at will without suffering adverse effects, either under the GATT system or through the very interdependence of trade relations. Something similar has been happening with respect to international monetary affairs.

The implications of this should be thoroughly understood. By virtue of their own economic structure, the developed countries of small and medium size feel no need for the larger countries to adopt special measures for their benefit, but participate in the steadily expanding world trade flows, to whose changing requirements they adapt themselves. Very different is the situation of the Latin American countries in the transitional phase through which they are passing. They are not in a position to gain by participating in the major world trade flows. They are largely dependent upon the decisions adopted by the developed countries for the reduction or removal of the impediments that hamper their export trade in primary commodities. And they are likewise dependent upon the developed countries where their exports of industrial products are concerned, since in addition to their own endeavors they need special measures to offset the competitive disadvantage at which they find themselves in the world market at present.

Thus, the countries of Latin America, like the other developing countries, are in a very special position within the world trade complex. This is why the application of GATT principles has not signified the same guarantees for them as for the advanced countries. What is more, it is no exaggeration to say that if at any time one of the developed countries has wished to deviate from those principles, there has been nothing to stop it from doing so.

To eliminate the disadvantages under which the developing countries are laboring, their own efforts alone are not enough. The cooperation of the industrialized countries is an inescapable necessity, and will continue to be so until the two groups have built up between them a trade structure which will guarantee a relative balance of reciprocal benefits such as already exists among the developed countries. Hence the supreme inportance of joint action on the part of the Latin American countries within their own hemisphere and, in concert with the other developing regions, at the world level.

There can be no doubt that reciprocal benefits do attach to the expansion of trade between the countries of Latin America and the developed countries. The unhindered development of trade would be advantageous to both groups from the outset. Here as in other respects, however, it is not long-term considerations but immediate interests that usually prevail. What generally carries the day is the opposition put up by specific activities in the developed countries which might be affected by the growth of the developing countries' exports. It is true that these exports would be encouraged, and that the aforesaid benefits of world trade would thus be secured. But they are potential benefits, not immediately visible or palpable. The influence exerted by interests which fear they may be injured is therefore disproportionate.

On the contrary, once a new trade structure had been established, and the period of transition left behind, the interplay of reciprocal advantages would be plainly evident. In the meantime, the developing countries will continue to be dependent on the goodwill of the developed countries. This dependence is not imputable to trade in itself, but to the fact—which must be stressed yet again—that the structure of international trade has undergone no change in response to the direct and indirect impact of technical progress. Thus, the problem lies in transforming it until it ensures that practical balance of reciprocal benefits by which trade among the developed countries is characterized.

The transitional period through which the Latin American countries are passing is therefore marked by certain relationships which, however different from those existing in the past, are still forms of dependence, in the domain of trade and finance as well as at the technological level. What the Latin American countries should seek to do is to modify this dependence by gradual degrees, without waiting until they reach the stage at which they can be termed developed countries. If the process is to acquire certain basic attributes other than those of a strictly economic nature, the modifications in question must be introduced during the transition period itself, not after it is over. Hence the importance of multilateralism both in financial matters and in trade.

## INTERNATIONAL FINANCIAL COOPERATION

### Political Importance of Multilateralism

Where finance is concerned, multilateralism means that the granting of financial resources depends in each specific instance on the decision adopted not by a single country, but by a group. The Inter-American Development Bank (IDB) and the International Bank for Reconstruction and Development (IBRD), with its affiliated organizations, afford cases in point. The idea that these multilateral institutions should be used as the means of channeling an increasing proportion of financial resources is gaining ground.

The idea is one which the developing countries have long been striving to propagate. It has been taken up in all the reports mentioned, as representing an objective to be attained by progressive degrees. The Government of the United States has also endorsed it. Furthermore, the Peterson Report suggests that even United States funds for bilateral aid, to be extended through an autonomous institution, should be channeled within a multilateral framework.

Undoubtedly, this represents a significant step forward, inasmuch as neither IDB nor IBRD has anything to do with the immediate political interests of the countries that provide financing. But it must not be forgotten that these countries virtually hold the power of veto in the institutions named. Whatever might be the arguments in favor, it would be unrealistic to suppose that matters could be otherwise, at least for a longer period that the present study envisages. Were it not so, moreover, the indispensable expansion of the flow of resources might be seriously jeopardized. Other ways of tackling the problem must therefore be sought.

First and foremost, mention must be made of the experience of IDB. During the first 10 years of its existence it has done a very great deal to promote Latin American interests. In reality, in an international credit institution, the developed countries supplying the resources should not take precedence over the countries receiving them, and vice versa. What is needed is to arrive at a consensus, and that is no easy task. I believe IDB is managing to accomplish it. In this respect moral authority is as important as technical competence.

Consequently, it seems to me that convergent action on the part of IDB and of IBRD would be a significant factor in the practice of multilateralism in Latin America. As I have just pointed out in another text,[2] IDB possesses a telluric virtue: it has deep roots in the Latin American countries, and sees men and events in the region in a light in which, naturally, only Latin Americans can view them.

This last point is of great importance in relation to the analysis of development plans and of progress in their implementation. The idea of planning is tacitly or explicitly accepted in the reports to which reference has repeatedly been made. It is now strongly supported by IBRD as well. But this task of analysis has always posed a delicate problem. A development plan is the expression of a country's development strategy, and strategy is of course a private matter, a manifestation of an autonomy which must be inviolable. On the other hand, international credit institutions could hardly earmark resources for the financing of a plan without analyzing its content, without making sure that the use to which those resources are put will really contribute to the more rapid attainment of the state at which the development process can be carried on without special international cooperation measures.

As already stated, in the past two decades external resources have not helped the Latin American countries to draw gradually nearer to this objective; nor have convergent internal development measures been adopted, at any rate in an adequate scale. The mobilization of domestic resources has not been stepped up, and the external bottleneck has certainly not been relieved, to say the least. Essential importance must be attached to these two objectives in the analysis of a plan. What is more, they are among the aims which justify the need for planning, both from the standpoint of the Latin American countries and from the angle of the international credit institutions.

Although these aspects of the problem seem straightforward enough, they are not really so, for the mobilization of domestic resources and the relief of the external bottleneck would alike require a number of internal measures, in respect of which the risk of intervention in what is exclusively the business of the country concerned could not be obviated altogether. In the light of their experience, the international credit institutions have been able to establish certain evaluation criteria. But there is not always a clear-cut dividing line between objective and subjective considerations. Accordingly, the definition of such criteria and their application to individual cases should be the object of mutual agreement, so as to ensure that national autonomy is not impaired.

No formulas exist in which the solution of this problem could be crystallized once and for all. But it must be recognized that the experience of the institutions referred to has been very valuable. It has taught many lessons. If we call to mind the opposition put up to industrial development, the doctrinaire objections to planning, the reluctance to issue loans to public enterprises on grounds of principle, and other attitudes such as, for example, those which formerly prevailed with regard to inflation, we can see how long a road has been traveled. Much more is now known about development problems than before, and extremely able personnel have been formed in the multilateral institutions. But perhaps the time has come for these institutions to share with others the responsibility of analyzing development plans.

### The Practice of Multilateralism

Just as governments are jealous of the autonomy of their decisions, so also are the international credit institutions, for they could not tolerate outside influence in the exercise of their power to take those financing decisions which are pertinent to their nature and their responsibilities.

These institutions, however, should avail themselves of the authorized opinion of experts who are neither on their own staff nor dependent upon the governments whose plans are under consideration. The International Bank for Reconstruction and Development has just given proof of its receptivity to outside opinion by asking a group of independent personalities to give their views on the form that international cooperation should take. This was the origin of the Pearson Report. And the present report, requested by IDB, bears witness to the same tendency. Of course, the institutions in question are under no obligation whatever to accept such opinions. They are obviously entitled to endorse them, modify them, or dismiss them altogether.

The desirability of hearing these independent views which do not necessarily reflect the opinions of governments and credit institutions was the consideration borne in mind in the Charter of Punta del Este, when a group of experts was established to review development plans submitted by the Latin American countries for the purpose of obtaining international financing. Thus the "Panel of Nine," as it was called, came into being. The weakness of that group was largely due to the concern evinced to prevent it from becoming a supranational agency—which had never been anyone's intention. It was not an organic body, and lacked the indispensable cohesion.

To this innate defect was added another, possibly more serious. Owing to what was perhaps overanxiety to ensure the complete independence of the group, it did not include representatives of the international credit institutions that had to grant the resources for financing plans. The unwisdom of this exclusion was soon demonstrated by facts. Because of it, the Panel could not invoke the authorized opinion of the representatives of the institutions in question. And these agencies went on making their own analyses, which took precedence over those of the Panel of Nine, and which, from a practical standpoint, were much more important, since upon them the granting of financial resources depended. I have observed a justifiable anxiety on the part of the Latin American governments to avoid the duplication of plan evaluations, inasmuch as this double filter through which their aspirations are screened may be not so much a help as a hindrance in obtaining development resources.

In any event, it may well be asked, in the light of this recent experience, whether the Latin American governments might not appropriately consider the desirability of establishing multilateral groups of recognized technical competence to review their development plans and their requirements in respect of international financing in order to facilitate plan implementation. To be effective, and to obviate the risk of duplication, the groups would have to include experts representing the financing agencies. They should comprise, on the one hand, experts from IDB, from IBRD, and from the Development Aid Committee (DAC), representing the countries members of the Organization for Economic Cooperation and Development (OECD), as well as from the International Monetary Fund; and, on the other, experts independent both of the governments and of the international financing agencies.

In this connection, it would be essential for the credit institution experts to be empowered to make final pronouncements on behalf of their agencies at the technical level, in order to pave the way for the institutions' executive organs to take the necessary decisions with respect to granting the development funds required.

The verdict of these groups on each of the development plans reviewed would be submitted to the consideration of ICAP, an agency in which, by its very nature, political points of view as well as technical considerations, might carry weight. Needless to say, however greatly ICAP might be strengthened in this way—which is a very important point— the final decisions would have to be made by the international credit institutions in question.

It would also be highly advisable for the expert groups to take part in the annual analysis of the progress made by the various Latin American countries in the implementation of their development strategies and plans. The opinion of the groups would be of great value to the members of ICAP, who could then base their pronouncements on this impartial technical analysis, with due regard to broader political considerations.

To ensure proper linkage between the expert groups and ICAP, it would be an excellent thing for them to have the same chairman, by which means the indispensable liaison between the technical and political levels would be established in the most natural way.

Through their periodic reports on the development of Latin America and its problems, too, the expert groups should help ICAP to fulfil its delicate functions with maximum efficacy. Experience suggests that the success of the action of such groups would depend essentially upon their power of persuasion at different levels. It would be all the greater if everything that might smack of monitoring were eliminated, so that emphasis was placed on the group's true nature as a body of experts cooperating with countries in the study and solution of their development problems. This would help to banish all anxiety on the grounds of dependence or subordination in negotiations for international financing.

The following would be another very important function of these groups of experts. In recent times, various ideas have been put forward as to the need for a technical body—operating, of course, at the level of the United Nations—to discuss development problems and international cooperation and to formulate the relevant recommendations. Members of the technical groups could contribute their experience in Latin America to the deliberations of such an international body, in addition to that of the regional agencies of the United Nations and the Organization of American States (OAS).

One further observation is worth making here. If plan financing is to be obtained, it is only natural that the development plans should be analyzed by those who have to assume the responsibility of granting resources. Much the same thing applies to major projects: credit institutions study the payments capacity and the financial policy of the country concerned before adopting decisions.

Any given country may legitimately be anxious to see that this analysis does not lead to results which may violate its sovereignty. Such risks are largely—if not altogether—obviated in the case of a multilateral analysis affected with the balanced participation referred to in the foregoing pages. It is understandable that in specific cases the path of bilateralism may be chosen on the grounds that it might be more favorable at a particular juncture. But perhaps this detracts from the weight which should in any event be carried by economic considerations, and to safeguard which is the aim of multilateralism, since in the long run it protects all concerned against damaging political interference.

## THE VOLUME OF INTERNATIONAL FINANCIAL RESOURCES

The proposals of the recent reports on international financial cooperation coincide so closely with what the countries of Latin America and the other developing countries had been suggesting that there would be no point in dwelling on any but a few of the important issues involved.

The need to increase the volume of financial resources transferred and to lighten the unduly heavy burden of remittances abroad is universally recognized. Universally recognized, too, is the absolute necessity of reducing the service payments in relation to the present debt and to avoid repeating the mistakes of the past in future operations.

It is likewise recognized that tied loans, which greatly raise the cost of certain operations, should be abolished. The Government of the United States has already allowed the resources it grants bilaterally to the Latin American countries to be used for purchasing capital goods in any of the countries of the region. The Peterson Report goes still farther, inasmuch as it suggests that all the countries granting international financial resources should agree to untie credits altogether. And it proposes that in the meanwhile credits should be freely usable in any of the developing countries, even outside Latin America.

As has just been noted, the need to increase the flow if international financing is fully acknowledged. The Pearson Report endorses the UNCTAD recommendation according to which net transfers of official funds of various kinds should amount to 0.7 percent of the gross product of the developed countries. The Pearson Report proposes that this should be the target for 1975, whereas in UNCTAD shorter time limits had been mentioned, and it had been recommended that the target should be raised to 1 percent of the gross product, including transfers of private capital as well as public funds.

Although the Peterson Report also unequivocally recommends that the flow of such funds should be expanded, it mentions that the Task Force "has reservations about the usefulness of any formula to determine how much assistance the industrial countries should provide." It suggests that "instead, the starting-point and the test" for transferring such funds "should be the determination of developing countries to mobilize their own resources and to adopt policies that will ensure the effective use of funds." And it adds that if results prove satisfactory, "the industrial countries should be prepared to make available the necessary amount of development assistance," pointing out that "in the end, this may mean greater or less assistance than would be called for by any predetermined formula."[3]

Experience seems to indicate that there is no real conflict between the two ideas. It has been pointed out that one of the disincentives to planning in Latin America, over and above the shortage of resources, is the great uncertainty felt as to the possibility of relying on international funds during the lifetime of the plan. A commitment on the part of the industrial countries to increase the amount of funds they transfer until the above-mentioned targets were reached would be highly significant. For it would enable bilateral and multilateral financing agencies likewise to plan their own commitments with the developing countries, which has hitherto been done only in exceptional cases.

The Peterson Report is quite right to link the transfer of funds to the measure adopted by the developing countries, as a means of ensuring good results. But it would be a mistake to wait until such measures became effective before determining the amount of international funds required. There would be a risk that further delays might seriously affect plan implementation and, above all, that by force of circumstances a relatively low order of priority might once again be assigned to international financial cooperation, just as at present.

The possibility that the opposite might happen—i.e., that the international funds to be transferred in accordance with a predetermined formula exceeded the amount of which the countries could make effective use—would seem remote on the whole, if the targets referred to were met; should it materialize, nothing would be lost, since the granting of the funds in question could simply be postponed.*

I do not think concern on this account is justifiable, since it is common knowledge that even today the capacity to absorb external loans would suffice to deal with a volume of resources approximately equivalent to 1 percent of the gross product of the industrialized centers.

Undoubtedly, targets of this nature are far from perfect. A refinement upon such formulas is conceivable; for instance, transfers might be related to average per capita income in the developed countries. But so much progress has been made in the acceptance of the proposed targets by a considerable number of countries that it would be a pity to turn back in quest of better formulas. This should be left until international financial cooperation policy is consolidated.

However great the defects of the formulas suggested, they have the twofold merit of providing both for continuity and for the expansion of resources as the product of the industrialized countries increases. With regard to continuity, the Peterson Report says that "foreign assistance, like domestic programs, cannot be changed drastically from year to year,"[4] adding later that "it involves continuing programs, the actions of many other nations and a functioning international framework—for all of which the position of the United States is of the greatest importance." And—a still more significant point—attention is drawn to the fact that "disruption of the United States [foreign assistance] program could undermine the entire system of international cooperation in this field." For all these reasons, the report categorically declares that "the downward trend in United States development assistance appropriations should be reversed."

Furthermore, the idea of continuity is implicit in the proposal to set up an International Development Bank in the United States which would be initially endowed with real or potential resources for which annual authorization by Congress was not required.

The content of the Peterson Report is in general so positive that it is a pity to find certain reservations still maintained with regard to the targets for the transfer of resources. It is understandable that the difficulties through which the United States is passing should have counseled great caution. But perhaps it would not have been incompatible with such caution to establish a period of five years in which to reach the 1 percent target recommended by the United Nations, together with that of 0.7 percent for public funds suggested in the Pearson Report.

All this is bound to be of supreme interest to the Latin American countries. For if increasingly wide acceptance is accorded to the idea of setting up development targets whose attainment will gradually give the economy the additional dynamism it lacks, it would seem essential to be

---

*This should not be confused with the negative effects on the external debt produced by delays in making use of credits already granted. Such delays, besides unduly deferring enjoyment of the benefits that would accrue from the use of the funds concerned, saddle the country with an extra financial burden.

reasonably sure of obtaining enough international cooperation to support an intensive effort to mobilize domestic resources.

It is therefore worthwhile to take a brief glance (on the basis of Table 15) at what would be implied if the two targets mentioned above were met in respect of net financial resources from all the OECD countries, if they were reached by 1975, and if the Latin American countries retained the minimum share of about 15 percent which fell to their lot in 1964-1967. In 1960-1967 the corresponding proportion was 16.5 percent, and in 1956-1959 it was 26.4 percent.

In the projections presented in Chapter 4, Table 22, and on the basis of certain reasonable assumptions there set forth, it was calculated that the net transfer of capital to the Latin American countries would gradually increase during the current decade until the sum of about $4,100 million had been reached in 1980.

These figures, besides providing orders of magnitude of unquestionable interest, point to the road that it would be rational to take during the 1970's. It is a road for two-way traffic. On the one hand, the Latin American countries

TABLE 27

Projection of Net Transfers of Capital from OECD Countries Through
Multilateral Agencies, and Possible Share of Latin America
(thousands of millions of dollars)

| Year | Total Net Transfers | | Transfers to Latin America | |
|---|---|---|---|---|
| | Target: 0.7 Percent of Product | Target: 1.0 Percent of Product | Target: 0.7 Percent of Product | Target: 1.0 Percent of Product |
| 1967 (present amount) | 11.3 | | 1.8 | |
| 1975* | 15.4 | 22.0 | 2.3 | 3.3 |
| 1980* | 19.3 | 27.5 | 2.9 | 4.1 |

Note: It is assumed that the product of these countries would grow at the same average annual rate as in 1957-1967 (4.5 percent); that the share of the Latin American countries in transfers of resources would be 15 percent; and that the targets would be reached by 1975, the same level being maintained in subsequent years.

*Projection.

Source: Latin American Institute for Economic and Social Planning.

would gradually project, in the course of time, the amount of international capital they needed in order to reach certain development objectives; and, on the other hand, the industrial countries would determine, in accordance with the targets referred to, the resources they would place at Latin America's disposal to stimulate its development.

It is common knowledge that in this field of the transfer of international financial resources there has been retrogression rather than progress (see Table 28). Whereas in 1960 the resources transferred by the OECD countries represented 0.89 percent of their gross product, this proportion had fallen to 0.77 percent by 1968. It should be noted that these figures include private capital, as well as transfers of official resources.

## THE CONTINUITY AND TERMS OF FINANCIAL COOPERATION

It was shown above that recognition is accorded to the need for continuity in financial cooperation. This is highly important because of the contradiction existing at the present time. On the one hand, the Latin American countries are urged to pursue a realistic development policy, with clearly defined objectives and an appropriate order of investment priorities. On the other hand, institutional limitations are maintained which make it impossible to commit financial resources for the whole of the period covered by such development plans.

This is an aspect of the problem to which special consideration should be given, in order to increase the effectiveness of international financial cooperation by combining it with internal effort. The enlargement of the sphere of multilateral operations, in the first place, and, second, the experience acquired by ICAP in its functions relating to the analysis of external financing requirements, may help to overcome the difficulties indicated above.

As a planning incentive, the international credit institutions and the bilateral credit mechanisms should be empowered to assume financing commitments for periods ranging from three to five years. The idea of consortia of international, regional, and bilateral credit institutions seems much to be recommended in this connection, so that their action and responsibilities could be coordinated at a level transcending the mere approval of individual projects; but this would undeniably call for considerable effort both on the part of the interested countries and on that of the international financing institutions and agencies.

Another aspect of the question, linked to the foregoing, is that of the financing of the domestic expenditure component in a country's investment. It is essential to introduce greater flexibility in the financing of local expenditure. From a rational viewpoint, external financing should bridge the gap between investment requirements and the domestic resources that a country engages, in principle, to mobilize intensively under a development plan, if this plan is judged acceptable. What matters is that all investment should be covered by saving, whether foreign or domestic, without recourse to inflationary expedients and without detriment to essential projects, and that saving should

## TABLE 28

### Net Flow of Capital from OECD Countries to Developing Countries

| Country | Total Net Flow of Official and Private Capital | | Share of Each Country in Total, 1968 | Per Capita Gross National Product, 1968 |
|---|---|---|---|---|
| | 1960 | 1968 | | |
| | (percentage of gross national product) | | (percentage of total) | (dollars) |
| France | 2.19 | 1.17 | 12.0 | 2,510 |
| Netherlands | 2.11 | 1.09 | 2.0 | 1,980 |
| Federal Republic of Germany | 0.88 | 1.26 | 10.2 | 2,190 |
| Belgium | 1.59 | 1.17 | 1.4 | 2,150 |
| United Kingdom | 1.21 | 0.75 | 7.8 | 1,850 |
| Switzerland | 1.83 | 1.41 | 1.1 | 2,790 |
| Japan | 0.58 | 0.74 | 7.6 | 1,410 |
| United States | 0.75 | 0.66 | 49.6 | 4,380 |
| Australia | 0.38 | 0.67 | 1.6 | 2,330 |
| Sweden | 0.37 | 0.50 | 1.1 | 3,230 |
| Austria | 0.09 | 0.65 | 0.4 | 1,550 |
| Canada | 0.39 | 0.49 | 2.3 | 3,000 |
| Italy | 0.88 | 0.73 | 2.5 | 1,360 |
| Norway | 0.23 | 0.64 | 0.3 | 2,360 |
| Denmark | 0.64 | 0.59 | 0.2 | 2,540 |
| Total | 0.89 | 0.77 | 100.0 | 2,770* |

*This average includes Portugal.

*Sources: Partners in Development: Report by the Commission on International Development* (New York: Praeger Publishers, 1969), p. 145; OECD, *Development Assistance: 1969 Review*, p. 293.

not be used to finance consumer expenditure. It has been the practice of external sources of financial cooperation to confine themselves to financing the import content of specific projects. But there is nothing in this procedure to prevent a country's internal resources from being used for investment or expenditure which has not a high priority. Only an investment program enables the country itself to determine an order of priorities, which, in addition, facilitates evaluation of the plan. This idea has been making headway, but not yet sufficiently for so sound a principle to be generally applied.

By these means it would be possible to eliminate another of the difficulties that usually arise. As the external providers of financial cooperation feel a very understandable interest in participating in the financing of important or attractive projects, there are other projects left which, however properly integrated in an investment program, can usually rely neither on external financing nor on a share in the inadequate supply of domestic resources.*

From another standpoint, a development plan is indispensable for the effective application of supplementary financing. The continuity of a development plan, as regards its investment objectives, is often broken because of the external vulnerability of the Latin American economy. The purpose of supplementary financing is to provide additional resources so that the plan can be implemented without major setbacks when an unforeseen decline in exports occurs.

This matter has been the subject of lengthy discussion. In the end, the Trade and Development Board (in June, 1969) decided to request IBRD to put into effect a supplementary financing program in line with certain suggestions formulated in its report. The idea finally adopted was that IBRD should have discretionary powers to grant such financing, without the previous commitments envisaged in the original plan. It is to be hoped that the Bank will shortly be in a position to announce the terms on which supplementary financing will be granted.

Supplementary financing is not incompatible with stabilization agreements relating to primary commodities, partly because stabilization would not in any case be absolute and would leave an appreciable margin for fluctuations in a country's external income, and partly because there are some commodities on which such agreements cannot be concluded. It would be a good thing if international financing were also available for buffer stocks. This is an idea which ICAP and, of course, UNCTAD firmly support.

It would not entail any more resources than were needed for supplementary financing, since the greater the extent to which prices were stabilized, the less would be the external vulnerability of the producer countries and, therefore, the less also their supplementary financing requirements. IBRD and the International Monetary Fund (IMF) would appear to be willing to take positive action in this respect.

---

*The Chairman of ICAP has drawn attention to the necessity of meeting these residual financing requirements.

## INTERNATIONAL MONETARY REFORM AND
## FINANCIAL COOPERATION

In view of the difficulties presently encountered by some countries—the United States, for example—in attaining the targets for transfers of funds, it is a pity that advantage has not been taken of the creation of international monetary reserves to augment the flow of financial resources into the developing countries. It is estimated that in the next three years the reserves will be built up to about $9.5 billion of which, under the distribution procedure now adopted, about $2.5 billion would be available to the developing countries. Latin America's share in this amount would be close to $870 million.

Prior to this reform, it had been suggested that at least 50 percent of the new monetary resources thus created should be earmarked for increasing financial transfers to the developing countries through the international credit institutions.[5] Unfortunately, no decision was adopted to this effect. And it must be admitted that the Latin American countries—with a few exceptions—did not show much energy or persistence in supporting the idea.

As is common knowledge, the reform encountered serious difficulties, which were fortunately overcome. Possibly it would not have been wise to add an extra complication prematurely. But the position is different now, and perhaps the time is ripe to urge the proposal in question.

There is nothing in it that could affect the satisfactory operation of the new system. It is beyond question that even if the new monetary resources were transferred as suggested, they would have to be created in accordance with strictly monetary considerations, and not as a function of the financial needs of the developing countries. Moreover, the voting system established for the adoption of the relevant decisions forestalls the possibility of any deviation from this principle.

It must also be borne in mind that the proposal to which we refer is more closely in line with what has always happened. New gold from the mines has never been distributed in accordance with a preestablished procedure. Countries have had to purchase it by means of their exports of goods and services. If the monetary resources now being created were channeled into the developing countries, through the international credit institutions, the developed countries would have to tap them too by means of the competitive power of their exports.

In these circumstances, the developed countries would clearly not be able to secure additional monetary resources at little cost, any more than in the case of their reserves of bullion. They are, of course, in a position to acquire the resources in question through their export trade. Equity is certainly not much in evidence when the developing countries have to shoulder an oppressive burden of service payments in return for the resources lent them, while the developed countries obtain substantial resources free of charge to augment their monetary reserves.

## FOREIGN PRIVATE INVESTMENT

### Need for New Formulas

At the beginning of the present chapter reference was made to foreign private investment and to the problems it poses in the Latin American countries. This subject has been dealt with in a number of reports requested by ICAP, the findings of which have been assembled in a document in which the main ideas are set forth and discussed.[6]

The starting point is the idea that former investment patterns, which were dictated by the requirements of the outward-looking phase of development, are no longer consonant with the existing circumstances. But efficacious formulas to solve the problem have not yet been devised. Except in cases where extreme doctrinaire positions are adopted, foreign private investment is recognized as desirable when it implies a positive contribution in the shape of production techniques, organization, and knowledge of foreign markets. On the other hand, as was likewise pointed out above, Latin American enterprise clearly wants to acquire the know-how that at present it does not possess, at all those levels of technology.

Development is basically the responsibility of the countries which are proposing to develop. If this is so, private or public enterprise in these countries must progressively make up its deficiency as regards its ability to make use of technology. Otherwise, there will be a flagrant contradiction between the sense of responsibility and the existence of activities whose technical complexity renders them inaccessible to domestic enterprise.

Thus, it is of the greatest importance to discover formulas whereby foreign private investment will help to remedy the region's technological inferiority instead of prolonging it indefinitely, though of course this does not imply disregard of the significant role that must be played by other methods of transferring techniques.

This aspect of the problem is very important in itself, but there are others which are also causing serious concern. It has already been pointed out that a process is taking place in Latin America whose gravity is beyond question. In fields of economic activity where the technology is already familiar in the country concerned, local firms are passing into foreign hands, sometimes for want of enough domestic credit to finance their current operations. The psychological and political effects of such take-overs are of great consequence. And if we want to find sound and mutually beneficial cooperation formulas, some way of preventing the continuance of this process will also have to be devised.

Moreover, the change of hands affects remittances abroad. This is not a fact to be lightly dismissed when—as shown in Chapter 4—external constraint is and will continue to be a formidable problem. Investment policy must help to relieve it rather than to aggravate it.

Apart from these considerations, the take-over of domestic enterprises by foreign concerns arouses keen anxiety when decisions are made abroad which are of importance for national life. This applies particularly to enterprises which have long been exploiting natural resources. Here a very significant process of evolution has begun in those cases where a country seeks to negotiate agreements under which domestic control of such enterprises can be acquired immediately, or in a reasonable space of time.

Another motive of concern is the infiltration of foreign investment into a given country's bank system, together with foreign take-overs of banks which used to be in national hands. The foreign bank or its branch office has a specific and limited function when it is linked to external investment or trade operations. But the extension of this function to other activities creates unnecessary problems against which it is advisable to take precautions in good time. Some countries have very farsighted legislation in this field, and perhaps the most stringent is that of the United States, with respect not only to take-overs but also to the establishment of foreign banks.

There are other mainsprings of national life which are equally unsuited to handling from abroad. Mass communication media afford a significant case in point. In Chapter 8 attention is drawn to what these media imply when they are at the service of any form of concentration of power. And the implications are all the more serious when foreign influences prevail.

## Some of the Formulas Suggested to ICAP

Reference will next be made to the main conclusions to be drawn from the report on private investment and development mentioned above.[7] But one remark must come first. With regard to foreign private investment, a country may take the very serious decision to do without it altogether, or may choose to throw the doors wide open to it. Again, the country concerned may draw up a foreign investment policy. But what it cannot do, if it wants such a policy to be successful, is to disregard the other party. Consequently, frank discussion is indispensable as a means to the discovery of formulas which, while helping to dispel the anxieties aroused by foreign investment, will not discourage it in cases where a country is interested in attracting it.

This interest should be clearly and explicitly expressed. Governments should demarcate those fields in which they deem foreign investment to be desirable, either because of the inflow of funds it signifies, or because it brings with it know-how which for the time being is not accessible to domestic enterprise.

In this demarcation of the areas of interest, primary importance attaches to balance-of-payments considerations. Foreign investment must contribute to the expansion of exports and to import substitution. And as substitution possibilities at the national level are becoming seriously limited, industrial integration agreements will have to be concerted in which domestic enterprise will be called upon to play a leading role, except in those cases where, in order to incorporate new technologies—not only technical know-how proper, but the techniques of organization and of gaining a foothold in foreign markets—it is felt that the doors should be opened to foreign private investment. This does not mean that such investment cannot be useful outside the selected fields; but balance-of-payments considerations, in addition to those already mentioned, must always be borne in mind.

As regards investment itself, the idea of the mixed or joint enterprise has made great progress, although not yet enough. There are important foreign firms which are still reluctant to associate themselves with domestic enterprise. It is in these cases that powers of persuasion will have to be intensively exercised.

In this connection, the procedure recommended to ICAP is the stage-by-stage approach to association of interests, when it is not considered advisable for foreign enterprise to operate by itself. For a reasonable period of time, the foreign enterprise would hold all the share capital if it did not wish to enter into association with Latin American initiative straight away. But from the very outset a procedure would be established whereby a major proportion of the capital would eventually pass into the hands of domestic enterprise.

Another possibility envisaged is that of agreeing upon the transfer of all the capital. It is argued, however, that the foreign enterprise would lose interest in contributing its continually evolving technology, although there would be cases in which full domestic ownership might be accompanied by agreements on technical cooperation and use of trademarks. In this connection, an adequate degree of flexibility would be essential to the attainment of the end pursued.

Some such formula, it may be hoped, would help to overcome one of the biggest of the obstacles that are holding up the advance toward a Latin American common market. It is thought, and not without justification, that in industrial integration or complementarity agreements foreign enterprise would play the leading part, to the detriment of Latin American initiative. Multinational enterprises are being energetically developed. The industrial estate, i.e., the combination of heterogeneous activities in a single large-scale enterprise, has also come to the fore and is expanding. But an understanding must be reached as to terms. Generally speaking, the executive arm is multinational, but the decision-making center is at the national level.

All these enterprises are formidable for their size, their power, and their efficiency. They are a source of misgiving even in the advanced countries, which are observing with understandable apprehension these new forms of concentration of economic power. Much more understandable still, therefore, is Latin America's anxiety as to the influence of these enterprises in a common market. Hence the importance of a formula whereby Latin American enterprise—after the reasonable period of time alluded to above—could acquire control of the share capital in those cases where the admittance of foreign enterprise is considered desirable.

### Support for Latin American Private Enterprise

But to devise foreign investment formulas is not enough. It is also necessary to ensure their feasibility. To this end, financial support for Latin American private enterprise is indispensable. This applies not only to concerns operating in association with foreign investment, but to Latin American private initiative in general. State enterprise is not, of course, excluded. But it already has access to international financial resources. On the other hand, there is no suitable machinery for international financing of the region's private enterprise. It is true that loans can be obtained from international credit institutions; but these agencies cannot underwrite share capital except in the very limited case of the Finance Corporation of IBRD.

Hence the idea of setting up a subsidiary or affiliated branch of IDB, empowered to underwrite shares both in the case of entirely Latin American enterprises and in that of enterprises partly based on foreign capital. This subsidiary might initially take over part of the capital and gradually transfer it into Latin American hands, in conformity with special agreements under which the personnel of an enterprise or, more broadly, its workers would be given the opportunity of purchasing shares. In cases where a major proportion of the share capital was to be transferred, the support of this new institution might prove of decisive importance. Among other possibilities, it is conceivable that from the date of entry into operation of a joint enterprise, the IDB subsidiary might underwrite preferential shares without voting rights, which would afterward be converted into ordinary shares in the proportion it needed in order to hold most of the capital. These shares, preferential or ordinary as the case might be, would gradually be transferred into Latin American hands.

All this necessitates a long-term outlook. In relation to the interplay of immediate interests, it may perhaps be difficult to understand how an advanced country could contribute financial resources in order to enable Latin American private initiative to obtain control of undertakings which would otherwise remain in the hands of the developed country's private enterprise. But this would be too short-sighted a view. From the longer-term standpoint, it is essential to discover formulas whereby a basic identity of interests can be established between foreign private enterprise and national development. The continuing process of technological improvement will leave foreign enterprise ample scope for action, since as soon as domestic initiative has acquired a controlling interest in certain enterprises, new opportunities for association on a basis of reciprocal benefits will supervene.

It is unlikely, of course, that these possibilities will be exhausted as Latin American enterprise gradually makes up its technological deficiency. On the contrary, better cooperation patterns will have been arrived at, more reciprocally advantageous than in the past. Plurality of interests is very important in all this; and the more the sources of private foreign capital are diversified, the greater will be the efficacy and the political viability of its cooperation.

## INTERNATIONAL COOPERATION IN TRADE

### UNCTAD Recommendations and Concerted Latin American Action

For the Latin American as for all the other developing countries, the expansion of their foreign trade is of vital importance. This is no longer called in question. The ideas which had long been under discussion in the United Nations, and which in recent years have been crystallized in the UNCTAD recommendations, are at last making headway. The Pearson Report has endorsed them and, in addition, they are among the noncontroversial issues in the Rockefeller Report.

The Latin American countries, in conjunction with the other developing countries, struggled hard to get negotiatory groups set up in UNCTAD, with a view to the formulation of a program under which the customs duties and nontariff restrictions hampering their export trade would be gradually eliminated.

At the time they were unsuccessful. But good ideas are gaining ground. Not long ago, at a session of the Inter-American Economic and Social Council (IA-ECOSOC), the Latin American Governments and the Government of the United States agreed that the Council should establish a special committee to assume these negotiatory responsibilities. This is one of the positive results of the action of the Special Committee on Latin American Coordination (SCLAC).

Another promising development is the decision of the Latin American governments to extend SCLAC's sphere of influence to relations with the other developed countries, including the socialist countries. Thus important conversations will have to be held with the European Economic Community (EEC).

The significance of such a step is great. Up to a short time ago there was patent reluctance to undertake concerted action of this kind. Preference was accorded to bilateral arrangements. Now it has been recognized that far from being incompatible with multilateral action, bilateral agreements find in it their most solid framework.*

This is what was lacking: an effort to get the developed countries to adopt the political decisions required in order to put the UNCTAD recommendations into effect. Such concerted action on the part of the Latin American countries should in no wise weaken the solidarity of their relations with the Third World. There are a number of common denominators on which this solidarity is based, despite marked differences in degrees of development and in economic and social systems.

---

*When the European Economic Community was constituted, the governments of the member States sent a joint note to the Latin American countries, to each of which it was transmitted by a single common representative. Despite repeated negotiations, it was impossible to arrange for the note to be answered in common as well. Each Latin American country sent a separate reply.

The Community's note was not merely protocolar. It declared EEC's willingness to cooperate and proposed a kind of standing committee to consider problems of common interest. The bilateral attitude of some of the Latin American countries was among the reasons why this proposal was never implemented.

More recently, when I was working in UNCTAD, I had several opportunities for discussion with EEC officials. As at a certain meeting I had leveled severe criticism, in my personal capacity, at some of the Community's attitudes toward Latin America, a high official told me frankly that if matters stood thus, it was largely due to the Latin American countries' failure to join forces in determined defense of their interests. I record these facts to underline the significance of the course of action which has now been embarked upon.

Concerted action is an imperative need both at the level of the hemisphere and at that of the world at large, since the advances achieved in the realm of ideas are far from marking the end of a long campaign. They are barely the beginning, for in the developed countries formidable obstacles stand in the way of the developing countries' primary exports and exports of manufactures alike. Competition with domestic production is feared. In reality, the liberalization of trade will entail certain adjustments in the developed countries' production which will have to be introduced sooner or later in any event, if the developing countries—as is maintained elsewhere in the present report—are to be incorporated in a new world trade structure on a basis of reciprocal benefits.

The fear of competition is exaggerated, and there are various ways of preventing serious distortions, especially when the expansion of consumption allows imports to grow without undue ill effects on domestic production.

It must be recognized, however, that the Latin American countries are not in a very strong position to dispel the exaggerated apprehensions of the developed countries, when similar and equally exaggerated misgivings are holding back the movement toward a Latin American common market.

All this is extremely serious, because no alternative solutions exist. As contended in Chapter 4, if Latin America is to speed up its growth rate—as it inevitably must—the progressive restructuring of its exports is a sine qua non. While everything possible should certainly be done to encourage its exports of primary commodities, the proportion of its total exports represented by its external sales of manufactures should steadily increase, both in inter-Latin American trade and in trade with the rest of the world. This calls for an exceptionally energetic and persevering effort, until a change has been brought about in the composition of Latin American exports which will enable them to participate normally in world trade flows.

## The Problem of Preferences

The trade measures which the developed countries are being asked to apply are too well-known for mention of them to be warranted in the present report. All that will be dealt with here is an important aspect of the problem of perferences. The widespread acceptance of the idea of general and nondiscriminatory preferences, which formerly encountered so much opposition, encourages the hope that the relevant political decisions may shortly be adopted. What matters is to get a system going, even if its content still leaves something to be desired. Experience will show how it can be gradually improved. But this, at best, will barely afford a margin for the developing countries' own effort. As far as Latin America is concerned, this effort will have to be strenuous and sustained. Nobody will come from outside the region to look for the products of Latin American industry. We shall have to manufacture them well and sally forth to sell them on competitive terms.

In view of the possibility that the system referred to may not be established at an early date, however, the idea of vertical preferences crops up here and there. This offshoot of the problem is so thorny a question that it calls for brief comment.

As is common knowledge, in Latin America support of preferences of this type represents a very understandable reaction to the discriminatory preferences granted by the European Economic Community to some of the African countries and to other European countries in the Mediterranean area.

The Community carries a responsibility of great historical importance. Obviously, its system of preferences could not simply be dismantled without replacing it with a definite policy to promote the development of the African countries apparently benefiting by the discriminatory preferences régime; and I say "apparently" because they find they have to pay more dearly for their imports in an anachronistic context of reciprocity. The Community has not only maintained this policy, but has widened its radius of application; this may perhaps be partly attributable to the reluctance of the Latin American countries to join forces in collective action vis-à-vis EEC, as has already been pointed out.

The Community's adherence to this course incurs the risk of a recrudescence of those trends of thought which, both in the United States and in Latin America, advocate a system of hemispherical preferences. Under such a system, the developing world would be divided into areas of influence of major developed countries of the North. Nobody has set forth this thesis of a vertical division of the world with greater force and clarity than a former Undersecretary of State and ex-United States Ambassador to the United Nations, George Ball. In effect, what Mr. Ball says is that "there is a large body of support in Latin America for the United States to set up a special trading system for the hemisphere," under which it would grant Latin American products favorable treatment in its market, possibly in return for similar preferential treatment for the products of the United States, on a basis of reciprocity. He adds that "the governments of the industrialized North can never efficiently work together in assisting the poor nations of the South unless they reach some common agreement as to the substance and architecture of the whole structure of North-South relations." This leads him to ask whether the United States "should deliberately move toward some tacitly or explicitly agreed allocation of geographical responsibilities, which cannot and should not be disassociated from the whole question of spheres of influence." And he ends by saying: "If the European Economic Community continues to expand its system of preferences for Africa, we should, I think, make it emphatically clear that we will look to the nations of the Community to carry the burden of economic assistance and, where necessary, political tutelage for those African countries."[8]

It must be said in Mr. Ball's favor that this leaning toward the system of hemispherical preferences is attributable to his having reached the conclusion, in the light of his own experience, that there would be no possibility of the Community's altering its policy.

These opinions gave rise to deep concern among the developing countries in UNCTAD. In a recent article, however, this distinguished statesman and diplomat has been candid enough—to his honor, be it said—to call attention to what a system of hemispherical preferences would imply: "Yet for us to create a closed system with Latin America would, it seems to me, have certain obvious disadvantages. First, it would tend to generate a kind of commercial claustrophobia, since, if we were to grant Latin America preferred access to our markets as against the products of other developing countries, our own producers would certainly press for preferred access to Latin American markets as against the producers of other industrialized countries."[9]

It is gratifying that in the Consensus of Viña del Mar the Latin American countries categorically declared that it was necessary "to make joint efforts to eliminate, within the near future, discriminatory preferences militating against the sale of Latin American primary commodities in the markets of certain developed countries, and to suggest measures or actions which will enable and encourage developing countries favored by those preferences to give them up"; and likewise "to stress the urgent need to put into effect, within the specified periods, and in accordance with the timetable of scheduled meetings, a general, nonreciprocal and nondiscriminatory system of preferences to facilitate the exportation of manufactures and semimanufactures from the developing countries. Within this framework, measures should be considered which will allow the relatively less developed countries to make full use of the ensuing advantages."

The United States continues to sustain the thesis of multilateral trade as against vertical arrangements. This is in accord with the long-term interest of the Latin American countries. There is also a basic identity of interests between the Latin American countries and almost all the countries of the European Economic Community. There, too, powerful forces are opposed to vertical preferences. We must have the skill to enlist their support, for EEC's potential in Latin American trade is considerable.

Nevertheless, the danger of a system of hemispherical preferences is far from having vanished, and it is imperatively necessary to lose no time in coordinating Latin American action for the purposes of effective negotiation. It is not only the lot of such-and-such a product which is at stake—important though that is—but a design which cannot and should not be jeopardized for the sake of obtaining certain advantages: the design of building up an international trade structure which will be fully compatible with the Latin American countries' development objectives and autonomy in decision-making, on a plane of genuine international cooperation.

## INTRA-LATIN AMERICAN COOPERATION

### The Movement Toward a Common Market and the Montevideo Treaty

However determined the Latin American countries may be to speed up their rate of development, they will never be able to do so unless they counteract the persistent tendency toward an external bottleneck. This is where intra-Latin American trade has an extremely important part to play. Accordingly, the whole subject needs to be frankly discussed in the light of the experience of the last 10 years.

Advocacy of the expansion of intra-Latin American trade implies the pursuit of two primary objectives. The first is to make the import-substitution process more rational and economic, by looking beyond the narrow horizon of the individual country markets; and the second consists in the progressive introduction of competition into Latin America's industrial development process.

With these objectives in view, the idea of a Latin American common market, or rather of a movement toward such a market, was conceived long ago. The distinction just drawn is necessary to prevent confusing misapprehensions. In ECLA's initial recommendations,[10] the common market was conceived as a target to be reached by gradual stages. The first stage, in the light of pragmatic criteria, was envisaged as a preferential area which would be built up by means of industrial complementarity or integration agreements—whichever term is preferred—and also agricultural agreements, in line with a program for the gradual and automatic reduction of tariff duties and the conversion of nontariff into tariff restrictions. The idea was not to eliminate duties completely, but to reduce them within specified limits, which would be different for three categories of countries, according to their stage of economic development. This phase was expected to last 10 years, and when it was over the governments would decide how to follow up the movement toward a common market, in the light of the experience acquired.

While the Montevideo Treaty was based on these recommendations, and adopted the idea of industrial integration agreements, it deviated from them in other respects, in particular where the automatic nature of tariff reductions was concerned. A more cautious procedure of selective negotiations was considered preferable.

The application of the Montevideo Treaty has resulted in a significant increase in trade between the signatory countries, and a few integration agreements have been concerted. But agreements of this kind have not yet been concluded in relation to those dynamic industries which are of major importance in the development process.

## The Action of the Latin American Free Trade Association (LAFTA)

On the other hand, a considerable number of selective negotiations— micronegotiations, as it is the fashion to call them—have been conducted. But their number is tending to decrease, although the possibilities for new negotiations are still far from having been exhausted.

This fact, which had been causing concern for some time past, revived the idea of programmed or automatic tariff reductions. For example, at the Punta del Este Conference, the Presidents of the Latin American countries that are members of the Organization of American States (OAS) mentioned the need to devise a formula in which this idea could take concrete shape. The aim would be to bring a common market into full operation by 1985, with the total elimination of tariff duties and restrictions among the contracting parties.

Perhaps this was going too far, and it might have been better to take up the other idea of progress by stages. It is not surprising, therefore, that the decision of the Chiefs of State is not being implemented. What is more, there has actually been a retrocession, for at a subsequent meeting of LAFTA it was decided to go back to the starting point, i.e., to make a study of the possibility of establishing a common market, the conclusions of which would be considered by the Governments in 1974.

What has been achieved in LAFTA is undoubtedly significant. But there is no denying that progress toward the common market is weak and hesitant. And there have been important instances in which the advantages of reciprocal trade would seem to have been forgotten altogether. A conspicuous example is afforded by the motor vehicle industry, which has been established in several of the member countries—in some cases proliferating on an antieconomic scale—without any attempt to concert integration agreements. This was done later in respect of parts and spares—a slight and belated palliative for an ill which still persists.

### The Andean Group and the Central American Common Market

It would seem to have been the above facts that prompted the formation of the Andean Group, the importance of which can be seen in Table 29.

The objective pursued is a subregional common market based on the two essential requisites envisaged for the regional market, i.e., the conclusion of integration agreements and the automatic reduction of tariff duties within a reasonable space of time, in addition to the elimination of nontariff restrictions.

The Andean Group goes farther than the Montevideo Treaty not only in this respect but in relation to other points worth mentioning. Only two of them will be dealt with here: first, the more advanced countries' assumption of responsibility to support the industrialization process of the relatively less developed countries, i.e., Bolivia and Ecuador; second, the establishment of the Andean Corporation for the financing of common projects.

It is understandable that Venezuela should be reluctant to join the Andean Group. In many of its lines of production, its cost and price structures would prevent it from standing up to the competition of the other members. But in relation to other products, it could enter into reciprocally beneficial integration agreements with the other members of the Group. The fact that Venezuela is a full member of the Andean Corporation is encouraging.

Looking to the future, it is a ground for satisfaction that the Cartagena Agreement was concluded in the context of LAFTA. In reality, the aim of the parties to it is to advance toward the regional common market at a brisker pace than the other LAFTA countries. It is highly important that the Andean Group is an economic unit should be closely linked up with the other members of the broader Association. But this depends upon both groups. It is to be hoped that in one way or another the possibility of acceding to the integration agreements concluded by the Andean Group will be left open to other LAFTA countries. Clearly, however, if LAFTA takes much longer to decide upon adopting a system of automatic or programmed reduction of duties, the gaps will be gradually widened rather then narrowed, and the passage of time will make it harder to reconcile interests.

TABLE 29

Latin America: Significance of the
Andean Group and of Other Countries in
Relation to Product and Population

| Country or Group | Product 1968 | | Population 1970 | |
|---|---|---|---|---|
| | Millions of Dollars at 1960 Prices | Percentage | Thousands of Inhabitants | Percentage |
| Andean Group | 19,830 | 17.4 | 56,212 | 20.4 |
| Argentina | 20,103 | 17.6 | 24,352 | 8.9 |
| Brazil | 27,830 | 24.2 | 93,244 | 33.9 |
| Mexico | 29,990 | 26.3 | 50,718 | 18.4 |
| Other Countries | 16,566 | 14.5 | 50,409 | 18.4 |
| Total Latin America | 114,102 | 100.0 | 274,935 | 100.0 |

*Source:* Latin America Institute for Economic and Social Planning.


It is also desirable for all concerned that links should be forged between the Central American Common Market and LAFTA. This was one of the recommendations of the Chiefs of State at Punta del Este. Despite the Common Market, Central America's economic space is limited and requires expansion. This is a clear case of relatively less development. The bigger countries will have to grant concessions which will encourage the industrial development of the Central American countries on a basis of reciprocal benefits.


### Obstacles to the Latin American Common Market


We will now examine the obstacles to the movement toward a Latin American common market. Some are imaginary; others, real. All of them must be taken into account. Those that are imaginary include the myth of supranationality. It is a great pity that such an idea should have grown up, since no supranational mechanism is required in order to set up the common market. Neither in the original suggestions first put forward by ECLA, nor in the Montevideo Treaty in which these ideas are crystallized, is any explicit or implicit reference made to such a concept. One cannot help being surprised at the insistence with which objections to supranational mechanisms are urged, when the simple truth is that such mechanisms neither exist nor are necessary.

In the progressive advance toward the common market and in its final organization, it is unthinkable that decisions of importance for the economic and social development of an individual member country should be subject to the rule of the majority, with the consequent prejudice to national sovereignty. Everything will have to be the object of an agreement, except in the case of minor issues regarding which the governments, in the light of experience, may decide that they will all alike establish procedures whereby prompt and flexible action can be taken.

These considerations lead me to speak of another objection which is also apt to crop up when the common market is discussed. There are some who dream that political unity may one day be achieved in Latin America. Since the time of Simón Bolívar this idea has been intermittently resuscitated. Whatever its merits and the possibilities of putting it into effect, there is no reason for it to be confused with the concept of a common market. As proposed in Latin America, the common market would serve no political ends. But if at some future date it were brought into full operation, such close Latin American cooperation in the economic field might undoubtedly constitute—should the governments so decide—a firm foundation on which to build up political unity. Even so, what is the point of starting now to discuss an issue that in any case will be the business of future generations? The effective operation of a Latin American common market is perfectly conceivable irrespective of any idea of political unification.[11]

Admittedly, however, it is essential to remove some political obstacles whose mere existence is not only a barrier to economic understanding between countries but also embroils their whole range of relationships. I refer to certain frontier difficulties which it has not yet been possible to settle.

There have also been misunderstandings as to the scope of the concept of an intra-Latin American division of labor. For example, there are some who believe it to mean that Argentina would have to confine itself to exporting primary commodities to the common market and importing industrial goods. It would be completely irresponsible to think in these terms. With or without a common market, Argentina, like the other Latin American countries, must energetically develop its manufactures and in particular its basic industries. There is no question of returning to the trade pattern of the 19th century.

The problem is completely different today. The iron and steel industry will serve as a case in point. There may be other Latin American countries which have better iron or coal; but that would not constitute an impediment to the installation of this basic industry. As world experience teaches, if a country did not possess those resources and needed to import them, it could still have an economic and efficient steel-making industry, based on substantial present consumption and above all on potential consumption. The best way to reach a high degree of economic validity and efficiency, however, would not be to manufacture products of all types, but to specialize in selected lines, both for domestic consumption and for export—in particular to other Latin American countries—and to import from those countries other products manufactured by their iron and steel industries. The whole proceeding would have to be the subject of integration agreements.

Neither, incidentally, are national defense considerations irreconcilable with a sound policy for the development of the iron and steel industry. The point is to state clearly what absolutely must be produced within each country in the light of defense requirements, and what could be covered by integration agreements.

It has repeatedly been declared that no Latin American country would accept industrial integration formulas imposed upon it from outside. To be more exact, it is not for an international financing institution to determine, through its operations, what a country is to produce or to refrain from producing.

So obvious a point is not worth discussing. This is not the role of international credit institutions, however powerful. It is the sole prerogative of governments to adopt such decisions freely, and under no form of pressure, in accordance with their countries' interests. And it is on the basis of these decisions that the international credit institutions should conduct their operations, cooperating with governments, at their request, in the corresponding studies. Of course the role of international credit institutions is highly important, particularly in the case of IDB, and above all where integration projects are concerned.

Let us take a look at another argument which is often adduced to combat the idea of integration. First we must integrate within each country, it is said, and only when this objective has been achieved should the economic integration of Latin America be tackled. Needless to say, the solution of this internal integration problem is of decisive importance for the Latin American countries. Elsewhere in the present report it is contended that that without regional or subregional integration of the dynamic industries (apart from other measures), it will not be possible to speed up the rate of development; and failing that, the essential objective of internal social integration could not be attained.

### Latin American Enterprise

Among the really significant arguments that are advanced in connection with the common market there is one in which I fully concur. It is feared that by their very technical and financial superiority foreign enterprises may come to carry preponderant weight in the utilization of Latin America's vast economic space. We have already recognized the existence of this danger. With or without a common market, our countries are increasingly exposed to the risk that foreign private investment may assume a preeminent role in their development. The problem is not insoluble, however, and it would be possible to find the common ground of interest between Latin American initiative and foreign private enterprise to which allusion has several times been made.

But to this end Latin American enterprise must be given energetic backing, as was expressly recognized at the second Punta del Este conference. The Chiefs of State declared on that occasion that "integration must be fully at the service of Latin America. This requires the strengthening of Latin American enterprise through vigorous financial and technical support that will permit it to develop and to supply the regional market efficiently." And they agreed "to mobilize financial and technical resources to undertake specific feasibility studies on multinational projects for Latin American industrial firms, as well as to aid in carrying out these projects."

Careful consideration must also be given to another misgiving expressed in the relatively less developed countries whose markets are unduly small. The more advanced countries are naturally in a better position to establish complex industries manufacturing intermediate and capital goods. This is true, but only up to a point. The relatively less developed countries with small markets could also be parties to integration agreements, especially if a policy of definite technical and financial support to this end were established, both on the part of the other countries and on that of international credit institutions.

But there is no denying the probability—I would almost say the certainty—that the relatively more developed countries will take the lead in these complex industries. Thus, in many instances other countries would have to purchase intermediate and capital goods at prices higher than those of similar imports from the rest of the world. Obviously they would obtain some compensation if they could in their turn export manufactured goods whose prices would also be higher. But this takes time, and in the meanwhile an equitable situation would arise which would have to be set right. It is quite conceivable that the integration industries which sell the aforesaid intermediate or capital goods to relatively less developed countries or to countries with unduly small markets should do so at world market prices. I do not think this would be difficult, in view of the relatively small fraction of total sales which these exports represent.*

### Reciprocity, Protectionism, and Competition

If new trade flows are to develop smoothly, to implant the concept of reciprocity is not enough. It must be nurtured by practical measures which will encourage industrial development in those countries in which this process is only just beginning and which may therefore lag a long way behind in the movement toward the common market. Technical and financial support would have to be extended to all the national industries that could be developed for export purposes.

Furthermore, the concept of reciprocity is of basic importance for all the countries of the region. It cannot be put into practice simply through the forces of competition; a deliberately applied policy is needed, especially with respect to industrial integration agreements. Any imbalance of benefits would prove impossible to maintain in the long run, and would militate against

---

*At the Punta del Este meeting, President Johnson referred to the possibility of establishing a regionally integrated fertilizer industry. I understand that this idea was put forward with an eye to the situation of the relatively less developed countries.

progress toward the common market. Integration agreements could stem only from express decisions by the governments, in which the distribution of benefits had been carefully weighed. I would stress that this applies to the most important cases, to the major dynamic industries, for there would be a wide variety of instances in which private enterprise would have to be given a free hand and official action would only introduce complications that defeated its ends.

This does not mean that competition has no part to play in the cases referred to above. It has a role to fill, and a very important one. Industrial integration agreements, whatever the level at which they are concerted, must leave a reasonable loophole for outside competition, since otherwise they might be conducive to monopolistic practices. The most effective way of obviating this risk would be a gradual reduction of protection vis-à-vis the rest of the world to a level which would permit external competition if and when the difference between the prices of domestically produced and imported goods rose beyond certain limits.

Let us now consider the significance of competition outside the sphere of integration agreements. Owing to a number of all-too-well-known circumstances, the industrial development process has evolved in the shelter of an excessive degree of protectionism, which may have been justified in the initial stages but is no longer warranted. In those early days, protection was a great incentive to the installation of new industries. Now it has become a factor which—when overprotection is prolonged unduly—discourages efficiency in production, since industry develops without the powerful stimulus of outside competition. I do not of course believe that it will be possible at the present stage, except in cases like that of the risk of monopolies, to think of opening the market unconditionally to competition from the great industrial countries, but it could be done with respect to competition from other Latin American countries.

To this end, tariff duties would have to be gradually reduced in intra-Latin American trade until a moderate level was reached which, in conjunction with transport costs, would imply a resonable degree of protection in the first stage of the advance toward a common market. The time allowed for the full implementation of such a policy could be quite long—10, 12, or 15 years. This would give industries enough time to adapt themselves with foresight to the new situation, avoiding major disruptions. In my opinion, the only way of inducing entrepreneurs to improve productivity is by developing this kind of competition.

This policy would have to be applied on a basis of reciprocity, with due regard to the necessity of giving special consideration to the relatively less developed countries. It would certainly be regrettable if a country were to take steps by itself to reduce its tariff duties for the other Latin American countries without receiving similar treatment from them, since an imbalance might be created which would have serious effects. Hence, the machinery of the Montevideo Treaty should be utilized for concerting the policy in question.

To enable it to be satisfactorily implemented, technical and financial assistance would have to be given to the industries concerned so that they could fit themselves to face increasing competition. But, as the experience of other countries shows, it would be a mistake to attach too much importance to this aspect of the problem. The gradual development of competition within the European Common Market has not given rise to any of the distortions which were previously feared; and the same could be said of the European Free Trade Area.*

From another standpoint, if the Latin American countries are to increase their exports to the developed countries, it is essential for their industries to improve in efficiency and productivity, and this will not be fully achieved without the spur of tariff reductions.

Perhaps the more developed Latin American countries might first apply the reductions to imports from the relatively less developed countries. But tariff reductions alone are not enough. To facilitate imports an active policy is needed in LAFTA, i.e., measures on the part of the more developed countries to encourage the establishment of industries in those which are relatively less developed, so that these latter can take advantage of the tariff concessions. In all this the cooperation of international credit institutions, and in particular of IDB, could be highly efficacious.

However gradually competition is introduced, it will indubitably necessitate a number of adjustments in Latin America's industrial production. These are needed in order to increase productivity. But competition alone is not enough; another requisite is technical and financial action on the part of the State, to enable the adjustments in question to be introduced with a minimum of trouble. Otherwise, a number of unfavorable conditions which must be done away with might be perpetuated for an indefinite length of time. There are cases in which high production costs—even taking into account the small size of the domestic market—are due to inefficiency on the part of the enterprises themselves. In others, however, they are attributable to factors beyond the industry's control, above all the high price of the raw materials, intermediate products, or capital goods which the enterprises concerned have to use. All these failings are usually covered up by the high level of protection; and as tariff duties are gradually reduced, they will come to light. A little thought will show that this is not a bad thing. Quite the contrary. It is favorable to the productivity of the economy as a whole that weaknesses

---

*Perhaps I may be allowed to describe what happened to me in Finland in this connection. A little over 10 years ago I had the pleasure of visiting Finland in my capacity as an ECLA official, and I returned there before relinquishing my post as Secretary-General of UNCTAD. On the first occasion I found that great anxiety was felt as to the adverse effects on Finland's incipient industries which might be produced by imports from Sweden and Denmark, countries at much more advanced stages of industrial development than Finland. On my recent visit, I happened to meet some of the people with whom I had conversed before, and had an opportunity of asking them how many industries had suffered or been forced to close down as a result of the tariff reductions. They were astonished by my question, as those early fears had long been left behind. Not a single industrial establishment had closed down, inasmuch as the gradual reduction of tariff duties had led industrialists to improve the efficiency of their enterprises; and this had enabled them not only to stand up against competition from the other member countries, but also to start exporting manufactures to the countries in question, thus strengthening, in addition, their competitive power vis-à-vis the rest of the world.

should be detected so that they can be cured. And far from constituting an argument against introducing competition, it is a reason for doing so, but—we would repeat—the process must be gradual.

It may possibly happen that competition is falsified in certain cases. The most serious of these—which sometimes causes a great deal of concern—is that of undervaluation of the currency. Undervaluation enables the country practicing it to obtain, in given circumstances, export advantages which might be injurious to others in the flow of reciprocal trade. The country affected might seek relief by applying compensatory measures; but if several countries had undervalued currencies, it is easy to imagine the serious complications that would supervene. On the contrary, it should be the responsibility of countries with undervalued currencies to impose export surcharges to counteract the effects of undervaluation. This is a mere suggestion regarding a problem which, despite its importance, has not yet been the subject of careful analysis. Where overvaluation exists, the country which practices it has measures to offset its effects within its reach. They could be adopted only under major provisions previously agreed upon by the governments that are parties to reciprocal trade systems.

Clearly, as it becomes possible to coordinate the countries' monetary and exchange policy, difficulties of this type will tend to become less important. In this connection, the payments agreements concluded and administered by the Central Banks, first in the Central American Common Market and later in LAFTA, are very encouraging. It is to be hoped that such agreements can be extended, not only on monetary grounds but also because they may generate incentives to putting the principle of reciprocity into practical effect. This example also shows how concrete solutions can be reached without the least suspicion of supranationality.

### The Meeting of Chiefs of State at Punta del Esta

To revert to the adjustments which would have to be made in industry, enterprises would need cooperation in order to carry them out without disruptive effects. This was recognized by the Chiefs of State at Punta del Este when they decided "to mobilize financial and technical resources within and without the hemisphere to contribute to the solution of problems in connection with the balance of payments, industrial readjustments, and retraining of the labor force that may arise from a rapid reduction of trade barriers during the period of transition toward the common market."

In this context, it should also be recalled that President Johnson sent a message to Congress in March, 1967, shortly before he went to the Punta del Este meeting, in which he recommended the allocation of additional resources to an amount ranging between $250 and 500 million over a period of three to five years, which would begin in about 1970. These resources would be used to strengthen Latin America's economic integration process. At the same Punta del Este meeting, the Chiefs of State laid great stress on the need to complete and modernize the physical infrastructure of Latin America, and decided to step up the multinational action required for execution of the projects involved. Bearing in mind that the availability of special financing operates in favor of the execution of infrastructure projects, they decided "to mobilize, within and outside the hemisphere, resources in addition to those that will continue to be placed at the disposal of the countries to support national economic development programs, such resources to be devoted especially to the implementation of multinational infrastructure projects that can represent important advances in the Latin American economic integration process. In this regard, the IDB should have additional resources in order to participate actively in the attainment of this objective."

In recent years IDB has been acting in practice as a bank for Latin American integration. For such purposes, it has assumed considerable financing commitments in respect of intraregional exports of capital goods; multinational projects, in particular highways, hydroelectricity works, and telecommunications; preinvestment studies; and training, research, and support for the economic integration process. With expanded resources, IDB should pursue and extend this work, for which it already posesses a most valuable store of technical and financial experience.

Multinational projects of such far-reaching scope call for substantial preinvestment expenditure. To this end, the Chiefs of State also agreed to "allocate sufficient resources to the Pre-investment Fund for Latin American Integration of the IDB for conducting studies that will make it possible to identify and prepare multinational projects in all fields that may be of importance in promoting regional integration. In order that the aforesaid Fund may carry out an effective promotion effort, it is necessary that an adequate part of the resources allocated may be used without reimbursement, or with reimbursement conditioned on the execution of the corresponding projects."

At the Assembly of the Board of Governors of IDB held shortly after this recommendation had been formulated, a resolution to the same effect was adopted, making it possible to strengthen the research and preinvestment work which the institution was already undertaking. This is a matter in which the United Nations Development Program is also interested. Unfortunately, the setback which has occurred since the meeting of Chiefs of State has been unfavorable to the application of these important recommendations.

The advance toward a Latin American common market is not easy. But there is no other alternative. It is indispensable for the acceleration of development. In turn, the development process, as the favorable effects of economic expansion make themselves felt, will tend to lessen the difficulty of the adjustments involved.

A few last words on trade in agricultural commodities. The speeding up of development will call for a considerable expansion of production. In view of the lack of satisfactory research, this question is not dealt with in our projections. It is extremely important, however, and should be given top priority among the subjects to be studied. Agricultural integration possibilities, too, are matters that should not be left at the mercy of the interplay of the forces of competition.

## NOTES

[1] See *U.S. Foreign Assistance in the 1970s: A New Approach*. Report to the President from the Task Force on International Development (Washington, D.C.: U.S. Government Printing Office, March, 1970), p. 2.

[2] See my author's introduction to *Raúl Prebisch, Una década de lucha por América Latina. La acción del Banco Interamericano de Desarrollo* (Mexico City: Fondo de Cultura Económica, 1970).

[3] See *U.S. Foreign Assistance in the 1970s, op. cit.*, pp. 36, 37.

[4] *Ibid.*, p. 36.

[5] See UNCTAD, *International Monetary Reform and Co-operation for Development*, United Nations publication, Sales No. E.70.II.D.2; *A Proposal to Link Reserve Creation and Development Assistance,* Report of the Subcommittee on International Exchange and Payments, Joint Economic Committee of the United States Congress (Washington, D.C.: U.S. Government Printing Office, 1969); and *International Monetary Reform and Latin America,* report to ICAP by a group of experts, ICAP/4, (March 9, 1966), pp. 24-25.

[6] The conclusions are condensed in a report which I submitted to the Chairman of ICAP under the title "La inversión privada en el desarrollo latinoamericano." Roberto Campos and Aldo Ferrer submitted different points of view.

[7] Raúl Prebisch, "La inversión privado en el desarrollo latinoamericano," a report submitted to the chairman of ICAP.

[8] See George W. Ball, *The Discipline of Power* (Boston: Little, Brown and Company in association with the Atlantic Monthly Press, 1968), Chapter 12, pp. 236-241.

[9] See *The Washington Post* (December 14, 1969).

[10] See *The Latin American Common Market,* United Nations publication, Sales No. 59.II.G.4, Part Two, pp. 28 *ff.,* the reports of the first and second sessions of the Working Group on the Latin American Regional Market. These sessions were held at Santiago, Chile, on February 3-11, 1958, and at Mexico City, on February 16-27, 1959. On both occasions, the chair was taken by Galo Plaza. The members of the Working Group included, on one occasion or the other, Carlos D'Ascoli (Venezuela), José Garrido Torres (Brazil), Rodrigo Gómez (Mexico), Flavian Levine (Chile), Carlos Lleras Restrepo (Colombia), Eustaquio Méndez Delfino (Argentina), Raymond F. Mikesell (United States), Juan Pardo Heeren (Peru), and Joaquín Vallejo (Colombia).

[11] I set forth these and other considerations more fully in articles published on June 13 and 14, 1969, in *La nación* (Buenos Aires).

PART IV THE ECONOMIC SYSTEM
AND ITS TRANSFORMATION

CHAPTER **6** THE SPONTANEOUS FORCES
AND DEVELOPMENT STRATEGY
IN THE ECONOMIC SYSTEM

Much emphasis has been placed so far in this study on the considerable development potential of the Latin American economy. However, its expansionist forces—which have demonstrated their vigor so often in the past, and continue to do so at present—are being seriously obstructed, to the detriment of the vast possibilities offered by scientific and technological progress for improving the lot of the population. Clearly, the development patterns that have been prevalent in Latin America must be discarded. They are already obsolete. A new type of development is required, imbued with great vigor and a strong sense of social equity. To achieve this, sweeping structural changes are needed to clear the way for the expansionist forces. But they are not all that is needed—far from it. The State should take deliberate action to influence these forces, in order to resolve the contradictions stemming from the advance of science and technology. It is these contradictions that are mainly responsible for the serious disparity between capital formation and the growth of the labor force, and for the persistent tendency toward an external bottleneck. To eliminate these problems is an essential requisite for speeding up the rate of development.

In brief, the present chapter will discuss changes in structures and attitudes, and also the need for discipline in order to act upon the forces of development. The task of influencing these forces calls for a clearly defined strategy, with planning as its fit instrument of implementation. Admittedly, there is some opposition to planning, not so much as a technique but—and this is the worst of the business—precisely because it is the instrument of a strategy which also arouses opposition.

## THE STRUCTURAL BASES OF THE SYSTEM

### The Agrarian Structure

The structural obstacles standing in the way of economic development are of great significance. They weaken the incentives to technical progress and deprive the economy of the degree of social mobility that is demanded by such progress, as well as by considerations of equitable income distribution. It is therefore justifiable to devote some attention to these obstacles, since neglect of them would mean failure to comprehend the dynamics of Latin American development in all their complexity.

It is a well-known fact that the concentration of land ownership and the proliferation of minifundia in Latin America are factors which over the generations have militated against the introduction of improved techniques and the efficient use of the production potential of the land, and have also been a major cause of social disparities. Moreover, even where technology has managed to penetrate into these outmoded land tenure systems—as has happened in export-oriented activities and is now happening in agriculture for domestic consumption—it has generally not been able to break them down, but has, rather, helped to buttress them. It is paradoxical indeed that in such cases technical progress should strengthen the traditional concentration patterns. Even in countries where the land has been redistributed, there is still some tendency for small and medium-sized units to join together to form large estates. While the advantages of this process in terms of productive efficiency cannot be disregarded, its aggravating effects on concentration of ownership and on social disparities are equally impossible to deny.

Further explanation is in order here. Technical progress—either through mechanization or through the introduction of farm practices that raise yields per unit of land—increases the product per agricultural worker. This does not mean, however, that there is a corresponding rise in the income of the masses working on the land. In the contrary, if labor is abundant and land ownership is concentrated in a few hands, the gains deriving from more advanced techniques, insofar as they are not absorbed by entrepreneurial profits, will tend to be incorporated into the rent of the land and thus increase its value.

Furthermore, the rapid growth of the labor force makes it very much easier for the landowner to arrogate to himself the gains accruing from technical progress. And the more this happens, the harder it becomes for the rural masses to obtain access to the larger amount of land they would need to be able to share in these benefits.

Thus the pressure of the active population on the land increases, minifundia are divided up into ever-smaller plots, and the number of landless peasants grows. In this incredible process of division and subdivision, there are some parts of Latin America where peasants inherit a single furrow. The people multiply, but the amount of land available does not.

It is not only the special way in which the benefits of technology are appropriated that intensifies income concentration and social disparities. Even without technical progress, the rent of the land tends to rise when agricultural demand is brisk. And it also rises—to a very marked extent—as a result of the means of communication and other infrastructural works constructed by the State with resources whose provenance is not usually rural property.

For all these reasons, it is understandable that the increase in the product per worker in agriculture—which has certainly taken place—has not led to a corresponding increase in the income of the rural masses, although in some countries movements to organize rural wage earners, minimum wage regimes, and social security systems are bringing about certain changes. Nonetheless, there is no reason to assume that matters will improve to any significant extent until the agrarian structure is changed so as to give land to the rural worker who has none at all and to increase the holdings of those who have some, to the extent permitted by population pressures. This would ensure the rural masses a fairer share in the benefits of technical progress, provided that nonagricultural activities make productive use of the redundant manpower in agriculture and that the indispensable improvements are introduced in marketing methods. Otherwise, social disparities will continue to increase.

## Old and New Structures

The system of land tenure exerted a dominant influence on the social structure of Latin America during the period of outward-looking development, before the world depression. Industrial development gained great impetus as a result of the depression, and simply superimposed itself on this structure, to which it adapted itself to some extent, but which it did not radically transform. It did not—as happened in other cases in the past—necessitate a redistribution of the land, for as a general rule easily accessible land was available for the expansion of agricultural production. Nor was any need felt until recently to open up the vast potential market of the underprivileged masses and extend the social range of demand, because an industrial development process based on import substitution found a market already in existence that grew in step with urban growth. But now there are clear signs that this process has already begun to lose its dynamic impetus. And that impetus cannot be renewed by credit expedients which are designed simply to stimulate demand and which, moreoever, adversely affect capital formation.

What is more, industrial development is taken place in watertight compartments, under the strong protection of high tariff barriers and of restrictions and prohibitions that elminate external competition and hamper the assimilation of technological progress and the efficient use of the factors of production.

Nor has industrial development changed the traditional structure of Latin America's foreign trade, which is still oriented toward the major industrial centers. Primary commodities continue to be exported and industrial goods imported in return, although the pattern is less rigid than it used to be. Only the composition of such imports is changing, as a result of the import-substitution process, which is taking place separately in each country, for the traditional trade structure did not encourage intraregional trade, except in certain primary commodities.

Import substitution is steadily progressing within a number of industrial microcosms, as the ratio of the capacity to import to the overall product of the economy gradually decreases. Industrialization on these lines is inefficient and costly for the all-too-well-known reasons: markets are small and the spur of competition is lacking. The process bears within itself the seeds of its own loss of dynamism, since industrial development takes place within a closed circuit of costs and prices which, because it has no contact with the world market, discourages exports of manufactures; and these are really essential, for industry needs to stretch outward in order to develop inward in depth.

Admittedly, in the 1930's it would have been unthinkable for the developed countries to relax their import restrictions in order to encourage imports of manufactures from the peripheral countries. They did not even do so later: the Second World War and its immediate aftermath were not propitious to such a policy. But more recently it has become a possibility, although nothing of any great moment has been done by the developed countries to change the structure of their trade with the Third World.

This point is of such significance that it warrants a brief digression. The developed countries have made notable efforts over the past two decades to reconstruct world trade, culminating two years ago in the success of the Kennedy Round. However, the developing countries have been virtually excluded from this process. The seriousness of this must not be disregarded, for the developing countries need to take their place in the new structure so that their commodities and manufactures can play an active part in world trade, and the adverse effects that technological progress in the major centers has had on exports of commodities can thus be counteracted. These effects are well-known: some are direct, resulting from increased production of synthetic substitutes; others are indirect, deriving from the fact that demand for commodities is expanding relatively slowly as income in the industrial centers rises, with very few exceptions, at a rapid rate. Added to this are the ill effects of these centers' overprotection of their own primary production, which is completely exempted from the movement toward trade liberalization.

To look at the other side of the coin, the Latin American countries for the most part have not yet evinced a firm determination to modify the aforesaid structure based on industrial microcosms. Quite rightly, they are insistently urging the developed countries to give their manufactures favorable treatment; but they have not displayed equal zeal in doing what they can themselves in relation to their own reciprocal trade. Gradually linking up the industrial microcosms—apart from all that it would involve in terms of structural improvements—is a basic essential if the Latin American countries are to enter the world market on a competitive footing and become effectively integrated in the new order of world trade that the industrial centers have been at such pains to construct. It is also essential if the region is to develop its trade with the socialist countries, especially once these are fully incorporated in the opulent flow of the world trade.

It is no exaggeration to say that these structural changes in Latin America's industry and foreign trade are of decisive importance. Without them, it will not be possible to stimulate export expansion or relieve the external constraint that is holding down the rate of development. Moreover, unless development can be stepped up—and this warrants reiteration—it will not be possible to give the economic system the requisite dynamic strength or to make it meaningful from the standpoint of social equity.

This question of social equity has to do not only with the way in which income is distributed, but also with the actual sources of income in the prevailing social structure. If a large part of the income of the upper strata derives from privilege, from their dominant position in the system, the incentive to technical progress is weakened. The traditional case in point is the appropriation of land rents, both in the rural areas, as described earlier, and also in the cities, as a result of development itself and of the high rate of population growth.

Privilege also exists when excessive protectionism makes disproportionate profits possible, despite the high cost of industrial production; and when restrictions on competition or the backwardness of the domestic marketing system allows higher incomes to be obtained than would otherwise have been the case. Participation in the power structure, too, usually carries with it privileges of this kind. In such cases, there is no strict relation between the income of individual persons and their contribution to the production process in its broadest sense.

Consequently, in addition to stimulating the growth of income, the structural changes that pave the way for development will also gradually change the sources of income and thus increase the incentives to technical progress.

Social mobility has a very important part to play here. It is both a requirement for and a consequence of development, which it likewise tends to accelerate. From the standpoint of mobility, development requires that jobs be filled as far as possible by those most suited for them, to prevent the waste of potential talents. In Latin American societies, with their special structures, a number of factors limit mobility. Some are structural, such as the concentration of land ownership and of income in general; the weakness of incentives to improve industry, resulting from overprotection; industry's limited capacity to absorb manpower, with the consequent spurious absorption of labor in services; etc. All this means that the rate at which new jobs are created at the medium and high levels is relatively slow, and thus reduces the possibilities of social advancement. Furthermore, the extremely unequal distribution of income limits access to education even at the primary level for many groups, and makes it difficult at the secondary and higher levels, with all the waste of human talent that this entails. It should be borne in mind, however, that education and the development of skills at all technical levels are potential factors of social mobility. If this potential is to be realized, economic activity must have a keen sense of the need to increase productivity through technical progress. Thus, there is a close linkage between technology and social mobility.

It is worthwhile emphasizing this point because, in our eagerness to find simplified solutions to the very complex problems of development, we often forget that technical training cannot take place in a vacuum, outside the context of economic and social development. Unless the pace of development is stepped up, occupational opportunities will be too scarce for mobility to become effective. Not only will the effort expended on training be wasted, but further cause for resentment or frustration will be added to the motives already activating or troubling—as the case may be—the younger generations in Latin America. And there will be yet more reason for Latin American professionals to leave their own countries—mainly for the United States—at a considerable loss to the region in terms of resources and potential.

### The Power Structure, Immediatism,
### and Foresight

It is a well-known fact that the linkage between the economic and social structure and the power structure is very close. The two form a complex whole, whose different but mutually interdependent components can be separated only in abstracto, for when all is said and done, they are but different facets of a single reality.

In Latin America, some changes have occurred in the power structure as development has proceeded. The traditional groups of landowners and businessmen that characterized the period of outward-looking growth have been joined in the ensuing phase by new elements, their numbers varying from country to country, with industrialists accounting for a steadily increasing proportion. The middle strata are considerably strengthening their position: they have become larger and more diversified and, through high-level technical specialists and officials, are increasing their influence on the public administration. Thanks to their enhanced trade union and political power, workers are acquiring a manifest ability to defend their interests and aspirations. And in a number of Latin American countries labor leaders are beginning to form part of the power structure itself.

Notwithstanding all these changes, a special urban constellation has gradually evolved, in which the politically inarticulate and unorganized lower strata are not making the weight of their numbers fully felt—except at intervals, on particular occasions—in the struggle for income redistribution: a struggle that is being exacerbated as the dynamism of the economy falls increasingly short of what is required. For if the industry group absorbs such a small proportion of the increment in the labor force, and the volume of manpower in services is growing out of all proportion, to say nothing of unemployment, the imbalance thus created leads to ever-mounting tension.

It is politically and also socially understandable that this tension should be relieved through measures to redistribute income, by means of either wage increases or public spending. The steady expansion of the groups participating to some degree in the power structure, and the growing calls upon the State to satisfy social welfare aspirations, give rise to a complex set of commitments that, inter alia, conduce to immediatism in respect of income redistribution. However genuine its underlying concern for social equity, and however much it may do to alleviate social tension in the short term, this redistributional immediatism does not solve the basic problems. Neither does a repressive approach.

As the lower strata in the cities—which are today in such an underprivileged position—gradually become aware of their power, they will carry greater weight in the income struggle; and if they are joined by the rural masses, tension will inevitably tauten to a point at which it seriously jeopardizes the operation of a system which, moreover, is far from efficient.

Something more is involved here than the power structure alone. If representatives of the lower strata managed in one way or another to become part of it, there is no guarantee that their combative vigor would not also lead to immediatism, and again the basic problem would be bypassed: namely, how to combine immediate measures with others which would show results only after some time had passed. In other words, immediate measures must be merely the first step in tackling the basic problem. This is certainly not an easy approach, but is is perfectly feasible.

Immediatism cannot be assigned to any particular point in the political spectrum, for short-term solutions are sought not only by the staunch defenders of the status quo, but also by those who are at odds with it, and who find such expedients an easy substitute for radical changes to which there are powerful obstacles. The net result is that the ills inherent in the existing structure are intensified.

Basic solutions do not emanate spontaneously from the conflict of interests and aspirations, but require an enlightened and long-range view of the situation that can be achieved only through a thoughtful analysis of the major problems of development.

In the case of immediate solutions, each of the parties concerned sets itself specific and rapidly attainable objectives. This is not true of the longer-term approach. It can be clearly shown that, if the distortions in the structure of employment are eliminated and the distribution of income is made more equitable, there will be much greater scope for industry and agriculture to expand, as we noted in an earlier chapter; and the services sector, freed by this corrective process from its heavy burden of redundant manpower, will be able to participate actively in the benefits of accelerated development. But this is only a future prospect, and if nothing at all is offered in the immediate present, it will be difficult if not impossible to win acceptance for a continuing development discipline, except during spasmodic outbreaks of collective emotion.

Immediatism has frequently prevailed over foresight. Hitherto the latter has certainly not been a dominant feature in the present stage of Latin American development. It is true that there have been government leaders who possessed it, and that in some countries this has had lasting consequences. They were men capable of interpreting the course of events and facing the future with a strong sense of responsibility.

It must be admitted, however, that the problems which arose at the beginning of the present stage of development did not really appear to demand such a high degree of foresight. Industrial development is a case in point. Given the wide margin initially available for import substitution, simple measures, with immediate economic and social effects, sufficed to spur on the industrialization process. In agriculture, the availability of accessible land made it possible to expand production with no great difficulty, and population growth was not then as rapid as at present. It was natural that in those days immediate concerns should have taken the fore, and that anything demanding thought about the future should have been put to one side.

Now that this relatively easy stage has been completed, immediate expedients must inevitably be combined with longer-range measures that admit of no makeshift procedures, not only because of the nature of the problems involved, but also because our knowledge of them is greater today. Want of foresight would be inexcusable at our present stage. Furthermore, in all these measures it is essential to adopt a rational approach, to have a clear idea of the objectives and of the means available for attaining them. But, irrespective of the power structure, the longer it takes to get results, the more difficult it is to exercise rationality.

## CONTRADICTIONS IMPLICIT IN SCIENTIFIC AND TECHNOLOGICAL PROGRESS

### State Action and the Market Mechanism

The first section in this chapter discussed the major structural changes that are needed to facilitate the introduction of technical know-how and clear the way for the expansionist forces of the economy.

Although State action is still a highly controversial issue in Latin America, it is now undisputedly acknowledged to be an essential requirement for economic stability. In this respect, a very important change took place in the developed countries as a result of the great world depression—and in the developing countries, too. It became necessary to take deliberate action to influence the forces of the economy in order to bring about first recovery and then development without serious fluctuations. Today all this seems quite natural and beyond dispute. But it was not so in those days of ardent doctrinal controversy.

It is also beyond question today that if the economic system is left to its own devices, it does not promote equitable income distribution. What is more, even large and affluent countries are discovering that huge sectors of their own populations are among the ranks of the underprivileged. But this is not the whole story. In these same countries, concern about the adverse effects of technological progress is mounting to a dramatic pitch. At last, public opinion is coming to realize that not everything is for the best, either for society itself or for its physical environment. For in these large countries the physical environment is deteriorating while the indexes of prosperity are steadily rising. It is not just that the ecological balance has been interfered with, as has been observable for some time past, by technological advances in agriculture. Lack of awareness of these problems, or indifference to them, has allowed the free play of economic forces to result in large-scale pollution of water and atmosphere, systematic destruction of the natural environment, and urban congestion with all its economic and social implications. With the help of the electronic brain, the cost-benefit analyses guiding these forces have become more and more precise. But the calculations do not yet take account of one factor which is of enormous significance in human terms: the huge social costs that industry and the internal combustion engine have brought in their wake.

The farther science and technology progress, the more unavoidably necessary it becomes to influence the spontaneous movements of the economic forces. This is the great problem whose urgency is progressively increasing in the developed countries, whatever their power structure: namely, how to do this and yet ensure that the State does not interfere with the decisions of individuals and subject them arbitrarily to its growing authority.

These, like other problems posed by scientific and technological progress, have come to Latin America before their time, before the resources and skills needed to deal with them have been created. The problems of the developed countries are thus being superimposed on those characteristic of development—which are difficult enough to solve in themselves. However, one and all are problems that cannot be avoided and that must be tackled in one way or another.

Despite the marked change that has taken place in ideas on the role of the State in the advanced countries, in Latin America such matters are not always approached with as much clear-sighted objectivity as they might be. In addition to the very understandable opposition to changes in structures and attitudes, there is often some confusion about the role of the spontaneous forces of the economy. Efforts to act upon or influence these forces are confused with State interference in the market mechanism. But there is no basic incompatibility here. The proper functioning of the market mechanism depends in large measure on the efficacy of the changes made.

The market mechanism is based upon the prevailing economic and social structure and responds to its needs. It can neither be held responsible for the consequences of the structure, nor be supposed capable of changing it. It must not be expected to do more than it actually can. If the economic and social structure preserves a very unequal distribution of income, then the market simply reflects good or bad consumer preferences; and in accordance with these preferences, it channels the use of investment resources, thus giving a particular configuration to the production apparatus. If this configuration does not coincide with the interests of the society as a whole, the blame must be laid not on the market mechanism, but on the underlying structure and the income distribution inherent in it. What is essential is for consumers to be able to manifest their preferences through the market mechanism, and for activities serving consumers to be able to respond to these preferences under the stimulus of the economic incentive and of competition.

From another standpoint, a patent truth must be recognized. Consumer preferences are influenced by increasingly .subtle and pervasive forms of advertising, which, in the Latin American countries, are promoting the systematic dissemination of consumption patterns that militate against capital formation. Even if income were distributed more equitably, it would still clearly be necessary to tackle this problem. There is not very much evidence that this has been done effectively, for in the most obvious case—namely, bans and restrictions on imports of nonessential goods—domestic investment has been encouraged to produce the self-same goods, despite the shortage of capital.

Nevertheless, the market mechanism continues to be of great value because it operates in a completely impersonal way. However much the size of disposable income and certain forms of consumption may be influenced by the State, it still leaves consumers with a wide range of choice, without prescribing what should or should not be done in specific cases. This is very important, as is also the fact that, under the market mechanism, responsibilities are diffused and decisions scattered throughout all the various activities of the economy. Concentrating decision-making in the hands of a single supreme authority does not give the flexibility and efficiency required in the increasingly intricate complex of economic life; and this is something which the socialist economies are now recognizing, as was pointed out in Chapter 1.

With this clarification, then, we can now consider the various fields in which State action is needed. It was said earlier that the State, in addition to carrying out the requisite structural changes, has to act upon the forces of the economy in order to resolve the contradictions that derive from scientific and technological progress and thus help to achieve a rate of development that will imbue the economic system with the degree of dynamism that is required. In this respect, there are two fields in which action by the State is essential: capital formation and foreign trade.

## Capital Formation

At the present stage of Latin American development, no spontaneous forces exist that can raise the investment coefficient. The rate of capital formation must be appreciably stepped up in order to reconcile the incompatibility engendered by scientific and technological progress between the population's soaring growth rate and increasing consumption aspirations and the steady rise in the capital/worker ratio which more advanced techniques generally entail. The State has to take deliberate action to encourage personal and company saving, or, by means of the tax system, to increase its own savings, either for direct investment or for channeling into private enterprise.

Such deliberate action is essential, since interest rates respond satisfactorily only to an increase in real demand for investment resources; they are completely untouched by the considerable potential demand that would have to be met in order to absorb the redundant labor force and step up the tempo of development.

Keynes showed during the world depression that the economic system did not spontaneously arrive at a position of equilibrium with full employment but at a whole range of positions of equilibrium with differing degrees of unemployment; similarly, it can be said that in Latin America positions of dynamic equilibrium are conceivable without full utilization of the labor force and with differing degrees of redundancy.* In such cases, the market mechanism is completely inoperative.

It then becomes essential for the State to intervene to raise the investment coefficient—admittedly a very difficult task. But once it is accomplished, the

---

*This is not the place to start a theoretical discussion, but I do wish to mention the concept of "positions of equilibrium" in order to draw a parallel with Keynesian thought that seems to me interesting. However, I do not think it appropriate to use this static concept to explain the dynamics of the system.

problem of capital formation becomes much simpler, for as a general rule the investment coefficient tends to remain at the level it has reached, although monetary or fiscal instruments may have to be used to counteract possible fluctuations.

## Foreign Trade

State action with respect to foreign trade is indispensable, both at the Latin American and at the international level, in order to change structures and also to resolve the very serious contradictions caused in this context by scientific and technological progress. In Latin America, this progress has the effect of promoting the rapid growth of demand for imports, while in the great industrial centers its effect has been to reduce demand for imports of primary commodities.

The conflict between these effects cannot settle itself spontaneously through the free interplay of economic forces. Structural changes are needed to enable these forces to expand, as well as to direct them toward the achievement of certain objectives. It is well-known that there is resistance to such changes in Latin America. There is also resistance in the developed countries, which have not yet decided to modify the structure of their trade with a view to facilitating the access of exports from the developing countries. In actual fact, the changes required in this latter respect are not of any great magnitude in comparison with those that have been and still are taking place in the development of the advanced economies.

Simply making all these structural changes, however, is not enough. Promotional action by the State is also essential. There are noteworthy instances of achievements elsewhere which are taking some time to have an impact on Latin America. They are in some cases having that impact now, and this shows how much can be done to promote new exports by combining State action with private enterprise. There must be a great deal of continuity of purpose, however, which has not always been in evidence. What is more, it has frequently happened that a change in regulations or overvaluation of the currency has disrupted serious efforts to promote new exports, besides affecting the traditional export lines.

## The Population Explosion

Obviously, the problems of capital formation and the external bottleneck also reflect the implications of the population explosion. Some rather odd attitudes exist in this respect. Recognition of the need to act upon the spontaneous forces of the economy does not signify acceptance of the need to do likewise with demographic forces, since many believe that the population problem will eventually solve itself of its own accord.

Admittedly, this is a very delicate topic. For birth control touches certain deep-rooted sentiments which cannot but be respected. Moreover, it is sometimes advocated with a degree of oversimplification that defeats the ends pursued. A suggestion commonly put forward is that family planning is a basic formula for economic development, if not an alternative to the international financial cooperation that Latin America needs in order to cope with the economy's lack of the required degree of dynamism. It has even been said that $1,000 spent on birth control would take the place of many thousands of dollars spent on capital investment. There is a risk that this singular comparison might be taken as the reason—even if it were not, if there were other motivations—for the attitude of certain non-Latin American bodies which spend substantial sums in disseminating information about birth control practices, not only in countries that approve of them but also in countries which are firmly opposed to them or which have adopted no definite position.

All this has given rise to a controversy in which it is very difficult to find one's bearings unless the terms of the problem are carefully defined. This is what will be attempted in the following paragraphs. First and foremost, population policy is only one of the components—admittedly a very important one—of an economic and social development strategy. It is obvious that the growth rate of the economy will not be speeded up simply by birth control, without anything being done to act upon the other factors on which the dynamics of economic and social development depend. Moreover, it would be absurd to think that a country with an overall growth rate of 5 percent, for example, could increase its per capita income at the same rate if there were no increase in its population. The mutual interdependence between population and development must not be disregarded. There may possibly be an optimum rate of natural growth for each country, falling somewhere between absolute demographic stagnation and the maximum now being approached by some Latin American countries which have already exceeded an average annual population growth rate of 3.5 percent.

Some thought must likewise be given to the length of time required to implement reasonable measures in respect of family planning practiced by carefully considered technical methods; and also to the time it would take to achieve specific results, since the effects of such measures on the labor force would not make themselves felt for some 15 or 18 years, and only subsequently would they become more marked as the new cohorts of working age were fully incorporated into the labor force.

Hence, in the initial stages, birth control would not help to correct the distortions in the structure of employment of the labor force or to relieve unemployment. What is more, as families became smaller, the proportion of women joining the labor force might rise, as has happened in the developed countries. Thus it would be still longer before demographic policy showed definite results in terms of the population of working age.

On the other hand, it would have immediate effects on household budgets, particularly in the lower strata, and on social investment by the State in health, housing, and education, in which the unsatisfied needs are considerable. Birth control would make this pressing problem more manageable. It should not be forgotten, however, that the factor that weighs most heavily on social investment by the State is the cumulative deficit in housing, health, and education services, rather than the natural growth of demand.

In any case, although the impact of population policy on the labor force may take some while to become evident, no time should be lost in considering this matter, nor should it be simply shelved. In Chapter 3, it was shown, for purposes of illustration, that if the rate of development could be raised to 8 percent per year, all that could be managed in a decade would be to prevent the structural distortion in the labor force from growing any worse. To correct it gradually would take still more time. Meanwhile, in 20 years' time average per capita income should have reached about $920, or 129 percent more than at present. But this average would continue to embrace widely differing situations, apart from the fact that it would still fall far short of satisfying increasingly insistent desires for betterment. Even more time would be required to attain a level compatible with these aspirations.

It is here that the fundamental significance of the population problem lies. Twenty years is a relatively short span of time in the development of a community. But within this period, the Latin American countries will have to make a major effort to ensure that the coming generations enjoy living conditions very different from the poverty-stricken lot of most of the population today. If the economic system could be imbued with the genuine dynamic vigor in which it is a good deal lacking at present, the time would then be ripe for the Latin American countries—some sooner, some later—to set themselves objectives that today seem beyond their reach.

It is not just a question of providing a better diet for a rapidly increasing population. Let us assume that the technological revolution in agriculture will be the decisive factor in this respect. But man's expectations for the future compass much more than this, and they will be continually expanded by new aspirations which, even though they transcend the purely economic sphere—and it would be well that this should be so—require a sound economic groundwork if they are to come to fruition. Whether these objectives can be attained will depend largely on the decisions taken in the coming years regarding deliberate action to influence the demographic situation.

These decisions cannot be left to those who come after. Economic and social development is basically something that demands foresight and a deep sense of collective responsibility. This responsibility will not be fulfilled if population questions are viewed through the narrow lens of the immediate future. The serious problems that Latin America has to tackle today are in great measure due to a lack of foresight. The population explosion and the difficulties that have arisen in the course of development were in fact new problems that it would have been difficult to anticipate 30 or 40 years ago. And if they had been foreseen, it would have been nothing more than an intellectual exercise on the part of a few. But now these problems are no longer new, much is known of them, and their effects are being felt. We cannot shirk our responsibility to tackle them with firm determination.

However, it is commonly argued that foresight is not needed in demographic matters, since the birth rate will fall of its own accord as development progresses. The experience of the industrial countries in general—and of Latin America itself in certain cases—shows that the birth rate has indeed declined as the economic situation of the family has improved. This has happened because a rise in income fosters changes in certain family habits. There should, therefore, be no objection if efforts to disseminate such habits were begun forthwith, provided that population policy were implemented as part of an economic and social development strategy.

In both cases, the fall in the birth rate is the result of deliberate action, the only difference being that in the first it is attributable to the new attitudes that economic development brings with it, while in the second it is due to appropriate persuasive action to influence the rate of population growth in advance. In other words, the question is to determine *when* the per capita income level is reached at which this deliberate effort to control family size is made: the more that is done beforehand, the sooner this level will be attained.

It is also often argued that in the Latin American countries, generally speaking, there is enough capacity for a much larger population than they have at present. This is true. But what is also important is the length of time needed to attain a given level and the economic conditions in which this larger population would live. The alternative is clear: either the period of time is shortened and the population increases to a given number of inhabitants, with the result that the problem of the economy's insufficient dynamism is aggravated; or the period is extended, and in the interim higher levels are achieved in terms of per capita well-being.

It must be stressed that all this has to be set in the context of a development strategy. But those who oppose population policy would not be unjustified if it were presented as a substitute for a development strategy, if it were advocated simply as an alternative.

Nor do those who oppose birth control measures for certain other reasons lack grounds for their attitude. If the population explosion is left to run its own course, the crisis in the system will become more and more profound. Thus, if it is believed that the system must be changed—and changed radically and even violently—then opposition to birth control is perfectly logical. The only trouble is that after the system had been changed, population policy would inevitably have to form part of the new order of things, if this too was to be imbued with sufficient dynamic force.


## TECHNOLOGY AND ITS ADAPTATION TO
## LATIN AMERICAN CONDITIONS


The second set of development problems that requires State action no longer has to do with the contradictions attendant upon scientific and technological progress, but relates to the rational use of technology in Latin American development.

A great deal of concern is felt in Latin America about the wholesale transfer of the production techniques developed in the great industrial centers. Awareness of this problem is growing, but it is so complex and so vast that study of it has not progressed as would be advisable in view of its great importance. In this respect, it should be noted that little has been done in the way of proposing solutions that take account of the particular circumstances of the developing countries. Several aspects of the problem warrant more systematic attention than seems to have been given them to date. We shall begin by considering the economic aspects, and then go on to analyze some of the special problems of the transfer of technology.

The effects of using technologies in Latin America that are not compatible with the region's shortage of capital, the relative abundance of labor, and the availability of factors of production in general are only too well-known. There is no automatic way out of this situation, which frequently leads to conflict between the interests of the individual entrepreneur and the interests of the community, as was noted earlier in connection with the mechanization of agriculture. In this typical case—as in many others—the entrepreneur saves labor by investing more capital, without considering whether the economic system has the capacity to absorb the manpower thus made redundant.

If the rate of interest on capital reflected potential demand for the capital needed to absorb this redundant labor, as well as current demand on the financial market, it is possible that certain highly capital-intensive investments would in many cases not be economically viable. But the market reflects actual demand at a given point in time, and not the potential demand that would have to be satisfied if the redundant labor force was to be absorbed. And even if this potential demand were reflected, one difficulty would be solved but another very serious problem would take its place, since a rise in rates of interest would have a regressive effect on income distribution.

In relation to all this, it is not enough to analyze the different technological options that are available; it is also necessary to consider what policy measures and procedures could be applied to encourage the adoption of technologies that would be more suitable from the standpoint of the economy as a whole.

The possibilities for the selection of technological alternatives would seem to be greater in public activities than in the private sector. In cost-benefit analyses relating to public investment, it might be possible to apply either a social or a shadow rate of interest, higher than the market rate, that would reflect to some extent the potential demand for savings. If this were done, more economic alternatives could be chosen. But this is not what happens. On the contrary, because loans are obtained from abroad at rates of interest which—although they may be high in terms of a country's payments capacity—are low if account is taken of the shortage of capital, the choice frequently lights upon alternatives which are excessively capital-intensive. The same applies to the use of budget funds that are interest-free, or of domestic resources obtainable at interest rates that not only do not reflect the potential demand for savings but are also usually lower than the prevailing market rate.

It is not possible, however, to force the private sector to make cost-benefit calculations of this type, favorable to the adoption of less capital-intensive alternatives. Quite the reverse: certain measures designed to stimulate investment have achieved their ends, but to the detriment of employment.

There have been cases where tax concessions have led to investment which has had virtually no direct impact on employment. Overvaluation of the currency, application of preferential exchange rates, or the granting of credit at low interest rates has had similar results.

International loans have usually had roughly the same effect, apart from the question of interest rates. It is natural that firms of consultants in the great industrial centers should favor technical solutions which are familiar to them rather than seek to devise others. How far can Latin American consultants divorce themselves from this attitude, if no well-defined policy exists in this respect?*

It is also understandable that in making their investments the large foreign companies follow the same course, although there have been some happy instances in which techniques have been adapted to Latin American conditions. This question has aroused great interest, as shown in a recent international document.** I do not believe that in this connection persuasion can be entirely effective. It can do a great deal, but in view of the magnitude of the problem it is perhaps not enough. Hence, thought will have to be given to the possibility of resorting to procedures that will foster the selection of options more favorable to development.

So far, this subject has not received the attention it deserves. An idea which has been broached is that of levying a tax on new fixed investment to make it more costly, which would have the same effect as raising the interest rate. The resources thus obtained would be used for additional investment, in order to prevent the total volume of investment from decreasing. It has also been suggested that tax concessions should be granted on the basis of employment of labor instead of on the value of investment. The prevailing method of financing social security systems constitutes in actual fact a tax on the use of labor, which in some countries is as high as 50 percent of wages. These are matters which, despite their importance, have not been studied in depth, at least in Latin America.

Let us now look at some further aspects of the problem of technology. First we must ask ourselves how much freedom of choice there is with respect to the options mentioned above. Given the current state of technology, do options exist which permit production on a smaller scale than in the great industrial centers, with a saving in the input of capital per worker and yet with no undue loss of productivity? In a number of cases, the answer to this question is in the affirmative. In this respect, satisfactory results appear to have been obtained from the technologies used by some of the small and medium-sized industrial countries in the developed world.

Irrespective of the scale of production, there are other factors to be considered that would make it possible to devise certain capital-saving combinations of technologies. It would be interesting to look into experience in this regard, from which useful conclusions might be drawn. In essence, the problem is how to use the available technology to the best advantage, and how to adapt and combine its components to respond more adequately to Latin American conditions. Obviously, this presupposes the possession of a stock of

---

*Recently, the activities of Latin American technical consultants have been stepped up, and this might lead to the adoption of techniques more in keeping with the supply of factors available in the region, given the existence of the well-defined policy referred to in the text.

**See Edwin N. Martin, *Development Assistance: Efforts and Policies of the Members of the Development Assistance Committee* (Paris: OECD, December, 1969).

knowledge on the basis of which our technicians would be able to make up their own minds. In other words, we need to develop the capacity to form independent opinions, instead of relying too much on the judgment of others.

Although the selection and adaptation of techniques is very important, this does not mean that we should not concern ourselves with the creation of technology as well. On the contrary, this is a matter which warrants serious thought. According to expert opinion, there are very interesting possibilities in this connection which have barely begun to be explored, not only as regards the exploitation of natural resources—where it is possible to develop new techniques or improve those already in use—but also in a vast number of areas in which new processes or combinations of existing processes could be invented. This cannot be done unless a scientific and technological structure suited to both functions is established. And, from the economic standpoint, it can be done only if basic criteria are defined for assigning priorities in specific fields. It must not be forgotten that virtually all technological innovations are directed toward highly specific ends. Moreover, for action to be effective, research programs must be undertaken that are in line with the priorities established; and one of the main aims of such programs must be to increase the capacity to create and adapt new techniques.

All this is very closely linked to education. It will be necessary to promote educational programs that, in addition to fostering the dissemination of techniques, have as one of their main purposes the stimulation of the capacity to create them.

Some steps are already being taken in Latin America, mainly in the field of industrial and agricultural technology, but resources are limited and the efforts made are far from concentrated. Such moves must be given full support, as must all the other endeavors to promote more efficient use of natural resources. So far, there does not seem to have been enough coordination between the State, the universities, and private enterprise in this respect.

Furthermore, given the magnitude of the resources required for technological research and the similarity of conditions in many Latin American countries, this is an obvious opportunity for pooling effort. Frankly, it is surprising how little progress has been made in a field which offers so much scope for integration.

As regards agricultural technology, there is conclusive proof of what perseverance can achieve. Cases in point are the astonishing results obtained in Mexico with wheat and corn. It must be asked, however, whether Latin America is doing all it should in this respect, especially as regards agriculture in the tropics.

A similar question might be asked with regard to technical training at all levels. It is inadmissible to take a static view of this question. If the rate of development is to be much higher than in the past, technical training efforts will have to be based on what will be needed over the years to ensure that this objective is achieved. At present, with an overall product that is far from satisfactory, there are serious stumbling blocks: the shortage of research workers or extension service personnel in agriculture, and of intermediate and high-level technicians in industry and other activities. In other words, there is a marked contrast between the ample supply of unskilled labor and the lack of the skilled personnel needed for its efficient utilization.

What is required is systematic action by the State and the organs of the community, guided by perspicacious forethought. Otherwise, it will also be impossible to deal with the adverse effects of technological progress. As noted earlier in this chapter, excessive reliance on the market forces has been the reason why the developed countries have taken so long to recognize the growing seriousness of these effects. Public opinion in the developed parts of the world is now becoming aware of such concepts as ecology and the preservation of the environment. It is to be hoped that the same thing will happen in Latin America.

## STATE ACTION TO SMOOTH OUT SOCIAL AND GEOGRAPHICAL DISPARITIES

### Disparities and the Lack of the Required Degree of Dynamism

After these very general comments on technology, let us pass on to the great disparities apparent in the way in which income is distributed among the various social strata and among geographical areas because of the unevenness with which technical advances are introduced and their benefits distributed, given the prevailing economic and social structure.

It was noted above that in the developed countries the free interplay of economic forces has not led to an equitable distribution of income. The problem of income distribution is complicated in the Latin American countries by the fact that their economies lack the required degree of dynamism. And it is this lack of dynamism that must be combated, in order to ensure that redistribution policy is effective.

The terms of the problem have already been defined. As a result of the relative weakness of the rate of development, a sizable proportion of the increase in the labor force has not found really productive employment, and in addition, the masses in the lower income strata have been unable to move up into higher strata at a satisfactory rate.

The existence of a redundant labor force which it has not been possible to absorb in productive employment tends to depress the real income of the part of the labor force that is productively employed, and consequently to cause steadily mounting social tensions. For these tensions the usual escape valve is inflation, and anti-inflationary policies will always be on a shaky footing so long as nothing is done to to strike at the roots of the economy's lack of dynamism.

The existence of a redundant labor force and the evident incapacity to absorb it hitherto displayed by the economic system, together with the concentration of land ownership, account for the poverty-stricken situation of the rural masses. The gains accruing from technical progress—insofar as this has been achieved—usually end up in other hands. They go to the landowner or the agricultural entrepreneur and are spent in the cities. Some of them also find their way to the cities when they are absorbed by the middleman. And, of course, this applies only to such part as is not transferred abroad through a deterioration in the terms of trade.

The cities, in contrast to the rural areas, have shown that they are capable of retaining the benefits of their own technological progress, even though these gains are distributed very unevenly within the urban areas themselves. Thus, the income accruing from industrialization also tends to remain in the cities, and its effects do not spread out into the countryside. On the contrary, it grows partly at the expense of the rural masses, since the prices of the few manufactures reaching them, which were formerly imported, are higher as a result of protection. Moreover, when protected industries increase their productivity, there is no corresponding drop in prices; the extra income is divided up in varying proportions between urban activities and the State.

To this must be added the fact that the coverage of social security systems is generally confined to urban areas; and that in the few cases where rural areas are covered by labor legislation, the legal regulations are not always properly applied. Rural areas have also profited less than the cities from the social benefits won by popular effort in the fields of health, housing, and education, from which many of the urban marginal population are also excluded.

Lacking in political power and trade union organization, and debarred from access to productive land, the rural masses have not obtained their proper share in the benefits of technical progress, and have barely been able to take advantage of it in their own agricultural activities.

### Concentration in the Cities

Thus, the spontaneous forces of the economy, in combination with institutional factors, have driven more and more people to live in the cities. It is well-known that the process of urban concentration is much more intense in Latin America than it was in the industrialized countries when they were at a similar stage in their development. Income and demand have been concentrated in the big towns, while in rural areas they have been too weak to promote the installation of industries and a better spatial distribution of the labor force.

Had this been otherwise, might the structure of employment have been different too? Would the distortion of which we have spoken with so much concern have been attenuated, if not eliminated? There are no grounds for thinking so, for the distortion, as well we know, is the result of the inadequate rate of development. The redundancy problem would have been the same in the economy as a whole, although perhaps services and local industries might have developed more in rural areas and the volume of redundant labor moving to the cities might have been smaller.

A distinction must be made between the outflow of redundant labor from agriculture and the inflow of redundant labor into the big cities. There is no valid reason to suppose that a substantial proportion of the redundant agricultural labor could not be retained in farming areas, in activities associated with agriculture itself, or in the scattered towns of small or medium size that already exist in such areas or that might be created to meet the needs of a properly devised spatial policy. A policy of this kind would clearly have to aim at improving the rural environment, for which economic and social investment is required on a large scale. Without such investment, the cities would continue to be the dominant center of attraction, even if the income of the rural masses were to increase.

As has been repeatedly stressed, if land were distributed more equitably and were better developed, it would be possible to raise rural incomes, not only because of the direct effects of such changes, but also because they would facilitate the introduction of more advanced agricultural techniques. Experience everywhere shows that special measures are needed to ensure that the benefits of such technical progress are retained in the agricultural sector. It must not be thought—as it sometimes is—that the main reason for increasing agricultural productivity is to lower the prices of agricultural products in the cities. Higher productivity is needed for the social integration of the rural masses. If the rate of economic development were speeded up, there should be no real difficulty in respect of equitable income distribution.

In any case, it is important to see that the interplay of economic forces and of structural and institutional factors does not continue to encourage overconcentration of the population in the cities. The problem is of disquieting dimensions. Suffice it to bear in mind that if redundancy is combated in the way suggested in the present report, the rate of the exodus from agriculture will be higher than at present. The figures given in an earlier chapter tell the story: the nonagricultural labor force, which is to be found mainly in the cities, expanded at an average annual rate of 3.5 percent during the period 1950-1965; but this figure will probably rise to 3.9 percent by the end of the 1970's and during the following decade. Nevertheless, an effort should be made to prevent the process of urban concentration from intensifying.

It would appear that up to a certain point, which is different in each individual case, the advantages of urban agglomeration continue to increase. Once this point has been passed, the disadvantages begin to outweigh the advantages. Hence, for the Latin American countries great importance would attach to a policy deliberately aimed at strengthening urban centers of medium size. It may be that there is also an optimum level for investment in infrastructure—and for all the many other services required in urban development—and that above this level the subsequent growth of cities should be prevented. It is necessary to find out what these levels are and to devise effective means of implementing spatial policy.

There are no forces that emerge spontaneously to counteract urban concentration. On the contrary, the free play of market forces tends to aggravate it. A good example is the case of urban land: as concentration in the cities increases, the value of urban land rises rapidly, and it then becomes economically expedient to tear down existing buildings—with all the loss of capital that this entails—and erect taller ones, in order to take greater advantage of the high value of land.

In this way, urban congestion is increased and traffic problems become virtually insoluble, given the huge amounts of capital needed for development. Just as in the developed countries, in Latin America a truck possibly takes longer to cross from one side to another of a large town than a horse and cart used to take at the beginning of the century. And the income thus generated is, of course, included among the indicators of the welfare of the city dweller.

It is also necessary to take deliberate action to influence the forces that increase urban concentration beyond certain limits. Measures will have to be adopted that may seem antieconomic today, but which actually may not be so, or will cease to be so with the passage of time. Some of the current concepts relating to economic viability need revising with a great deal of forethought.

## STRATEGY AND PLANNING

### The Hard Experience of Planning

All the above forms of State action are superadded to the public sector's regular activities, which themselves are continually on the increase. They are not measures that can be adopted independently of one another, since they are closely interrelated. Hence, they must be linked together within an overall strategy which, besides taking account of their interdependence, will ensure that they are applied simultaneously or in succession, as the case may be.

Strategy must not be confused with planning. A development plan represents a quantification of strategic objectives—insofar as they are quantifiable—and of the means and resources considered necessary to attain them. A strategy without a plan is conceivable, but planning would be impossible without a strategy; although it is true that the plan, with its quantification of the various components of the strategy, is the only means of showing the scale of the effort to be made and the degree of compatibility of all the various forms of action that the State intends to take.

Moreover, unless the strategy or plan includes the formulation of a well-organized series of development policy measures and an outline of the main investment projects to support them, it will simply be an expression of aspirations, and nothing more.

It was desirable to clarify these points before considering what has been termed the planning crisis in Latin America. There can be no doubt that the first flush of enthusiasm for planning has now worn off; but there is something more involved than a critical juncture in the history of a method or a technique, for the obstacles in the way of planning are the same that impede progress in the formulation of development strategy.

It is true that, in certain cases, those responsible for planning—and also those of us who have disseminated the planning concept—did not take care to ensure that a specific and explicit strategy to guide development policy was formulated at the appropriate time. All too often, plans have followed imprecise and general long-term guidelines.

If, when a government comes into power, it sets itself the task of defining the main features of development policy, the planner then has a framework within which he can situate his methods and techniques. Planning, after all, is a tool for ensuring maximum efficiency in the implementation of a development strategy or policy. But if the opposite occurs, and the prevailing trend is to adopt short-term measures relating to immediate problems, experience shows that planning will probably become merely an academic exercise, which has little or nothing to do with the State's practical action.

Formulating a plan takes time, and governments cannot wait. On several occasions, the failure of planning efforts has been ascribed to such delays. But now that virtually all the countries of Latin America have been formulating plans for over a decade, it is surely legitimate to assume that governments can be provided at short notice with at least a statement of the main obstacles to economic development and alternative means of surmounting them.

This would enable the planning offices—if they were assured a minimum of continuity, which is not generally the case—to provide valuable technical advice for the guidance of policy-making. As this seldom happens, the question arises whether, political and institutional considerations apart, there have not also been shortcomings in the planning systems themselves.

Planners often have a certain tendency to prolong the gathering of data and their analysis, and the formulation of projections. They let themselves be carried away by a sort of econometric preciosity that generally distracts attention from the specific conditions on which government action must be based and the urgent needs that such action must satisfy. Meanwhile, a government has to act: it cannot wait too long for a new plan to be drafted and perfected. And by the time the plan is actually forthcoming, a policy is already being implemented that is formulated mainly in response to immediate circumstances, if not to the pressure of certain interest groups.

Even when a plan stands completed, careful thought has not always been given to the measures required to implement it, nor have preinvestment studies been made or the investment projects implicit in the plan itself formulated.

Furthermore, plan formulation and implementation involves more than simply superimposing the planning agency on the structure of the State administration. This structure, and also administrative attitudes, must be changed—admittedly a very difficult task, for it involves problems of a political nature, and more than once it has been sidestepped. As is clear from a perspicacious report by Cibotti and Bardeci, planners have often had to work in isolation, instead of as an integral part of the public administration machinery that formulates and implements policy measures and investment programs.

In this connection, account must also be taken of the disruptions that inflation causes in plan implementation. All the estimates are invalidated, and the measures dictated by immediate circumstances do not coincide with the provisions of the plan. This discourages planning precisely when it is most needed to remedy basic economic and social situations that spur on the inflationary process.

Nevertheless, the planning efforts made are far from having been wasted. Much valuable experience has been gained, and there have been marked improvements in certain of the instruments of planning, notably the national budget. More is known about fiscal and monetary instruments, and they are being handled with greater efficiency. The basic elements for formulating development strategy are now available, together with knowledge of the techniques for translating it into specific plans.

In addition, it must be noted that, generally speaking, the planning process has brought the Latin American countries to a clearer understanding of their own national circumstances. In pointing up the conflicts that characterize the developing societies of Latin America, planning has made a contribution of inestimable value. These conflicts can now be clearly seen, and the situations they give rise to are no longer considered natural phenomena, but social and cultural manifestations that can be corrected by changing the composition of the political forces and making their decisions more rational. The diagnoses prepared, and the overall and sectoral plans that have sprung therefrom, have helped to being these problems to light.

A plan has to be flexible so that it can be continually adapted to suit new needs or unforeseen circumstances; but a minimum number of conditions must be fulfilled. These include, in particular, a reasonable assurance that external financing will be both available and sufficient to meet specific demands imposed by actual fact. International development financing agencies—both bilateral and multilateral—have generally been reluctant to commit the financial resources required in the course of plan implementation to supplement the domestic resources mobilized. To commit them in principle, that is, for if the financing is based on a plan containing projects for execution, it is obvious that fulfillment of the commitment must be subject to the implementation of the essential measures envisaged in the plan.

International financing should also be capable of covering the domestic as well as the imported component of an investment project, if the domestic resources available are insufficient or if there are difficulties in transferring them from one budget appropriation to another. Moreover, it must be flexible enough to be able to supply additional international resources if the amount of domestic resources forthcoming falls short of expectations, owing to an unforeseen drop in exports or a deterioration in the terms of trade, or for other acceptable domestic reasons.

## Resistance to Planning

All these problems add new difficulties to those inherent in the State's necessary intervention in the development process. As noted earlier, the very idea of State intervention still arouses a great deal of resistance in Latin America. Admittedly, it has sometimes been unfortunate and self-defeating; a long and very instructive list could be made of measures that have created problems worse than those they were intended to solve. The most obstinate resistance is to State action in connection with the structural changes that are essential to clear the way for the forces of development. Apparently, State intervention is admissible to preserve the status quo, but not to change it.

There is also resistance of another kind. The need to take deliberate action to influence economic forces is often confused with arbitrary interference in the market mechanism. It is also assumed that planning is inseparable from the extension of the State's direct economic activities. This is a very serious misapprehension, which should be dispelled. Widespread State control of enterprises is not a requirement for planning, which is clearly compatible with private initiative. State control of enterprises has its own raisons d'être, whether they stem from doctrine or from the pressure of actual fact. In some cases, it is prompted by the idea of bringing in socialism by gradual degrees. In others, it derives from an approach that has wide currency in Latin America: the concept of the mixed economy, in which State enterprises coexist with private concerns.

The reasons for State control are well-known. Some have been in evidence for a long time. Cases in point are the public utilities, or enterprises that it is thought should belong to the State so that too much power is not concentrated in private hands. In other instances, the public enterprise is either a temporary expedient to enable the State to take promotional action before eventually transferring ownership to private initiative, or an alternative to the control of certain important activities by foreign private capital. It should be borne in mind that in the basic industries the only alternatives have often been in the past—and still are in the present—State ownership or foreign ownership of the major producer enterprises.

Furthermore, it must be recognized that the State enterprise has frequently proved to be an effective instrument for promoting development, and has also fostered technical training and the formation of management skills. In addition, it has been a means of absorbing men of drive and initiative who did not have access to private enterprise, or who would otherwise have been deprived of opportunities, because of the economy's lack of the required degree of dynamism.

It must be admitted, however, that in Latin America the State enterprise is not generally characterized by efficiency. It frequently runs at a loss, unless it sets the prices of its goods and services at an unduly high level. But this situation must be viewed in the proper perspective. Private enterprise too is usually inefficient. It is inefficient in traditional agriculture, the basis of which is the concentration of land ownership. And it is inefficient in industry as well—with laudable exceptions—because of the umbrella protection of excessively high tariffs. The social cost of all this is probably several times greater than that of the inefficiency of public enterprises.

In many cases, State enterprises have to tailor their tariff rates to the payments capacity of the bulk of the population, in order to make their services accessible. If income distribution is very regressive, it is unlikely that such rates will cover operating costs and the cost of replacing equipment. In such cases, subsidies are fully justified to bolster the current financing of the State enterprise, so that operating at a loss does not lead to the contravention of principles of good management.

Thus, the problem that Latin America has to tackle in this respect is vast and extremely complex. Industry must be kept on its toes by means of competition and at the same time helped through State incentives and promotion policy. In agriculture, agrarian reform and the introduction of more advanced techniques are needed. And the sphere of action of State enterprise must be demarcated either in terms of its significance from the socioeconomic or political standpoint, or in terms of its necessity on the ground of national autonomy.

All this has a bearing on deliberate State action to influence the forces of the economy and of technological progress, as described earlier in the present chapter. The task is inherently formidable, and it should not be unnecessarily complicated by direct economic activities on the part of the State when no considerations of great weight are involved. The State is a better manager when it has control of the mainsprings of the economy and knows how to handle them, than when it fills its hands with a medley of activities that prevent it from operating efficiently.

For the State to be able to fulfill its role in the development process, it too must undergo a metamorphosis, and acquire efficiency. It must change its image in the eyes of society. It is not very likely that the rate of development of the Latin American economies can be stepped up if the State is regarded as the bastion of long-standing privilege or as a necessary evil. Herein lies another of the structural reforms of which we have been speaking.

It is not all up to the economists. For development strategy is in fact inseparable from the political art of development. Economists have an important part to play in the work of elucidation on a purely intellectual plane. This process is already under way in Latin America. The development crisis is not taking Latin America by surprise, as did the world depression of the 1930's. Everyone was unprepared at that time. Now a rigorous and genuinely self-reliant effort is being made to clarify the situation. It is rigorous because more is known about the problems, and improvisation and dialectical virtuosity are giving way to scientific objectivity; and it is genuinely self-reliant because there is a manifest desire to avoid doctrinal dependence and the mere transplantation of theories and formulas that have no relation to Latin America as it actually is.

Nevertheless, the substantial efforts being made are so far confined to a few groups of intellectuals, economists, and sociologists, perhaps because there is still lively controversy, and as yet no well-knit system of ideas has been developed, no systhesis of thought, that could illuminate and guide national strategies. Public opinion has been touched only on the surface, and, with very few exceptions, not enough weight is carried to influence the politicians.

It is a great task that lies ahead of us. The nature of the power structure is a highly important factor; and supreme importance attaches to the guiding principles of those who participate in it, to the conviction that it is possible, with a great effort, to overcome the present crisis and give a major impetus to development without continuing to sacrifice equity in income distribution and without seriously jeopardizing the very sense of national cohesion. Without that, development could never be based on firm and lasting foundations.

**7**

## FERMENT IN LATIN AMERICA


Dissidence and rejection are keynotes of the growing unrest among the youth of Latin America. It would be a mistake to ascribe these attitudes solely to the influence of ideologies, for events do not stem from ideologies as a rule. Ideologies catch on, take root, and thrive where events create a propitious climate and get out of hand in the absence of a farsighted policy to influence their course. In such cases ideologies enhance the significance of the existing facts and acquire great importance in the content of change.

This is how I am inclined to interpret the ferment working in some of Latin America's younger minds. Finding that the economic and social system offers no solutions for the problems which trouble them, they turn from it in vehement repudiation. In all this there is doubtless a sort of world contagion, with which mass communication techniques have a good deal to do. These techniques are a powerful factor in the creation of a certain emotional unity which recognizes no frontiers. And the successes or misfortunes that stir the hearts of men, the promptings of collective sentiment, thus gain a truly worldwide significance.

It would be a grave mistake, however, to see this unrest among the younger generations simply as a reflex of what is happening elsewhere. No contagion would spread, except in a superficial and incidental fashion, if all were going well. But things are going far from well in Latin America. We are faced with a genuine product of our own situation. The most that the tide of foreign-bred emotion can have done is to bring to the surface, with a measure of violence which may indeed be imitative, the undercurrents already latent in the depths of society. However, there is no denying the force of contagion, at least at moments of crisis. It works both ways, not always outward from the center to the periphery. Some of the troubles of the peripheral countries cast their shadow on the developed world as well, disturbing its social conscience and moral sense. Such is the emotional unity which is growing up in the world of today.

In this whole phenomenon men of a certain dynamic type play a prominent part in Latin America. They are the sort of men who, although comparatively few in number, set a characteristic stamp upon their generation.

216

They spring up in all the social strata. They are men of imagination and creative ability, full of drive and tenacity of purpose, capable of accepting risks and shouldering responsibilities. If the economic system is functioning vigorously and the degree of social mobility is high, these dynamic members of society make their way ahead until they have assumed leading responsibilities in all the manifold walks of community life: in politics and trade union movements, in science and literature, in productive activities, in the professions, everywhere. The system absorbs them, and they in turn give it greater momentum.

When the system cannot absorb them because social mobility is cramped by too slow a rate of development, these dynamic personalities find their horizon in life restricted. Attitudes of destructive criticism then supervene, which, although at first involving only a minority, may give decisive impetus to historic processes of change: processes in which the unbridled passions of the initial stages may undermine the rationality and the strictly objective outlook necessary for the inevitable task of construction.

It is essential, however, to beware of supposing the system's inadequate absorption capacity to be the sole reason why feeling is running high among the younger generations. That would mean overlooking the importance that may sometimes attach to other motivations, as the recent experience of developed countries has shown. There is, in reality, something that goes deeper than the sense of personal frustration. What is more, even before the encounter with practical life takes place, the imagination of the adolescent is stung by social inequity, and he begins to impugn the existing state of affairs, the type of society in which he lives, and the basic values inherent in it. And all these attitudes are fomented and strengthened later on by the economy's lack of the required dynamism.

In any event, there is a striking contrast between this mood and the passivity of the rural masses. It is a passivity that from time to time breaks out into sporadic acts of rebellion which are not always commensurate with the magnitude of the problem of social inequity. Seldom have spontaneous movements been led by men from the ranks of the rural population in Latin America. It might almost be true to say that the agricultural revolt in Mexico in the second decade of the present century constitutes an isolated episode. Instead, appeals to the masses have been made by leading groups desirous of obtaining occasional support in the conflict of their interests and aspirations.

But here again significant changes are taking place. Mass communication media are awaking and quickening the social consciousness of the rural sectors. History does not necessarily repeat itself. Conditions today are very different from those of yesterday. What is more, certain changes of attitude can be noted whose significance should not be underrated. Institutions which up to a short time ago had stood solidly behind the established order of things are now giving patent evidence of such a change. The sharp social contrasts and other flagrant evils of the system as it functions at present are arousing serious concern in the Church, which has even embarked upon internal discussion of the use of violence. The armed forces themselves have been unable to refrain from critical analysis of the situation; the vision of those who see in them a bulwark against drastic change is clouded, perhaps, by a false perspective of the present juncture of Latin America's history.

These attitudes of revolt might have salutary effects if they were to provoke an honest and objective restatement of our problems: a new approach, guided by an urge for genuine self-reliance incompatible with the unconditional adoption of what is being done and thought outside the region.

Criticism of the industrial societies, of their technology, and of their codes of values is another characteristic manifestation of the ferment brewing in Latin America. This is all very well if it expresses an aspiration on the region's part to project an image of its own, unadulterated by imitation. But, as has often happened in the intellectual experience of the Latin American countries, the fascination of other people's controversial issues keeps us from a proper understanding of our own, blinds us to what lies around us and prevents us from probing deeply into its significance.

The desire for a genuinely independent approach, which had long been latent, began to crystallize a couple of decades ago in an effort at original interpretation, in a persevering search for solutions consonant with economic fact in Latin America. Those were the days of assertion and debate. New ideas then began to emerge which have not yet been molded into a proper system. For a system of ideas cannot be confined to economic questions, but must also embrace social and political affairs, since all these are different facets of one and the same reality.

The lines of thinking which have been pursued must be critically reviewed, followed up in greater depth, extended to social and political questions with strictly scientific objectivity. In short, what is needed is a system of ideas, which should undergo continual revision to keep it alive and fruitful and avert the risk of its petrifying into hard-and-fast dogma. It is not enough to know what is happening in Latin America. It is also essential to define where we want to get, the type of society we should like to have, the values by which it will be sustained. This is an area of basic importance where we are barely starting to clear the ground.

The critical attitude of the younger generations in Latin America—within its special context of repudiation of the existing state of affairs—often leads them to question whether the transfer of technology from the great industrial centers to the Latin American countries will not foster a tendency to copy the developed countries' living patterns, their attitudes to life, and their basic codes of values.

Is all this inherent in technology? Is there an element of incoercible determinism in economic development, inevitably introduced by the uninterrupted advance of science and technique? It may seem strange that in this study, which expresses deep concern at the present course of Latin American development, such a question should be taken up in the final pages. But it is not out of place. Making the economic system really dynamic is only part of a much vaster enterprise. Undoubtedly, economic goals are of basic importance: a high degree of measurable welfare for the masses is in itself an objective which must be speedily attained. But they are also a means to other supremely important ends which call for definition and which, although they do not emanate from the operation of the economic system, might be utterly defeated by it.

## THE AMBIVALENCE OF TECHNOLOGY

What, then, is the role of technology? Some time ago there was a myth in common currency that man had become the slave of the machine. But it was shorter-lived than other myths of more lasting consequence. In point of fact, the machine had freed the human race from an age-old burden of crushing toil. The Utopian ideal of the liberation of man could also become a reality on the soil of Latin America. As technology advances with giant strides, the production, transport, and sale of goods will take up a progressively decreasing proportion of man's time. And the greater the efficiency of production, the wider will be the margin of free time that can be devoted to other activities outside the sphere of the economy proper.

What other activities? In this simple question lies the key to the future. Technology cannot provide the answer, because it is a two-edged instrument; it can be used for good or for ill. Everything depends upon man himself, upon his ability to direct it toward the good and away from the ill that is already assuming such disquieting proportions. For man, who has succeeded in creating this stupendous technology, has not yet made up his mind to expend the same energy and the same imagination on using it to build a better society.

A good deal of talk is heard nowadays about a computers' world and the inevitable subjection to the computer, as formerly about enslavement to the machine. It is true that the computer cannot think; but it does ensure precision and incredibly extend the range of the rational faculty of man. It is a potent instrument for the collection and combination of data in pragmatic tasks which the human brain could not perform without enormous expenditure of mental energy. And it is also the medium for new adventures of the mind in the realms of science and technique, in which undreamed-of frontiers are constantly being opened up.

But the computer can also be an agent of oppression if, for example, its fantastic memory is used to place indelibly on record all the events in a man's life, all his mistakes and weaknesses, precluding all hope of their effacement, every stimulating possibility of a new chance in life.

Ambivalent, like the computer, are radio and television. The problems which arise therefrom are very grave, and Latin America cannot, of course, escape them. The television set is rapidly invading the home and strongly influencing both today's and tomorrow's image of Latin American society. This is a new phenomenon, whose effects on the meaning of life are unpredictable. A child's parents always used to try to mold its personality in its early formative years; now, willy-nilly, they have to share this responsibility with television, which inevitably tends to override their influence.

It is not only the parents' educational effort that is at stake, however, but also that of the school. Let the State do its best to improve school textbooks! It will largely be wasting its time. For television takes it upon itself to give the child a different vision of life, in which ethical and aesthetic considerations frequently give way to the trivial or the grotesque, and in which all that is finest and most positive in his personality is exposed to contact with cheating and violence.

This applies not only to children but also to people of all ages. The point is to capture the attention of the maximum number of viewers, regardless of the legitimacy of the means to the eminently utilitarian end by which this medium of mass communication is generally guided. The commercial performance of an enterprise, the effectiveness of its publicity, is measured by the number of viewers, no matter what methods are used to attract them. Hence the waste and vitiation of what could be so tremendously potent an instrument of education, culture, and exaltation of the highest human values.

These and other products of technology reflect not only its own ambivalence but also that of the economic development which it brings in its train. Their indifference leaves all doors open. They may serve mankind in its pursuit of excellence or undermine human personality by causing spiritual erosion.

## THE ECONOMIC SYSTEM AND THE TRANSCENDENT VALUES

The material welfare of man, of the broad masses of the population, is no longer out of Latin America's reach. This is the welfare that can be measured. There are other values which defy measurement, which are sensed although they cannot be assessed in quantitative terms. These are the values that relate to fullness of life. Will fullness of life be attained through economic development alone?

In the course of history, it has been accessible only to a very small minority. The cultivation of personality, the exercise of critical ability and creative power, the formation and enjoyment of culture have been the privilege of a very few; just as very few have been able to indulge in a merely frivolous existence. If these things have been possible at all, it has been thanks to the unending drudgery of the many. The opportunities for fullness of life are now broadening out to an extent inconceivable before. And for the first time in history this is happening without recourse to the sacrifice, the exploitation, of other human beings. What is now coming into play is the exploitation of technology, the ability to control the forces it unleashes and to take advantage of the tremendous possibilities it is continually opening up for the human race: the exploitation of technology by man, not the subjection of man to technology.

To prevent such subjection is a matter outside the province of economic decisions. The economy should not be expected to give what it cannot or ought not to offer. Efficiency may be asked of it, because of what that signifies in terms of measurable welfare and because of the increasing margin of free time it leaves for other human activities. But nothing more. Economic activity should not encroach upon those other territories, or carry into them the material incentive which sets it in motion.

Closely linked though they are, the economic incentive as such must not be confused with competition. The domain of the latter stretches far and wide.

Whether it is called competition, emulation, or desire for self-betterment, it is a spur to sustained effort in all the fields of activity in which the human spirit finds expression. Material interests should not be allowed to invade these realms. Motives of a different kind must govern there, if they are not to be debased. Even sport is perverted if the economic incentive is preeminent. All this is of supreme importance, and of course transcends the sphere of the economy proper.

## DIFFERENT FORMS OF CONCENTRATION OF POWER

At the level of the economy, competition will be guided by the economic incentive unless and until a sweeping change is made in motives that are deeply rooted in human nature. There is no other alternative, if the concentration of decision-making power in a few hands is to be avoided. Even socialist systems are increasingly resorting to competition, to the economic incentive, and to the market mechanism in order to promote greater efficiency in production and consumption; and there has been no evidence of any incompatibility with collective ownership of the means of production. It is not a matter of efficacy alone. The significance of these reforms goes farther, for by extending the field of initiative to a large number of people, by distributing among them a responsibility which was formerly centralized, a sense of autonomy is developed that could seriously undermine the concentration of political power. This concentration of power was a doctrinal requirement in its day, imposed for the purposes of radically transforming the system and the power structure linked to it.

In Latin America's circumstances, the concentration of political power might well be generated by events themselves rather than imposed by an ideology. It might be the logical sequel of stubborn opposition to inescapable structural changes. What is more, the long spell of strenuous effort needed to strengthen the dynamic impetus of the economic system might also lead to the concentration of political power. If the Latin American countries were left to shift for themselves entirely during the difficult period of transition to a new phase of development, there would be more likelihood of their having to resort to coercive measures incompatible with the system of party politics.

The broad masses of the people, whom development has conspicuously failed to reach, have likewise been left behind in the political evolution of the Latin American countries. Their social and political integration is an imperative necessity, and for that very reason also greater dynamism must be imparted to the economic system. Can this objective be attained without a lasting setback in the long and vicissitudinous process of Latin America's political development?

Whatever avenues of thought may be adventured along in this exploration of the future—a not very distant future, perhaps, if events are left to run their own course—there can be no overlooking the political significance of certain different forms of concentration of power which, instead of effecting changes, are intended rather to prevent them. Latin America has a long history of experience in this respect.

In any event, it must not be forgotten that the concentration of power, whatever its origin, aims, and degree of intensity, now has at its disposal a formidable instrument which it used not to possess: mass communication media.

These media afford a few people ample opportunities of exerting a strong though sometimes imperceptible influence on the minds of others and even their very attitudes to life. And the significance of this is considerable.

Such is the intricate network of interrelationships between the various components of the existing situation. It would be impossible to speak of changing or completely transforming an economic system without explicitly and clearly expounding these vitally important political premises.

## IN PURSUIT OF GENUINELY INDEPENDENT THINKING

This is no mere matter of a hankering for originality, but an inescapable necessity imposed by facts themselves. It has already been pointed out that the transfer of technology devised in the great industrial centers to countries not yet ready to receive it poses problems which those centers themselves did not have to face, or which at least in their case did not loom so large.

To begin with, in the development process of the industrialized countries new techniques were introduced as capital formation progressed; whereas the Latin American countries have to assimilate a ready-made technique before they have accumulated sufficient capital.

Second, in the industrial centers consumption expanded in line with the growth and diversification of production; in the Latin American countries, on the other hand, consumer aspirations manifest themselves far in advance of the availability of means of production.

Last, in the industrial countries the psychological changes which development brought in its train helped to ensure that the birth rate followed close behind the gradual downward movement of the death rate; whereas in the developing countries—and particularly in Latin America—scientific and technological progress has brought about a marked decrease in the death rate, while the rate of development has been too slow to produce those psychological changes which modify family attitudes to birth rate problems. Thus Latin America's development effort is affected by the exceptionally high rate of increase of the population.

Moreover, structural obstacles would seem to have a different significance. In accordance with one of the basic theses of Marx, in the course of economic development, changes in production techniques made it essential to transform social, political, and institutional structures, as well as attitudes of mind and ideologies.* First came the development of techniques; after that the changes ensued. The developing countries, on the contrary, have to introduce internal structural reforms before the ready-made technology can be fruitfully

---

*What is called "superstructure" in Marxian terminology.

assimilated, and must also bring about the necessary changes in their relations with the industrial centers if they are to reap the full benefits of development.

Thus, Latin American development phenomena cannot be interpreted by unqualified reference to theories which relate to a different set of historical facts. But this is not the only reason for seeking original lines of though whence the region can evolve its own ways of influencing the course of events.

As a matter of fact, the advanced countries themselves are facing grim problems which technology has brought with it, and have not yet found satisfactory formulas for solving them. At such a hurried pace have innovations been introduced, and in so relatively short a space of time, in comparison with the tempo of the nineteenth century. The monstrous overcrowding in the big towns, together with the pollution of the atmosphere, as serious as that of seas and rivers; the disquieting tensions in social relationships; the adverse effects of technique on human personality itself: all these are harassing problems which are also arising—sometimes in an acute form—in the Latin American countries. They and others are preceding economic development and complicating it to an extent which would have been inconceivable at the time when the industrial centers were developing.

Further complications are introduced by the close interrelationships between these problems and political phenomena, which, together with popular participation, evolved gradually in the developed countries with the passage of time. But the formulas worked out there are not always adaptable to the economic and social situation of the Latin American countries or to their development requirements.

The quest for a path of our own thus becomes a necessity. It is essential to get rid of certain manifestations of intellectual dependence. The lessons of other regions' experience, the ideas that have been and still are being worked out elsewhere, can on no account be dispensed with. Genuine independence and originality do not signify fatuous self-sufficiency. But outside thinking must be analyzed in an alertly critical and selective spirit which, avoiding slick imitation, will make it possible to extract from world experience whatever is positive and usable in its content.

Thus, through observation of what is going on at home and abroad, a system of ideas can ultimately be built up which will cover all the various aspects of the Latin American scene and enable rational influence to be brought to bear on the course of events. Now more than ever will the creative ability of Latin American minds be put to the test, together with their capacity to express it in terms of lastingly effective action.

## THE COMMON INTERESTS OF THE LATIN AMERICAN COUNTRIES

If action is to be lasting in its effects, it should be guided by a clear awareness of the common interests of the Latin American countries: common interests which naturally call up a vision of their future unity. This long-term vision should not be allowed to distract effort from what is within reach today and cannot be set aside until tomorrow. The concept of unity has always been one which politically robust minds have entertained with profound conviction.

But it has also often been invoked at random, as occasion has decreed. A hundred and fifty years of high-flown sentimental eloquence, of painful divorce between stirring rhetoric and stubborn fact!

The Latin American countries have not been capable of cooperating systematically with one another. They are learning to do so now; they are increasingly realizing the need for such cooperation, not only in order to take a well-thought-out stand vis-à-vis the developed world, which is still far from grasping the true significance of what is happening here, but also in order to embark resolutely on certain forms of concerted action within Latin America itself, stemming primarily from the development of each country's own initiative and creative forces.

This is not merely a question of economics. It concerns all the various activities of mankind which need more space than any—however promising—that a single country can offer. To create a large economic space is of course an essential objective of intra-Latin American cooperation, but it is not the sole condition required for dynamic development. The economy is not the only field in which the lack of space restricts the expansion of vital forces.

Latin America's creative ability cannot be fully exercised within the microcosm of national life. Plenty of space is also needed for scientific activity, if the region is to make up its technological deficiency and turn to good account talents which are being wasted today. If privileged minds exist which cannot be confined within narrow bounds, let them be offered the whole length and breadth of the Latin American terrain.

The cultural space is likewise much broken up, despite common roots that strike very deep. There is not enough intercommunication. The spirit of every man of letters, of every artist of worth, can project itself more effectively at the Latin American level, and can gain in vigor and fertility by the reciprocal stimulus of contact with other creative talent. And this, over and above its intrinsic significance, could give culture-building in Latin America the cohesion and sturdiness that are indispensable if it is to withstand the inroads of certain exogenous elements which are gaining ground not so much by virtue of the cultural values they represent as by the technical and financial resources at their disposal. It is not a case of superiority in creative power, but of superiority in the power of diffusion. Yet another consequence of scientific and technological progress which must be tackled with clearly defined objectives in view.

The communications satellite is another two-edged instrument. It can be a means of assimilating what is of real worth, as well as of transmitting our own contribution abroad, if we are properly linked up; or it can serve to subordinate Latin American values to others that are highly debatable or definitely prejudicial to the formation of a genuine culture of our own, if in this field—as in that of the economy—each country continues to enjoy the privacy of withdrawal into its shell, to harbor this odd complex of reluctance to cooperate openly.

Latin American cooperation at the level of international affairs is also supremely important. Without it some of the manifestations of dependence cannot be converted into genuine long-term relationships based on mutual interest. Singly, the Latin American countries lose political weight and power of persuasion. Hence the significance of the Special Committee on Latin American Coordination (SCLAC). It must go farther than a felicitous document whose effects are already discernible: farther in time and in space. The time factor calls for firmness and constancy of purpose; while the common interests of the Latin American countries—and they will all have to come together again some day—counsel extending the struggle to other regions of the world.

Clearly defined objectives must be established in the context of an international policy for the stimulation of Latin American development. If the word "policy" is taken to mean a carefully concerted set of measures, such a cooperation policy has never existed. Measures, yes, but inadequate, unconnected, and intermittent, without plan or coordination. International cooperation is a very different matter.

## INTERNATIONAL COOPERATION POLICY

Let us be absolutely frank. The developed countries, and the United States in particular, must decide whether they have or have not a basic and lasting interest in Latin America; whether the course of its economic development and of its political evolution is or is not a matter of indifference to them. If a positive conclusion is reached as a result of this self-examination, the inevitable corollary is a systematic long-term effort, in which the scale of the means is in reasonable proportion to the magnitude of the ends pursued. This is what has been wanting. Just as immediatism has prevailed in Latin America, so in the attitude of the great industrial countries the interests of the moment have overridden far-reaching considerations.

The problem must be viewed in the right perspective. The developed countries neither have been nor are omnipotent or omniscient. In the hard school of experience they have gradually learned to take deliberate action to influence the forces of their economy and their social life. Rationality and foresight were not innate gifts. They had to be painstakingly acquired. The United States' astounding development in the past seemed to testify to the efficacy of the free and spontaneous interplay of economic forces, guided only by the "invisible hand" of the classical economists.

The world depression of the 1930's, however, forced the industrial countries to tackle these forces and try to modify their course, until by now they have acquired remarkable skill in this art. Remarkable at the internal level, but not yet at the level of the world economy. What is more, it is now being discovered that even internally, despite the existing affluence, huge sectors of the population are still underprivileged; and deliberate measures to remedy this situation are no longer adopted with reluctance. It is also understood nowadays that, as already pointed out, the overcrowding in the large towns, the disruptions of every sort which it involves, and the pollution and deterioration of the physical environment cannot be dealt with by means of the price mechanism, however effective this may be within the strict domain of ordinary economics. And at the international level the lack of rationality and foresight has been patent. Unequivocal warnings of very dangerous defects in the international monetary machinery were bootless. It required a crisis which might have assumed grave proportions for the first steps—or rather strides—to be taken in the organization of a true international monetary system.

It is not surprising, therefore, that in practice new cooperation patterns have not crystallized to take the place of relationships of an outworn type which the growing sense of autonomy renders unacceptable to the Latin American countries. Immediatism and opposition on the part of certain interests are not a sufficient explanation. Here too there is a lack of rationality and foresight. It is not that breadth of vision has been wanting in relations with Latin America; but this breadth of vision on the part of the few has been frustrated by the incomprehension and the skepticism of the many. Nor has it been able to prevail over the negative approach that usually characterizes developed bureaucracy. In the Latin American countries, bureaucracy has been prevented by its very inefficiency from attaining as yet that internal cohesion which would protect it—as it is protected in the developed countries—against the onslaughts of imagination and of bold new ideas. Thus it is difficult for us to understand the immensity of the obstacle to change represented by certain die-hard attitudes in the advanced countries.

The only way to bring about a change in these attitudes is by concerted action on the part of the Latin American countries and the persevering exercise of their powers of persuasion: persuasion aimed at forestalling the defeat of farsightedness by immediatism. Nothing sound will be achieved unless momentary and transient considerations are dismissed in favor of the search for a common ground of interest, not only for today, but above all for tomorrow, a tomorrow which stretches on into the distant future. We must probe into it forthwith by the light of new ideas.

## THE ESSENTIAL WORK OF PERSUASION

New ideas are making headway. Disappointment was felt in the Third World when Latin America and the other developing regions secured the adoption of no more than a minimal proportion of the cooperation measures which had been evolved in UNCTAD. Today, only a short time later—as already mentioned in the introduction to this study—leading figures in the northern hemisphere are taking up, improving upon, and endorsing all the most important proposals, without exception.

Other examples of persuasive action could be cited. The main ideas expressed in the Charter of Punta del Este were first mooted in Latin America, and encountered tremendous opposition. The persuasive influence of argument and events gradually dispelled this opposition in the intellectual field. But a serious political error was committed: the Charter was initially presented as a United States master plan for Latin America. Later on, basic ideas which to a large extent still hold good were vitiated, or have been only faintly reflected in the sphere of policy decisions.

This poses a grave question for those who, inside and outside Latin America, are watching the trend of events with deep concern. I share this concern, but not to the extent of letting myself be overwhelmed by apocalyptic forebodings. Latin America has plenty of *élan vital* which, in one way or another, will end by overleaping the obstacles in the way of its development. Changes in the system will not be preventable by force. The recommendation that the armed institutions of the Latin American countries—the army and the police force—should be endowed with the technical resources they need is understandable enough. Insurrection might be momentarily checked if the continuance of the present course of events were to provoke such reactions. But changes and the problems that ensue cannot be avoided. Besides, who can say how force would be used? Perhaps it might be employed as the instrument of change. And equally unpredictable are the direction the changes will take and the guiding principles that will dictate them. What can be foreseen is their social and political cost.

Huge, too, will be the political and social cost of changes which, if they are not introduced with rationality and foresight, may perhaps come without them. Should that happen, rationality would likewise be needed for the task of rebuilding.

Herein lies the deep political significance of international cooperation during the difficult period of transition to a new phase of development. If it is governed by long-term considerations, based on an enlightened conception of essential interests, it will help to ensure that the cost of the transition can be borne without causing a setback in the process of political evolution or enforcing a retreat in the arduous and often-halted advance toward consolidating the basic human rights already enjoyed by some, and extending them to the vast masses for whom they have as yet no real meaning.

Latin America needs to persuade others. But it also needs to persuade itself. It has not much time left to find its own path, obscured as this is by the persistent interplay of interests and by ideological confusion. The problem is not one of discovering a lucky formula and waiting for everything else to follow of its own accord. It is not a formula that is really needed. It is a process, guided by great steadfastness of purpose. The path must be found, and pursued intrepidly but not unthinkingly, with the strength of feeling that incites to bold feats, and with the rationality and foresight in default of which it would be impossible to convert the unrealism of today into the reality of tomorrow.

PART V SUMMARY AND CONCLUSIONS

# CHAPTER 8   CONCLUSIONS FOR ACTION

## INTRODUCTION

The aim of this report has been to consider the great task of change and development which Latin America must face in order to give its economy the additional dynamism it needs and to promote social equity. The emphasis has been placed on how much there is to do. But this does not mean that what is being done in our countries is disregarded. In some of them, important changes are being brought about in the land tenure system, and in more than one instance concern for income redistribution is very marked. Notable efforts are also under way in the field of export expansion. And it has been demonstrated that relatively high rates of development can be reached and maintained, although they are still below the level at which the redundant labor force could be satisfactorily absorbed. In other words, during the 1960's manifest headway was made in many fields, and the economic and social scene in Latin America has undergone significant modification. But the economies of the region have not yet succeeded in making good their lack of the required degree of dynamism.

This is the great problem. It is better understood nowadays. A backward glance reveals how the region is gradually becoming fully aware of its significance, and of the serious consequences—to a large extent already apparent—that must ensue if a laissez-aller policy is adopted. Moreover, the ability to influence the course of events is much greater now than it used to be. Latin America is already technically qualified, in the main, to seek new paths and devise more efficient economic combinations adapted to each country's real circumstances.

However, a paradoxical situation seems to have arisen; despite the existence of this deeper awareness, it does not yet seem to have permeated the political art of development as it should. Decisive progress must be made in this respect. To achieve it is no easy matter, nor a mere academic exercise. For all this in fact implies a great collective undertaking which calls for the intensive mobilization of the Latin American communities.

This regional awareness has also failed to spread to the international field. It is true that increasingly frank recognition is accorded to the limitations of the cooperation effort made so far, to the fact that its role must necessarily be complementary to national development policy, and to the need for revising

231

the terms on which it is extended. But the major political decisions convergent with national measures have not yet been adopted. Accordingly, there should be no further delay in drawing up the basic outlines of a development and international cooperation strategy.

The purpose of the present report is to collaborate in these tasks, which can be put off no longer. The main conclusions which might serve as guides to practical action are presented below.

## THE LACK OF THE REQUIRED DEGREE OF DYNAMISM IN THE LATIN AMERICAN ECONOMY, AND ITS SOCIAL AND POLITICAL EFFECTS

There are considerable expansionist forces in the Latin American economy, but they are held in check by an unfavorable constellation of internal and external factors. The way must be cleared for them so that the rate of development can be raised, with a view to progressively imbuing the economy with the additional dynamism required.

The most serious symptom of insufficient dynamism is the steady growth of the redundant labor force. There is a great deal of redundant manpower in the rural areas; and the population migrating from the countryside to the town largely takes its own redundancy with it, for as it cannot be productively absorbed in the industry group (industry, construction, and mining), it either finds its way into all sorts of urban services where income is very low and where it is not really needed beyond a certain point, or else goes to swell the ranks of the unemployed. This involves an enormous waste of human potential, even in relation to the prevailing production techniques. The indispensable improvement in these techniques will increase productivity per worker, thus aggravating the redundancy problem, unless the rate of development of the whole economy is energetically speeded up. Absorption of redundant manpower, technical progress, and acceleration of the rate of development are thus inseparable objectives.

The inability of the economic system—as it operates at present—to absorb the redundant labor force at a satisfactory level of productivity is one of the reasons why the increase in income in Latin America has benefited the lower income strata only in a minimal degree. Instead of growing narrower, the gap between these strata and the middle and, above all, the upper income groups has been gradually widening. This is a very grave matter, for these lower strata would seem to constitute some 60 percent of the Latin American population, while their share in consumption is only 22.5 percent. On the other hand, the urban intermediate strata have expanded and have raised their level of living, although it still falls far short of their growing aspirations for higher standards of welfare.

Owing to the spurious rather than genuine absorption of manpower, employment in goods-producing activities has been increasing less than it should. A serious deficit is thus created, since not enough goods are produced to meet consumer requirements.

Such is the background of the social tension in the cities and the ceaseless battle for the distribution of what will not go round. Despite the hardships of their living conditions, the rural masses take only a sporadic part in this struggle for redistribution. But there are manifest signs of a change in attitudes, as a result of which the tensions are spreading to all social strata.

With some differences from one country to another, the social integration of the underprivileged masses is a fundamental problem throughout Latin America. Not only is it an urgent social and political need; it is also an imperative economic necessity. For a progressive rise in their purchasing power will extend industrial development possibilities by broadening the domestic market.

This potential market is immense, both for industry and for agriculture. If the income levels of the lower strata are rapidly improved by virtue of the progressive absorption of the redundant labor force and an increase in its productivity, there will be a noteworthy expansion of domestic demand, whose inadequacy, besides being one of the principal causes of the slow growth of agricultural production, hampers the progress of industrial development, as the impetus resulting from import substitution slackens.

## STRUCTURAL CHANGES AND THE RATE OF DEVELOPMENT FOR THE CURRENT DECADE

The dynamics of agricultural and industrial production and—in a broader sense—of development itself also call for changes in the economic and social structure. The defects of the land tenure and land use systems are all too well known. Those of an industrialization process which, with very few exceptions, is broken up into isolated microcosms with a high degree of protection are also becoming increasingly patent.

The structure of industry must be changed, concomitantly with that of foreign trade. These changes are indispensable if the way is to be cleared for technical progress, equitable income distribution furthered, and social mobility promoted.

Better land use and technical progress will tend to aggravate the problem of redundant manpower in the rural areas and intensify the need to transfer labor from agriculture to other activities. This is a universal phenomenon from which Latin America is not and cannot be exempt. The trouble is that here the exodus from the countryside is accompanied by overconcentration of the population in a few large towns, with the resultant grave problems.

In consequence of the economy's inability to absorb this manpower in productive urban activities, the disquieting problem of urban marginality—in which the redundancy of labor finds striking expression—is becoming yet more acute. In Latin America as a whole, the proportion of the nonagricultural labor force employed in the industry group has declined over the last two decades instead of rising. In 1950 it was 35 percent, and today it is estimated at about 30 percent. This implies a serious loss of ground which can be recovered only if the rate of development is speeded up. In two countries only the aforesaid proportion reaches 40 percent. This should constitute a reasonable goal for the development process in Latin America. There can be no solution for the problem of insufficient dynamism unless exceptional impetus is given to the industrial development of the Latin American countries.

The attainment of this objective will entail the expenditure of steady and vigorous effort during the coming decade. It is estimated that in Latin America as a whole, with due regard to the well-known intercountry differences, an overall rate of development of 8 percent would have to be reached within the space of 10 years and kept up during the following decade, in the first place to prevent the distortion in the occupational structure of the labor force from becoming more serious, and then to correct it by gradual degrees.

During the past two decades the average annual rate of development was 5.2 percent. To form a clearer idea of the exertion involved in reaching a rate of 8 percent, it should be noted that this virtually implies raising the growth rate of the per capita product from 2.3 percent in 1950-1965 to 3.6 percent in the 1970's and to 5 percent in the 1980's. This would mean increasing the per capita product in Latin America as a whole from about $400 (at 1960 prices) to $900 in the course of the next 20 years.

The sole purpose of presenting this quantitative development target is to indicate the dimensions of the problem, the requirements it entails, and the results that might be achieved. There is no question of formulating an overall strategy for Latin America as a whole. Development strategies and programs must be the business of each individual country, and drawn up in line with its structure, its stage of development, and the special character of its problems. The target serves, however, to give some idea of the internal effort required and at the same time to permit of a first rough estimate of international cooperation requirements.

## THE CONVERGENCE OF THE INTERNAL EFFORT AND SUPPLEMENTARY INTERNATIONAL COOPERATION

Such a rate of development necessitates a considerable capital formation effort. The investment coefficient, which is 18.3 percent, should rise to approximately 26.5 percent by the end of the 1970's and be kept at that level during the 1980's.

Domestic saving must be the mainstay of this investment effort. International financial resources cannot take its place, but should help to encourage it, especially in the initial stages. Latin America's aim should be to raise its level of domestic saving high enough for external resources not to be indefinitely required.

In the past two decades external funds have failed to play this promotional role, both because of grave shortcomings in international financial cooperation and because of the weakness of the internal development measures taken by the Latin American countries.

The amount of financial resources transferred has been inadequate and the burden of the corresponding service payments excessive. In the case of public funds, it is estimated that annual amortization and interest payments have now come to represent about 19 percent of the debt outstanding. In recent years, these heavy service payments have exceeded the gross inflow of funds from abroad. In combination with the deterioration of the terms of trade, they have had a highly prejudicial effect on the mobilization of domestic resources and on investment. If Latin America's rate of development is to be speeded up, this situation must be substantially altered.

Convergent international and internal measures are needed to modify the trend of events in this respect. The United Nations has recommended that the industrial countries should contribute the equivalent of 1 percent of their gross product to financial resources for transfer to the developing countries, a proportion which in the case of public funds would amount to 0.7 percent. The Pearson Report firmly supports the latter recommendation and proposes that this percentage should be gradually approached, and attained by 1975. If with the inclusion of the contribution made by private capital the target of 1 percent were reached, and Latin America maintained at least the minimum share in resources of this type that has fallen to it in the past, the financial resources required to support domestic capital formation would be secured, provided that the burden of service payments was lightened and no sharp deterioration in the terms of trade supervened.

In order to attain this objective, it would be desirable for the developed countries to engage to earmark for such financial transfers a steadily increasing proportion of the additional monetary resources they obtain from the International Monetary Fund (Special Drawing Rights).

Another indispensable requisite is that this cooperation should be permanent and should be reflected in commitments to finance development plans. Permanent, and also flexible enough to be adapted both to development requirements and to any contingencies which may arise in the development process.

On the other hand, a great responsibility is implied for Latin America: that of progressively improving its savings capacity until it attains self-sufficiency and no longer needs special cooperation measures. And this also involves making an almost unprecedented effort to generate exports which will enable the region to cope with external debt servicing, as well as with its increasing import requirements, without the creation of major tensions.

In all this the collaboration of the international financing institutions, in particular IDB, is of basic importance. And it is to be hoped that the developed countries will support their efforts to tap resources in the international capital markets, by abolishing the restrictions which still persist.

All this will help to pave the way for a stage at which the Latin American countries—some earlier and others later—will be able to gain free and direct access to the capital markets in question in order to obtain the financial resources they need.

It is increasingly recognized that this international cooperation policy cannot and should not be based on considerations dictated by particular political or trade circumstances, but on a long-term view of the relations between the countries of Latin America and the developed countries—especially the United States—which seeks to discover a common ground of interests in relation to fundamental economic and political issues.

It is of primary importance that this external financial cooperation should be accompanied by steadfast action on the part of the Latin American countries to raise the domestic savings coefficient. Otherwise it would be virtually impossible to accelerate their rate of development. The consumption or the consumption increment of the strata possessing real savings capacity would have to be restricted, especially as the rate of income growth increased.

Despite this savings effort, by the end of the decade the average consumption of the population would have expanded much more rapidly than in the 1950's and 1960's, especially in the lower income strata.

In order to raise the level of domestic saving a firm development discipline is an inescapable necessity during the difficult period of transition to an 8 percent growth rate of the product. In this phase, not only the structural changes which will release the expansionist forces of the economy are needed, but also special measures to provide the resources indispensable for their operation, or, in other words, to foster investment and discourage the expansion of consumption beyond certain limits.

## THE ROLE OF FOREIGN TRADE: A NEW TEMPO, AND STRUCTURAL CHANGES IN ITS COMPOSITION

During the transition period foreign trade will have to fulfill a highly important function: that of preventing the external bottleneck from frustrating internal development efforts. Imports in this period will tend to increase faster than the product. This will be impossible without a substantial expansion of exports and other external resources. It would be unwise to assume that current exports, a large proportion of which consists of primary commodities, will increase much more rapidly in the 1970's than in the 1960's.

Consequently, powerful impetus will have to be given to new export lines comprising both primary commodities and manufactured goods. But however successful export promotion measures may prove, it will be indispensable to step up the import substitution process with exceptional vigor, mainly in respect of intermediate and capital goods, for which demand will expand at a very rapid rate. Generally speaking, these are goods whose manufacture entails a complex technology and heavy investment and calls for specialization and broad markets. Thus, if import substitution in respect of such goods is to be an economically sound proposition, it should be effected in the framework of the regional market or of subregional markets linked to it.

Accordingly, integration agreements are a sine qua non for the industries producing intermediate and capital goods. Unfortunately, up to now no really significant agreement of this type has been concluded.

It is a very encouraging fact that the Andean agreement makes provision for this type of integration. The countries forming the Andean Group constitute a sizable economic space, comparable to that of the Latin American countries with the largest markets. This will enable them to make rational progress in substituting domestic production for major import lines. But for other items it will be essential to pursue the import substitution process in the much broader setting of LAFTA. It is clearly realized that this linking up of the subregional markets with that of the region as a whole is of great importance as a precaution against slipping into new forms of fragmentation of the Latin American economy.

It is likewise necessary that links should be forged between Latin America as a whole and the Central American Common Market, whose success might be somewhat undermined by recent regrettable events.

All this brings us to the problem of the countries which, because of the size of their markets or owing to special circumstances, are not reaping the full benefit of reciprocal trade. It is essential that the more highly industrialized Latin American countries should resolutely assume responsibility for cooperating in the development and the industrialization process of the rest. There are reasons of definite economic expediency for doing so, as well as supremely important motives of political and social solidarity.

The import-substitution effort on these new bases, and the promotion of exports, especially of manufactured goods, are matters of primary importance. If the Latin American governments reach agreement on a policy with these ends in view, great significance will attach to the coordinated action of international credit institutions with respect to the financing of multinational Latin American enterprises.

The Inter-American Development Bank, which is called upon to play an essential role in this field, is in a privileged position to support integration agreements, concurrently with other credit agencies, in particular the International Bank for Reconstruction and Development (IBRD). This latter in its turn could play a very important part in the financing of projects designed to increase exports to the rest of the world. Consideration of the IDB proposals under study, in respect of contributing to the more intensive promotion of Latin America's exports, should be given priority by the countries of the region.

## EXTERNAL COOPERATION IN THE FIELD
## OF TRADE

In Latin America, imports tend to expand rapidly as development proceeds, while the growth of exports is relatively slow. Hence the persistence of the tendency toward an external bottleneck. The developed countries have not cooperated effectively with the developing countries in counteracting this process. On the contrary, in many instances they have helped to intensify it by restrictive measures.

What is more, the Latin American countries have been lent less than they needed; very heavy amortization and interest payments have been required of them, in addition to the remittances of profits on foreign private capital; and the major industrial centers have not adopted export promotion measures of any significance under which these payments could have been made without involving the serious problems that have hampered the development of the Latin American countries.

Hence the inescapable need for a trade policy which will facilitate the expansion of the developing countries' exports. In this connection it is encouraging that the Pearson Report has endorsed the principal UNCTAD recommendations. The Rockefeller Report, in its turn, has also placed emphasis on trade policy requirements, although not on financial questions.

Thus, financial cooperation must be combined with an enlightened trade policy. "Trade or Aid" is a false disjunctive, at any rate during the transition period. Both trade and financial resources are needed. Financing will be required until domestic saving has reached the necessary level. Trade, on the other hand, is a permanent factor in autonomous development.

The autonomy of development must be founded on multilateralism, not only in financial matters but also in trade. The Latin American countries should diversify the composition of their exports, and their markets as well, at a multilateral level.

They might find the autonomy of their development and their ability to make their own major decisions seriously prejudiced if their foreign trade depended increasingly upon a single large market. Hence the long-term political significance of a system of general and nondiscriminatory preferences to encourage the developing countries' industrial exports.

The European Economic Community (EEC) carries a responsibility of considerable historical importance in all this, since the continuance and extension of the discriminatory preferences which it grants foment the idea of breaking up the world into areas of influence and, in the light of this principle, establishing a system of hemispheric preferences between Latin America and the United States.

Nor will it do to blind ourselves to Latin America's own share of the responsibility. For that reason the concerted action of the Latin American countries begun by the Special Committee on Latin American Coordination (SCLAC) with the Consensus of Viña del Mar is of great importance: not only as regards the United States, but also with respect to EEC and the rest of the developing countries, including the socialist countries, as was wisely decided.

Nevertheless, Latin American action is somewhat one-sided. The developed countries are urged to adopt measures which will help to enlarge the market for the region's exports; but the Latin American countries are not displaying the same zeal in opening up their own markets to one another.

Not only are indispensable industrial integration agreements deferred, but there is open reluctance to undertake the automatic or programmed reduction of tariffs in order to bring them down smoothly and gradually to a moderate level which will promote trade and competition in Latin American industry. This is an essential step toward increasing productivity, serving the consumer's needs more efficiently and on a more economic basis, and promoting exports of manufactured goods.

It is a grave mistake to contend that internal integration must come first, and then the regional or subregional integration of the dynamic industries and the adoption of other measures which will lead little by little to the establishment of a common market. For internal social integration and the opening up of wider possibilities for industry call for the acceleration of development, and its tempo cannot be quickened unless the integration of basic industries is embarked upon, in the context of intra-Latin American trade, and great impetus is given to exports to the rest of the world.

## THE ROLE OF DOMESTIC AND
## FOREIGN PRIVATE ENTERPRISE

The guiding principle in these operations should be the strengthening of Latin American enterprise, which today is at an obvious disadvantage both technically and financially. New formulas must be devised to enable it to combine with foreign enterprise in such a way that this disparity can be remedied and its indefinite perpetuation prevented.

The Inter-American Committee on the Alliance for Progress (ICAP) has undertaken studies of major importance on this subject, which should be carefully considered in order to arrive at formulas acceptable to all the interested parties.

According to one of these formulas, when foreign private enterprise—in cases where its admittance is considered to be desirable—is reluctant to associate itself with Latin American enterprise in the initial stages, a procedure should be established for it to do so after an agreed period of time. Once this period was over, the control of the enterprise would pass into Latin American hands.

To this end, great importance would attach to the approval of the project for the establishment of a subsidiary or affiliated branch of IDB empowered to promote and support Latin American initiative, both in national and in multinational enterprises.

Basic national development and balance-of-payments considerations make it advisable that the areas of activity in which the Latin American countries want foreign private enterprise to operate should be clearly demarcated. A selective policy is a necessity. Foreign enterprise should be regarded as desirable not in those fields where production techniques are already familiar to Latin Americans, but in those where they are not accessible for the time being or where foreign experience might be of great value, as, for instance, in the development of exports to the rest of the world.

In any event, foreign investment policy should be compatible with the basic principle of national autonomy in decisions that are important to a given country.

Another indispensable requisite to buttress Latin American enterprise is a strenuous effort in the direction of the adaptation and creation of technology, without which Latin America will not be able to take maximum advantage of its own resources, or make up its technical deficiency in the vast process of transfer of world technology.

With the clearsightedness called for in this connection, IDB and the United Nations Development Program (UNDP) would have to mobilize far more resources than are at present available for the purpose, so that our countries may be enabled to make bold use of their creative imagination and to join in the great march of contemporary science and technology.

## STRENGTHENING OF MULTILATERALISM

Multilateralism is consonant with the requirements of national autonomy. An idea is gaining ground that has long been battled for: namely, that international financial cooperation should be increasingly channeled through multilateral conduits. The Peterson Report likewise recommends that bilateral cooperation should be effected within a multilateral framework. Since it has roots in Latin America, IDB plays, and unquestionably must continue to play, an exceptionally important part in this multilateral action. And the same is true of the Inter-American Committee on the Alliance for Progress (ICAP).

Any world mechanism to guide a strategy for international cooperation with the developing countries is inconceivable without the active participation of these and other regional institutions pertaining to the inter-American system and to the United Nations, so that they can contribute what they have learned from experience and wield effective influence at the international level, where coordinated action on the part of the developing countries is an increasingly indispensable necessity.

Multilateralism acquires special significance in connection with the financing of the Latin American countries' development plans, for the implementation of which firm international financing commitments are essential. Naturally, this involves analysis of the plan and of the progress of plan implementation by the international financing institutions.

In the light of the experience of recent years it seems advisable that this analysis too should be multilateral. The suggestion put forward is that it should be undertaken by groups composed of experts from the financing institutions together with independent experts belonging neither to them nor to the governments concerned.

To obviate the duplication of this work of analysis, which has been hampering negotiations, it would be essential for the experts from the credit institutions to make final pronouncements at the technical level on behalf of the institutions to which they pertain, although this would not imply any intervention on their part in decisions as to financing, which would be the exclusive prerogative of the governing bodies concerned.

These groups responsible for evaluating plans and plan implementation should operate independently under the aegis of ICAP, to which they should present their recommendations so that it can pronounce an opinion on sound bases. This would help to strengthen the influence that its verdict might exert on the decisions adopted by the multinational and bilateral financing institutions.

It is of great importance to perfect mechanisms—both international and national—whereby the aims of multilateralism can be more effectively achieved. But multilateralism will not acquire its full significance unless the amount of financial resources transferred to Latin America is increased and, above all, unless steps are taken to lighten the burden of service payments, which have been absorbing an increasingly large proportion of export earnings and of the foreign exchange saved by means of import substitution.

## DEVELOPMENT OF DISCIPLINE

The acceleration of development is no light undertaking. None of the tasks of primary importance in the period of transition to a higher rate of development can be described as easy. A true development discipline is needed in competition, in reciprocal trade, in the promotion of exports, in capital formation, and in determined State action to further the changes required. In other words, a discipline for drawing up and implementing a development plan as the expression of a national strategy. Considerable obstacles are still placed in the way of a planning process based on a real strategy for change and development. Strategy and planning are not incompatible with the market mechanism, which cannot be effective if it is founded on structural bases that are inimical to the expanding operation of the economy's dynamic forces. The State must take conscious and deliberate action to influence these forces in order to accelerate development and make it socially meaningful.

This calls for a farsighted outlook which at the same time should not disregard immediate problems. It is equally wrong to be exclusively concerned with immediate needs and to ignore them. Short-term solutions must be the starting point for longer-term action. This is of decisive importance in the political art of development. It will take time to make up the economy's lack of the required degree of dynamism. But social tensions cannot wait. It is essential to begin the transition period with a carefully thought out expansionist policy which, while looking after the most pressing needs of the lower income strata, will at the same time enable the economy's idle capacity to be fully utilized, with the resulting impetus to the growth of the product. In this way consumption and saving can both increase simultaneously.

In such an expansionist policy a major role is incumbent upon investment in economic and social infrastructure. But international financial resources will be needed to supplement domestic efforts, especially as long as export earnings are insufficient to satisfy the increasing demand for imports which economic expansion brings in its train.

Without this combination of immediate action with measures that take time to bear fruit, it would be very difficult, if not impossible, to establish the essential development discipline to which reference has been made: a discipline which is needed both for structural changes and for rational action to influence the forces of the economy. And if this is not achieved, the sense of frustration will continue to grow: either the frustration of allowing the dynamic impetus of the economy to fall increasingly short of what is required, or the frustration of populism. However much it may have served to uncover major problems, populism—with its leaning toward immediatist solutions, and its want of strong convictions and of an organized system of ideas—has almost always shunned basic solutions.

Development discipline, or development by coercion. Coercion would not necessarily stem from an ideology, but might be the result of events themselves, of failure or inability to influence them with foresight. It has already been proved that the rate of development can be stepped up by coercive measures.

But there must be no misunderstanding as to the great social and political cost, the great cost in human terms, which this implies.

These problems are not always discussed in Latin America with the necessary objectivity, since the atmosphere is increasingly charged with emotion. There is a great deal of ferment and unrest among the youth of the region, which is not merely a form of contagion, although it involves some degree of violence that is imitative of what is happening elsewhere. The attitude of nonconformity apparent among the younger generations, as well as among those who have long left youth behind, has roots that strike very deep. Poverty in the rural areas, social marginality in the cities, glaring disparities in income distribution, limited opportunities for dynamic personalities in a wide range of human activities, all go to form the background of such attitudes of mind. But the phenomenon is too complex to be explained solely by reference to economic conditions.

Perhaps one of the principal problems arising in Latin America is that of resolving the contradiction between the rising generations' legitimate desire to take part in the solution of the major problems of community life and the hesitant or piecemeal response—if any—made by political and social movements with a view to translating their dynamic energy into effective forms of action.

Latin America must find its own path, its own solutions. The region's development phenomena are different in the main from those with which the advanced countries were confronted in their time. The promise of technology is tremendous. But the contradictions involved in the progress of science and technology are also very grave: the population explosion, and the assimilation of increasingly capital-intensive production techniques. And, also, techniques which ceaselessly inculcate consumption aspirations that in the upper and middle income strata militate strongly against capital formation.

This growing imbalance between the increase in the population and capital formation must be corrected. But let us not stumble into the oversimplified belief that birth control is an alternative to an energetic economic and social development strategy. This strategy must of course be the expression of sacrosanct national decisions, in which demographic policy is a component that must be clearly defined in the light of long-term considerations which by their very nature cannot be strictly confined to the economic sphere.

Rationality and foresight are essential in development strategy. And also in international cooperation. The movements gestating in the developing world are of vast dimensions and historic importance. The industrialized countries will not be immune to what is going to happen in Latin America and throughout the Third World if it is still left to drift along as best it can: much less will they be so in view of the conspicuous unity of feeling which mass communication techniques are helping to create on a worldwide scale.

The Latin American countries need to cooperate effectively with one another. They need to take common action carried out with great energy and strength of conviction. This concerted action should be based on a lucid conception of their objectives, targets, and resources in their economic and social development, as well as of their aims in their mutual relationships, and of the cooperation they need and the way in which they intend to use the resources provided.

And now a word for ourselves, for the peoples of Latin America: what is the image of the society we want to establish, and what are its political and human values? From the very outset, we must look beyond the economic system. But if such a society is to be built, the economic system will have to acquire complete efficiency, so that the kind of welfare which is measurable can be extended to the whole community, to the broad masses of the population. This in its turn is a sine qua non if values which are sensed, but cannot be measured, are to be consolidated at this supremely significant turning point in Latin America's history.

Complete mutual understanding has not been reached as yet in Latin America. To achieve it, dialogue is a pressing and indispensable requirement. A dialogue must be maintained with men concerned in politics, economics, and trade union organizations, with men who move in other spheres of thought and action, especially those who belong to the new generations. With all of them a fruitful dialogue must be sought, such as can lead to the discovery of common ground, to a pragmatic consensus conducive to the action that will brook no further delay.

STATISTICAL APPENDIX

**APPENDIX TABLES**

# APPENDIX TABLE 1

## Latin America:  Development Indexes

| Year or Period | Product (index:  1950=100) | External Resources (index:  1950=100) | Effect of Import Coefficient on Growth of Product (percentage of 1950 product) |
|---|---|---|---|
| 1950 | 100.00 | 100.00 | 0 |
| 1951-1953 | 110.36 | 114.32 | -3.96 |
| 1954-1956 | 129.62 | 125.82 | 3.80 |
| 1957-1959 | 152.05 | 143.91 | 8.14 |
| 1960-1962 | 179.03 | 148.64 | 30.39 |
| 1963-1965 | 204.59 | 153.78 | 50.76 |
| 1966-1968 | 236.45 | 183.83 | 52.62 |

*Source:* ECLA, on the basis of official data.

# APPENDIX TABLE 2

## Countries in Which the Import Coefficient Decreased:  Development Indexes

| Year or Period | Product (index:  1950=100) | External Resources (index:  1950=100) | Effect of Import Coefficient on Growth of Product (percentage of 1950 product) |
|---|---|---|---|
| 1950 | 100.00 | 100.00 | 0 |
| 1951-1953 | 110.41 | 111.55 | -1.14 |
| 1954-1956 | 131.13 | 120.68 | 10.45 |
| 1957-1959 | 154.89 | 137.73 | 17.16 |
| 1960-1962 | 183.25 | 136.57 | 46.68 |
| 1963-1965 | 208.24 | 129.92 | 78.32 |
| 1966-1968 | 240.41 | 149.54 | 90.87 |

*Note:* The countries are Argentina, Brazil, Colombia, Mexico, Uruguay, and Venezuela.

*Source:* ECLA, on the basis of official data.

249

## APPENDIX TABLE 3

### Other Countries: Development Indexes

| Year or Period | Product (index: 1950=100) | External Resources (index: 1950=100) | Effect of Import Coefficient on Growth of Product (percentage of 1950 product) |
|---|---|---|---|
| 1950 | 100.00 | 100.00 | 0 |
| 1951-1953 | 110.14 | 125.87 | -15.73 |
| 1954-1956 | 122.62 | 147.37 | -24.75 |
| 1957-1959 | 138.98 | 169.79 | -30.83 |
| 1960-1962 | 159.60 | 199.16 | -39.56 |
| 1963-1965 | 187.51 | 253.68 | -66.17 |
| 1966-1968 | 218.22 | 327.37 | -109.15 |

*Note*: The countries are Bolivia, Chile, Costa Rica, Dominican Republic, Ecuador, El Salvador, Guatemala, Honduras, Nicaragua, Panama, Paraguay, and Peru.

*Source*: ECLA, on the basis of official data.


## APPENDIX TABLE 4

### Latin America: Components of External Resources
### (index: 1950=100)

| Year or Period | Volume of Exports | Purchasing Power of Exports |
|---|---|---|
| 1950 | 100.00 | 100.00 |
| 1951-1953 | 102.54 | 98.82 |
| 1954-1956 | 121.14 | 113.29 |
| 1957-1959 | 138.46 | 117.99 |
| 1960-1962 | 156.77 | 124.69 |
| 1963-1965 | 180.41 | 140.15 |
| 1966-1968 | 204.45 | 156.69 |

*Source*: ECLA, on the basis of official data.

# APPENDIX TABLE 5

## Countries in Which the Import Coefficient Decreased: Components
## of External Resources
## (index: 1950=100)

| Year or Period | Volume of Exports | Purchasing Power of Exports |
|---|---|---|
| 1950 | 100.00 | 100.00 |
| 1951-1953 | 102.09 | 96.13 |
| 1954-1956 | 122.76 | 110.26 |
| 1957-1959 | 139.19 | 115.32 |
| 1960-1962 | 153.56 | 117.62 |
| 1963-1965 | 173.86 | 126.81 |
| 1966-1968 | 194.37 | 132.77 |

*Note:* The countries are Argentina, Brazil, Colombia, Mexico, Uruguay, and Venezuela.

*Source:* ECLA, on the basis of official data.


# APPENDIX TABLE 6

## Other Countries: Components of External Resources
## (index: 1950=100)

| Year or Period | Volume of Exports | Purchasing Power of Exports |
|---|---|---|
| 1950 | 100.00 | 100.00 |
| 1951-1953 | 104.22 | 110.48 |
| 1954-1956 | 115.13 | 126.39 |
| 1957-1959 | 135.76 | 129.51 |
| 1960-1962 | 168.67 | 155.28 |
| 1963-1965 | 204.69 | 197.85 |
| 1966-1968 | 241.81 | 260.13 |

*Note:* The countries are Bolivia, Chile, Costa Rica, Dominican Republic, Ecuador, El Salvador, Guatemala, Honduras, Nicaragua, Panama, Paraguay, and Peru.

*Source:* ECLA, on the basis of official data.

## APPENDIX TABLE 7

### Brazil: Development Indexes
### (1950=100)

| Year or Period | Product | External Resources | Effect of Import Coefficient in Relation to 1950 (percentage of product in each period) | Volume of Exports | Purchasing Power of Exports |
|---|---|---|---|---|---|
| 1950 | 100.00 | 100.00 | 0 | 100.00 | 100.00 |
| 1951-1953 | 113.02 | 131.76 | -1.66 | 101.55 | 98.16 |
| 1954-1956 | 137.38 | 111.34 | 1.88 | 105.20 | 97.20 |
| 1957-1959 | 165.89 | 126.69 | 2.35 | 114.97 | 96.13 |
| 1960-1962 | 210.15 | 131.24 | 3.73 | 129.40 | 95.18 |
| 1963-1965 | 234.28 | 108.17 | 5.35 | 140.11 | 104.88 |
| 1966-1968 | 267.15 | 147.96 | 4.44 | 175.41 | 122.25 |

Source: ECLA, on the basis of official data.

## APPENDIX TABLE 8

### Mexico: Development Indexes
### (1950=100)

| Year or Period | Product | External Resources | Effect of Import Coefficient in Relation to 1950 (percentage of product in each period) | Volume of Exports | Purchasing Power of Exports |
|---|---|---|---|---|---|
| 1950 | 100.00 | 100.00 | 0 | 100.00 | 100.00 |
| 1951-1953 | 111.66 | 121.98 | -1.19 | 103.93 | 104.34 |
| 1954-1956 | 131.94 | 133.11 | -0.11 | 141.26 | 125.06 |
| 1957-1959 | 157.30 | 150.60 | 0.55 | 144.46 | 121.27 |
| 1960-1962 | 184.68 | 162.94 | 1.52 | 158.18 | 137.59 |
| 1963-1965 | 231.16 | 181.47 | 2.78 | 185.15 | 153.82 |
| 1966-1968 | 285.04 | 216.63 | 3.10 | 210.51 | 177.22 |

Source: ECLA, on the basis of official data.

## APPENDIX TABLE 9

### Venezuela: Development Indexes
### (1950=100)

| Year or Period | Product | External Resources | Effect of Import Coefficient in Relation to 1950 (percentage of product in each period) | Volume of Exports | Purchasing Power of Exports |
|---|---|---|---|---|---|
| 1950 | 100.00 | 100.00 | 0 | 100.00 | 100.00 |
| 1951-1953 | 119.56 | 113.21 | -1.55 | 117.75 | 109.64 |
| 1954-1956 | 153.06 | 152.10 | 0.19 | 146.97 | 142.87 |
| 1957-1959 | 194.02 | 212.82 | -2.83 | 187.08 | 169.55 |
| 1960-1962 | 216.17 | 136.39 | 10.77 | 205.76 | 153.22 |
| 1963-1965 | 251.72 | 131.19 | 13.98 | 231.36 | 138.00 |
| 1966-1968 | 297.60 | 144.09 | 14.57 | 246.94 | 128.54 |

*Source:* ECLA, on the basis of official data.

## APPENDIX TABLE 10

### Average Annual Growth Rates of Product: Variation from
### One Period to the Next
### (percentage)

| Period | Brazil | Mexico | Venezuela |
|---|---|---|---|
| 1951-1953 | 6.3 | 5.7 | 9.3 |
| 1954-1956 | 6.7 | 5.7 | 8.6 |
| 1957-1959 | 6.5 | 6.0 | 8.2 |
| 1960-1962 | 8.2 | 5.5 | 3.7 |
| 1963-1965 | 3.7 | 7.8 | 5.2 |
| 1966-1968 | 4.5 | 7.3 | 4.5 |

*Source:* ECLA, on the basis of official data.

## APPENDIX TABLE 11

### Colombia:  Development Indexes
### (1950=100)

| Year or Period | Product | External Resources | Effect of Import Coefficient in Relation to 1950 (percentage of product in each period) | Volume of Exports | Purchasing Power of Exports |
|---|---|---|---|---|---|
| 1950 | 100.00 | 100.00 | 0 | 100.00 | 100.00 |
| 1951-1953 | 106.97 | 111.19 | -0.25 | 121.23 | 111.99 |
| 1954-1956 | 129.31 | 148.51 | -2.72 | 133.68 | 131.27 |
| 1957-1959 | 143.07 | 103.30 | 5.09 | 147.41 | 116.61 |
| 1960-1962 | 165.75 | 139.06 | 2.95 | 155.11 | 113.81 |
| 1963-1965 | 189.82 | 145.09 | 4.32 | 173.90 | 131.02 |
| 1966-1968 | 218.41 | 162.28 | 4.71 | 192.02 | 135.18 |

*Source:* ECLA, on the basis of official data.


## APPENDIX TABLE 12

### Argentina:  Development Indexes
### (1950=100)

| Year or Period | Product | External Resources | Effect of Import Coefficient in Relation to 1950 (percentage of product in each period) | Volume of Exports | Purchasing Power of Exports |
|---|---|---|---|---|---|
| 1950 | 100.00 | 100.00 | 0 | 100.00 | 100.00 |
| 1951-1953 | 101.94 | 83.97 | 2.48 | 79.45 | 68.24 |
| 1954-1956 | 113.85 | 85.97 | 3.44 | 100.72 | 72.22 |
| 1957-1959 | 127.48 | 97.39 | 3.32 | 114.42 | 77.56 |
| 1960-1962 | 140.79 | 128.46 | 1.23 | 129.45 | 95.29 |
| 1963-1965 | 148.77 | 117.64 | 2.94 | 150.48 | 125.34 |
| 1966-1968 | 166.23 | 116.13 | 4.23 | 161.06 | 125.88 |

*Source:* ECLA, on the basis of official data.

# APPENDIX TABLE 13

## Uruguay: Development Indexes
## (1950=100)

| Year or Period | Product | External Resources | Effect of Import Coefficient in Relation to 1950 (percentage of product in each period) | Volume of Exports | Purchasing Power of Exports |
|---|---|---|---|---|---|
| 1950 | 100.00 | 100.00 | 0 | 100.00 | 100.00 |
| 1951-1953 | 110.46 | 100.84 | 2.1 | 80.58 | 81.36 |
| 1954-1956 | 120.36 | 104.57 | 3.1 | 85.86 | 78.87 |
| 1957-1959 | 122.92 | 83.69 | 7.5 | 75.55 | 54.74 |
| 1960-1962 | 124.95 | 104.70 | 3.8 | 77.77 | 69.40 |
| 1963-1965 | 126.09 | 82.08 | 8.3 | 89.96 | 79.50 |
| 1966-1968 | 125.93 | 81.67 | 8.3 | 94.66 | 82.91 |

*Source:* ECLA, on the basis of official data.

# APPENDIX TABLE 14

## Average Annual Growth Rates of Product: Variation from
## One Period to the Next
## (percentage)

| Period | Argentina | Colombia | Uruguay |
|---|---|---|---|
| 1951-1953 | 1.0 | 4.7 | 5.1 |
| 1954-1956 | 3.7 | 5.6 | 2.9 |
| 1957-1959 | 3.8 | 3.4 | 0.7 |
| 1960-1962 | 3.4 | 5.0 | 0.6 |
| 1963-1965 | 1.9 | 4.6 | 0.3 |
| 1966-1968 | 3.8 | 4.8 | 0.0 |

*Source:* ECLA, on the basis of official data.

# APPENDIX TABLE 15

## Chile: Development Indexes
## (1950=100)

| Year or Period | Product | External Resources | Effect of Import Coefficient in Relation to 1950 (percentage of product in each period) | Volume of Exports | Purchasing Power of Exports |
|---|---|---|---|---|---|
| 1950 | 100.00 | 100.00 | 0 | 100.00 | 100.00 |
| 1951-1953 | 116.05 | 122.96 | 1.43 | 101.46 | 113.43 |
| 1954-1956 | 122.81 | 123.90 | 2.05 | 109.83 | 125.90 |
| 1957-1959 | 138.37 | 142.60 | 1.78 | 115.23 | 114.86 |
| 1960-1962 | 157.02 | 219.93 | -2.74 | 132.47 | 147.20 |
| 1963-1965 | 180.95 | 208.29 | 0.31 | 155.64 | 172.19 |
| 1966-1968 | 207.79 | 276.60 | -1.89 | 177.49 | 253.61 |

*Source:* ECLA, on the basis of official data.


# APPENDIX TABLE 16

## Peru: Development Indexes
## (1950=100)

| Year or Period | Product | External Resources | Effect of Import Coefficient in Relation to 1950 (percentage of product in each period) | Volume of Exports | Purchasing Power of Exports |
|---|---|---|---|---|---|
| 1950 | 100.00 | 100.00 | 0 | 100.00 | 100.00 |
| 1951-1953 | 114.16 | 136.49 | -3.72 | 121.32 | 120.03 |
| 1954-1956 | 134.54 | 159.41 | -3.51 | 154.10 | 144.54 |
| 1957-1959 | 147.70 | 183.94 | -4.67 | 187.16 | 154.31 |
| 1960-1962 | 182.11 | 212.93 | -3.22 | 288.41 | 229.30 |
| 1963-1965 | 218.54 | 296.45 | -6.78 | 324.04 | 291.16 |
| 1966-1968 | 256.50 | 390.46 | -9.92 | 345.81 | 380.97 |

*Source:* ECLA, on the basis of official data.

# APPENDIX TABLE 17

### Guatemala: Development Indexes
### (1950=100)

| Year or Period | Product | External Resources | Effect of Import Coefficient in Relation to 1950 (percentage of product in each period) | Volume of Exports | Purchasing Power of Exports |
|---|---|---|---|---|---|
| 1950 | 100.00 | 100.00 | 0 | 100.00 | 100.00 |
| 1951-1953 | 104.08 | 101.71 | 0.29 | 84.90 | 100.82 |
| 1954-1956 | 114.50 | 137.74 | -2.64 | 94.78 | 124.64 |
| 1957-1959 | 135.34 | 188.17 | -5.11 | 125.77 | 137.63 |
| 1960-1962 | 151.19 | 157.14 | -0.52 | 157.09 | 134.12 |
| 1963-1965 | 179.72 | 234.43 | -3.98 | 262.54 | 200.10 |
| 1966-1968 | 207.22 | 278.89 | -4.58 | 325.77 | 243.30 |

Source: ECLA, on the basis of official data.


# APPENDIX TABLE 18

### Average Annual Growth Rates of Product: Variation from
### One Period to the Next
### (percentage)

| Period | Chile | Guatemala | Peru |
|---|---|---|---|
| 1951-1953 | 7.7 | 2.1 | 6.8 |
| 1954-1956 | 1.9 | 3.3 | 5.6 |
| 1957-1959 | 4.1 | 5.7 | 3.2 |
| 1960-1962 | 4.3 | 3.8 | 7.2 |
| 1963-1965 | 4.8 | 5.9 | 6.3 |
| 1966-1968 | 4.7 | 4.7 | 5.5 |

Source: ECLA, on the basis of official data.

# APPENDIX TABLE 19

## Latin America: Investment with Domestic Resources and Gross Inflow of Foreign Capital
### (percentage of product)

| Year or Period | Total Investment | Investment with Domestic Resources | Gross Inflow of Foreign Capital |
|---|---|---|---|
| 1950 | 17.82 | 16.30 | 1.52 |
| 1951-1953 | 20.15 | 17.56 | 2.59 |
| 1954-1956 | 19.50 | 16.59 | 2.91 |
| 1957-1959 | 19.14 | 14.91 | 4.24 |
| 1960-1962 | 18.79 | 14.62 | 4.17 |
| 1963-1965 | 18.15 | 14.54 | 3.61 |
| 1966-1968 | 18.23 | 14.43 | 3.80 |

*Source:* ECLA, on the basis of official data.


# APPENDIX TABLE 20

## Argentina: Investment with Domestic Resources and Gross Inflow of Foreign Capital
### (percentage of product)

| Year or Period | Total Investment | Investment with Domestic Resources | Gross Inflow of Foreign Capital |
|---|---|---|---|
| 1950 | 14.2 | 13.8 | 0.39 |
| 1951-1953 | 18.8 | 17.2 | 1.68 |
| 1954-1956 | 17.0 | 18.1 | 1.95 |
| 1957-1959 | 17.1 | 14.0 | 3.06 |
| 1960-1962 | 22.5 | 17.0 | 5.51 |
| 1963-1965 | 18.5 | 15.5 | 2.92 |
| 1966-1968 | 18.1 | 15.7 | 2.43 |

*Source:* ECLA, on the basis of official data.

# APPENDIX TABLE 21

## Brazil: Investment with Domestic Resources and
## Gross Inflow of Foreign Capital
## (percentage of product)

| Year or Period | Total Investment | Investment with Domestic Resources | Gross Inflow of Foreign Capital |
|---|---|---|---|
| 1950 | 18.3 | 17.5 | 0.76 |
| 1951-1953 | 20.1 | 16.6 | 3.42 |
| 1954-1956 | 17.3 | 15.0 | 2.32 |
| 1957-1959 | 19.6 | 16.2 | 3.36 |
| 1960-1962 | 18.3 | 14.8 | 3.53 |
| 1963-1965 | 17.1 | 14.6 | 2.52 |
| 1966-1968 | 16.6 | 14.2 | 2.41 |

*Source:* ECLA, on the basis of official data.

# APPENDIX TABLE 22

## Colombia: Investment with Domestic Resources and
## Gross Inflow of Foreign Capital
## (percentage of product)

| Year or Period | Total Investment | Investment with Domestic Resources | Gross Inflow of Foreign Capital |
|---|---|---|---|
| 1950 | 21.8 | 20.1 | 1.71 |
| 1951-1953 | 20.8 | 18.5 | 2.25 |
| 1954-1956 | 25.2 | 21.7 | 3.49 |
| 1957-1959 | 19.6 | 15.8 | 3.85 |
| 1960-1962 | 20.3 | 15.5 | 4.73 |
| 1963-1965 | 18.2 | 11.8 | 6.44 |
| 1966-1968 | 18.1 | 11.9 | 6.21 |

*Source:* ECLA, on the basis of official data.

# APPENDIX TABLE 23

## Chile: Investment with Domestic Resources and
## Gross Inflow of Foreign Capital
## (percentage of product)

| Year or Period | Total Investment | Investment with Domestic Resources | Gross Inflow of Foreign Capital |
|---|---|---|---|
| 1950 | 17.6 | 15.8 | 1.79 |
| 1951-1953 | 17.2 | 14.4 | 2.77 |
| 1954-1956 | 15.7 | 13.5 | 2.18 |
| 1957-1959 | 15.1 | 10.2 | 5.04 |
| 1960-1962 | 17.8 | 9.5 | 8.37 |
| 1963-1965 | 18.1 | 10.3 | 7.80 |
| 1966-1968 | 17.0 | 9.6 | 7.08 |

*Source:* ECLA, on the basis of official data.


# APPENDIX TABLE 24

## Guatemala: Investment with Domestic Resources and
## Gross Inflow of Foreign Capital
## (percentage of product)

| Year or Period | Total Investment | Investment with Domestic Resources | Gross Inflow of Foreign Capital |
|---|---|---|---|
| 1950 | 10.7 | 10.5 | 0.17 |
| 1951-1953 | 8.9 | 9.3 | -0.36 |
| 1954-1956 | 12.4 | 9.6 | 2.78 |
| 1957-1959 | 13.5 | 9.0 | 4.56 |
| 1960-1962 | 9.2 | 5.3 | 3.97 |
| 1963-1965 | 11.5 | 5.8 | 5.75 |
| 1966-1968 | 11.6 | 5.9 | 5.70 |

*Source:* ECLA, on the basis of official data.

## APPENDIX TABLE 25

### Mexico: Investment with Domestic Resources and Gross Inflow of Foreign Capital
#### (percentage of product)

| Year or Period | Total Investment | Investment with Domestic Resources | Gross Inflow of Foreign Capital |
|---|---|---|---|
| 1950 | 16.8 | 13.0 | 3.73 |
| 1951-1953 | 18.6 | 16.7 | 1.92 |
| 1954-1956 | 20.0 | 17.2 | 2.77 |
| 1957-1959 | 17.8 | 14.8 | 3.03 |
| 1960-1962 | 18.8 | 15.1 | 3.74 |
| 1963-1965 | 20.3 | 16.6 | 3.71 |
| 1966-1968 | 21.3 | 17.1 | 4.24 |

*Source:* ECLA, on the basis of official data.


## APPENDIX TABLE 26

### Peru: Investment with Domestic Resources and Gross Inflow of Foreign Capital
#### (percentage of product)

| Year or Period | Total Investment | Investment with Domestic Resources | Gross Inflow of Foreign Capital |
|---|---|---|---|
| 1950 | 20.9 | 19.6 | 1.35 |
| 1951-1953 | 28.3 | 24.4 | 3.90 |
| 1954-1956 | 24.4 | 19.3 | 5.10 |
| 1957-1959 | 24.1 | 16.8 | 7.31 |
| 1960-1962 | 22.5 | 18.8 | 3.70 |
| 1963-1965 | 21.3 | 15.4 | 5.84 |
| 1966-1968 | 24.5 | 16.0 | 8.49 |

*Source:* ECLA, on the basis of official data.

# APPENDIX TABLE 27

## Uruguay: Investment with Domestic Resources and Gross Inflow of Foreign Capital
### (percentage of product)

| Year or Period | Total Investment | Investment with Domestic Resources | Gross Inflow of Foreign Capital |
|---|---|---|---|
| 1950 | 22.9 | 20.1 | 2.78 |
| 1951-1953 | 22.2 | 18.7 | 3.55 |
| 1954-1956 | 20.8 | 18.3 | 2.46 |
| 1957-1959 | 16.5 | 12.8 | 3.61 |
| 1960-1962 | 17.4 | 9.5 | 7.87 |
| 1963-1965 | 12.9 | 7.9 | 5.05 |
| 1966-1968 | 12.5 | 6.3 | 6.14 |

*Source:* ECLA, on the basis of official data.


# APPENDIX TABLE 28

## Venezuela: Investment with Domestic Resources and Gross Inflow of Foreign Capital
### (percentage of product)

| Year or Period | Total Investment | Investment with Domestic Resources | Gross Inflow of Foreign Capital |
|---|---|---|---|
| 1950 | 28.0 | 25.6 | 2.42 |
| 1951-1953 | 30.4 | 27.3 | 3.08 |
| 1954-1956 | 30.1 | 24.2 | 5.91 |
| 1957-1959 | 26.8 | 17.9 | 8.84 |
| 1960-1962 | 17.2 | 16.3 | 0.96 |
| 1963-1965 | 18.9 | 18.6 | 0.30 |
| 1966-1968 | 18.0 | 16.5 | 1.46 |

*Source:* ECLA, on the basis of official data.

## APPENDIX TABLE 29

### Latin America: Financial Resources, Consumption, and Investment
(percentage of product)

| Year or Period | Gross Inflow of Capital | Amortization and Debt Repayment | Interest and Profits | Total Service Payments | Net Inflow of Financial Resources | Consumption | Domestic Resources Available for Investment | Terms-of-Trade Effect |
|---|---|---|---|---|---|---|---|---|
| 1950 | 1.52 | 1.16 | 2.30 | 3.46 | -1.94 | 82.30 | 17.52 | 3.34 |
| 1951-1953 | 2.59 | 0.99 | 2.07 | 3.06 | -0.47 | 81.54 | 17.78 | 2.49 |
| 1954-1956 | 2.91 | 1.19 | 2.08 | 3.27 | -0.36 | 81.14 | 17.46 | 2.03 |
| 1957-1959 | 4.24 | 1.90 | 1.92 | 3.82 | 0.42 | 81.49 | 15.18 | 0.61 |
| 1960-1962 | 4.17 | 2.44 | 1.71 | 4.15 | 0.02 | 80.65 | 14.79 | -0.30 |
| 1963-1965 | 3.61 | 2.53 | 1.71 | 4.24 | -0.63 | 80.03 | 15.11 | -0.60 |
| 1966-1968 | 3.80 | 2.26 | 1.94 | 4.20 | -0.40 | 80.58 | 14.45 | -0.75 |

*Source:* ECLA, on the basis of official data.

## APPENDIX TABLE 30

### Argentina: Financial Resources, Consumption, and Investment
#### (percentage of product)

| Year or Period | Gross Inflow of Capital | Amortization and Debt Repayment | Interest and Profits | Total Service Payments | Net Inflow of Financial Resources | Consumption | Domestic Resources Available for Investment | Terms-of-Trade Effect |
|---|---|---|---|---|---|---|---|---|
| 1950 | 0.39 | — | 0.04 | 0.04 | 0.35 | 88.12 | 15.68 | 3.84 |
| 1951-1953 | 1.68 | 0.69 | 0.17 | 0.86 | 0.82 | 83.61 | 16.68 | 1.28 |
| 1954-1956 | 1.95 | 1.14 | 0.16 | 1.30 | 0.65 | 83.20 | 15.99 | -0.49 |
| 1957-1959 | 3.06 | 0.76 | 0.24 | 1.00 | 2.06 | 83.18 | 14.74 | -1.05 |
| 1960-1962 | 5.51 | 2.07 | 0.65 | 2.72 | 2.79 | 79.50 | 17.47 | -0.24 |
| 1963-1965 | 2.92 | 3.99 | 0.62 | 4.61 | -1.69 | 80.78 | 15.84 | 1.26 |
| 1966-1968 | 2.43 | 2.98 | 0.96 | 3.94 | -1.51 | 80.32 | 16.16 | 0.43 |

*Source:* ECLA, on the basis of official data.

## APPENDIX TABLE 31

### Brazil: Financial Resources, Consumption, and Investment
(percentage of product)

| Year or Period | Gross Inflow of Capital | Amortization and Debt Repayment | Interest and Profits | Total Service Payments | Net Inflow of Financial Resources | Consumption | Domestic Resources Available for Investment | Terms-of-Trade Effect |
|---|---|---|---|---|---|---|---|---|
| 1950 | 0.76 | 1.70 | 0.93 | 2.63 | -1.87 | 82.62 | 17.48 | 2.75 |
| 1951-1953 | 3.42 | 1.48 | 0.91 | 2.39 | 1.03 | 83.43 | 16.24 | 2.11 |
| 1954-1956 | 2.32 | 1.63 | 0.69 | 2.32 | — | 83.83 | 15.21 | 1.42 |
| 1957-1959 | 3.36 | 1.78 | 0.62 | 2.40 | 0.96 | 81.78 | 16.32 | 0.57 |
| 1960-1962 | 3.53 | 1.78 | 0.72 | 2.50 | 1.03 | 82.37 | 14.90 | -0.23 |
| 1963-1965 | 2.52 | 2.05 | 0.65 | 2.70 | -0.18 | 82.07 | 15.18 | -0.13 |
| 1966-1968 | 2.41 | 1.77 | 0.79 | 2.56 | -0.15 | 83.00 | 13.97 | -0.54 |

*Source:* ECLA, on the basis of official data.

## APPENDIX TABLE 32

### Colombia: Financial Resources, Consumption, and Investment
(percentage of product)

| Year or Period | Gross Inflow of Capital | Amortization and Debt Repayment | Interest and Profits | Total Service Payments | Net Inflow of Financial Resources | Consumption | Domestic Resources Available for Investment | Terms-of-Trade Effect |
|---|---|---|---|---|---|---|---|---|
| 1950 | 1.71 | 0.59 | 1.77 | 2.36 | -0.65 | 81.64 | 20.64 | 4.68 |
| 1951-1953 | 2.25 | 1.10 | 0.91 | 2.01 | 0.24 | 81.41 | 20.23 | 3.53 |
| 1954-1956 | 3.49 | 1.01 | 0.51 | 1.52 | 1.97 | 80.47 | 22.47 | 4.48 |
| 1957-1959 | 3.85 | 3.58 | 1.04 | 4.62 | -0.77 | 78.34 | 17.70 | 0.62 |
| 1960-1962 | 4.73 | 3.08 | 1.13 | 4.21 | 0.52 | 81.23 | 14.12 | -0.48 |
| 1963-1965 | 6.44 | 3.39 | 1.53 | 4.92 | 1.52 | 82.21 | 12.86 | -0.12 |
| 1966-1968 | 6.21 | 3.09 | 1.69 | 4.78 | 1.43 | 82.47 | 11.80 | -0.96 |

*Source:* ECLA, on the basis of official data.

# APPENDIX TABLE 33

## Chile: Financial Resources, Consumption, and Investment
### (percentage of product)

| Year or Period | Gross Inflow of Capital | Amortization and Debt Repayment | Interest and Profits | Total Service Payments | Net Inflow of Financial Resources | Consumption | Domestic Resources Available for Investment | Terms-of-Trade Effect |
|---|---|---|---|---|---|---|---|---|
| 1950 | 1.79 | 1.11 | 2.49 | 3.60 | -1.81 | 78.50 | 15.95 | -1.93 |
| 1951-1953 | 2.77 | 1.21 | 1.89 | 3.10 | -0.33 | 81.70 | 14.96 | -0.22 |
| 1954-1956 | 2.18 | 2.08 | 2.20 | 4.28 | -2.10 | 82.22 | 13.60 | 0.13 |
| 1957-1959 | 5.04 | 2.44 | 1.45 | 3.89 | 1.15 | 84.05 | 10.64 | -1.64 |
| 1960-1962 | 8.37 | 2.84 | 1.94 | 4.78 | 3.59 | 85.69 | 9.42 | -0.30 |
| 1963-1965 | 7.80 | 5.53 | 2.10 | 7.63 | 0.17 | 82.11 | 10.05 | -0.36 |
| 1966-1968 | 7.08 | 4.43 | 3.47 | 7.90 | -0.82 | 85.53 | 10.20 | 3.55 |

*Source:* ECLA, on the basis of official data.

## APPENDIX TABLE 34

### Guatemala: Financial Resources, Consumption, and Investment
(percentage of product)

| Year or Period | Gross Inflow of Capital | Amortization and Debt Repayment | Interest and Profits | Total Service Payments | Net Inflow of Financial Resources | Consumption | Domestic Resources Available for Investment | Terms-of-Trade Effect |
|---|---|---|---|---|---|---|---|---|
| 1950 | 0.17 | 0.14 | 0.45 | 0.59 | -0.42 | 90.13 | 10.52 | 1.24 |
| 1951-1953 | -0.36 | 0.33 | -0.55 | -0.22 | -0.14 | 93.86 | 9.41 | 3.08 |
| 1954-1956 | 2.78 | 0.16 | 0.22 | 0.38 | 2.40 | 93.19 | 10.98 | 4.55 |
| 1957-1959 | 4.56 | 0.24 | 0.38 | 0.62 | 3.94 | 93.21 | 8.56 | 2.33 |
| 1960-1962 | 3.97 | 0.92 | 0.62 | 1.54 | 2.43 | 91.61 | 6.12 | -0.76 |
| 1963-1965 | 5.75 | 1.93 | 0.69 | 2.62 | 3.13 | 87.62 | 7.15 | -2.88 |
| 1966-1968 | 5.70 | 3.14 | 1.49 | 4.63 | 1.07 | 86.66 | 5.75 | -3.43 |

*Source:* ECLA, on the basis of official data.

## APPENDIX TABLE 35

### Mexico: Financial Resources, Consumption, and Investment
(percentage of product)

| Year or Period | Gross Inflow of Capital | Amortization and Debt Repayment | Interest and Profits | Total Service Payments | Net Inflow of Financial Resources | Consumption | Domestic Resources Available for Investment | Terms-of-Trade Effect |
|---|---|---|---|---|---|---|---|---|
| 1950 | 3.73 | 1.53 | 1.42 | 2.95 | 0.78 | 82.67 | 15.84 | 1.44 |
| 1951-1953 | 1.92 | 0.78 | 1.53 | 2.31 | -0.39 | 82.94 | 16.16 | 1.39 |
| 1954-1956 | 2.77 | 0.79 | 1.26 | 2.05 | 0.72 | 78.62 | 18.97 | -0.30 |
| 1957-1959 | 2.02 | 1.37 | 1.36 | 2.73 | 0.30 | 82.15 | 14.23 | -0.88 |
| 1960-1962 | 3.74 | 1.99 | 1.62 | 3.61 | 0.13 | 81.04 | 14.82 | -0.43 |
| 1963-1965 | 3.71 | 1.82 | 1.69 | 3.51 | 0.20 | 78.99 | 16.56 | -0.87 |
| 1966-1968 | 4.24 | 2.27 | 1.92 | 4.19 | 0.05 | 78.55 | 16.58 | -0.68 |

*Source:* ECLA, on the basis of official data.

**APPENDIX TABLE 36**

**Peru: Financial Resources, Consumption, and Investment
(percentage of product)**

| Year or Period | Gross Inflow of Capital | Amortization and Debt Repayment | Interest and Profits | Total Service Payments | Net Inflow of Financial Resources | Consumption | Domestic Resources Available for Investment | Terms-of-Trade Effect |
|---|---|---|---|---|---|---|---|---|
| 1950 | 1.35 | 0.83 | 0.88 | 1.71 | -0.36 | 82.50 | 19.60 | 3.61 |
| 1951-1953 | 3.90 | 0.27 | 1.53 | 1.80 | 2.10 | 77.87 | 24.23 | 3.62 |
| 1954-1956 | 5.10 | 1.10 | 1.64 | 2.74 | 2.36 | 80.23 | 20.17 | 2.78 |
| 1957-1959 | 7.31 | 1.91 | 2.14 | 4.05 | 3.26 | 79.79 | 17.21 | 0.31 |
| 1960-1962 | 3.70 | 2.48 | 2.65 | 5.13 | -1.43 | 75.08 | 19.42 | -0.50 |
| 1963-1965 | 5.84 | 2.21 | 2.79 | 5.00 | 0.84 | 81.42 | 16.28 | 2.47 |
| 1966-1968 | 8.49 | 2.86 | 4.08 | 6.94 | 1.55 | 83.47 | 17.33 | 7.50 |

*Source:* ECLA, on the basis of official data.

## APPENDIX TABLE 37

### Uruguay: Financial Resources, Consumption, and Investment
(percentage of product)

| Year or Period | Gross Inflow of Capital | Amortization and Debt Repayment | Interest and Profits | Total Service Payments | Net Inflow of Financial Resources | Consumption | Domestic Resources Available for Investment | Terms-of-Trade Effect |
|---|---|---|---|---|---|---|---|---|
| 1950 | 2.78 | 1.50 | 0.45 | 1.95 | 0.83 | 75.35 | 26.6 | 3.10 |
| 1951-1953 | 3.55 | 1.12 | 0.38 | 1.50 | 2.05 | 80.83 | 19.93 | 2.46 |
| 1954-1956 | 2.46 | 2.47 | 0.39 | 2.86 | -0.40 | 81.67 | 15.82 | 0.55 |
| 1957-1959 | 3.61 | 0.73 | 0.40 | 1.13 | 2.48 | 84.05 | 11.76 | -2.92 |
| 1960-1962 | 7.87 | 1.79 | 0.55 | 2.34 | 5.53 | 86.65 | 11.01 | 0.02 |
| 1963-1965 | 5.05 | 3.59 | 1.07 | 4.66 | 0.39 | 84.36 | 10.82 | -0.15 |
| 1966-1968 | 6.14 | 5.71 | 1.79 | 7.50 | -1.36 | 83.79 | 8.40 | -0.33 |

*Source:* ECLA, on the basis of official data.

# APPENDIX TABLE 38

## Venezuela: Financial Resources, Consumption, and Investment
### (percentage of product)

| Year or Period | Gross Inflow of Capital | Amortization and Debt Repayment | Interest and Profits | Total Service Payments | Net Inflow of Financial Resources | Consumption | Domestic Resources Available for Investment | Terms-of-Trade Effect |
|---|---|---|---|---|---|---|---|---|
| 1950 | 2.42 | 1.74 | 14.72 | 16.46 | -14.04 | 66.80 | 26.74 | 10.58 |
| 1951-1953 | 3.08 | 0.46 | 12.13 | 12.59 | -9.51 | 63.42 | 30.59 | 7.37 |
| 1954-1956 | 5.91 | 0.35 | 12.69 | 12.84 | -6.39 | 65.90 | 29.10 | 8.96 |
| 1957-1959 | 8.84 | 3.96 | 10.37 | 14.33 | -5.49 | 72.12 | 18.60 | 6.14 |
| 1960-1962 | 0.96 | 5.61 | 7.19 | 12.80 | -11.84 | 68.50 | 16.83 | -0.85 |
| 1963-1965 | 0.30 | 1.28 | 6.39 | 7.67 | -7.37 | 64.70 | 19.87 | -6.94 |
| 1966-1968 | 1.46 | 0.52 | 5.46 | 5.98 | -4.52 | 67.13 | 16.70 | -9.41 |

Source: ECLA, on the basis of official data.

## APPENDIX TABLE 39

### Countries in Which Import Coefficient Decreased: Financial Resources, Consumption, and Investment
(percentage of product)

| Year or Period | Gross Inflow of Capital | Amortization and Debt Repayment | Interest and Profits | Total Service Payments | Net Inflow of Financial Resources | Consumption | Domestic Resources Available for Investment | Terms-of-Trade Effect |
|---|---|---|---|---|---|---|---|---|
| 1950 | 1.54 | 1.17 | 2.29 | 3.46 | -1.92 | 82.09 | 18.12 | 2.94 |
| 1951-1953 | 2.62 | 1.01 | 2.12 | 3.13 | -0.51 | 80.92 | 18.31 | 1.87 |
| 1954-1956 | 2.85 | 1.16 | 2.13 | 3.29 | -0.44 | 80.22 | 18.11 | 0.81 |
| 1957-1959 | 3.99 | 1.88 | 1.99 | 3.87 | 0.12 | 80.67 | 15.90 | -0.22 |
| 1960-1962 | 3.79 | 2.43 | 1.70 | 4.13 | -0.34 | 79.86 | 15.49 | -0.29 |
| 1963-1965 | 2.87 | 2.36 | 1.66 | 4.02 | -1.15 | 79.02 | 15.98 | -0.03 |
| 1966-1968 | 3.02 | 2.08 | 1.73 | 3.81 | -0.79 | 79.38 | 15.20 | -0.42 |

*Note:* The countries are Argentina, Brazil, Colombia, Mexico, Uruguay, and Venezuela.

*Source:* ECLA, on the basis of official data.

## APPENDIX TABLE 40

### Other Countries:  Financial Resources, Consumption, and Investment
(percentage of product)

| Year or Period | Gross Inflow of Capital | Amortization and Debt Repayment | Interest and Profits | Total Service Payments | Net Inflow of Financial Resources | Consumption | Domestic Resources Available for Investment | Terms-of-Trade Effect |
|---|---|---|---|---|---|---|---|---|
| 1950 | 1.46 | 1.10 | 2.31 | 3.41 | -1.95 | 83.24 | 14.76 | 1.49 |
| 1951-1953 | 2.45 | 0.85 | 1.88 | 2.73 | -0.28 | 84.36 | 15.35 | 2.49 |
| 1954-1956 | 3.19 | 1.38 | 1.83 | 3.21 | -0.02 | 85.71 | 14.20 | 3.14 |
| 1957-1959 | 5.51 | 2.02 | 1.55 | 3.57 | 1.94 | 85.70 | 11.48 | 0.61 |
| 1960-1962 | 6.17 | 2.46 | 1.76 | 4.22 | 1.95 | 84.79 | 11.07 | -0.01 |
| 1963-1965 | 7.42 | 3.42 | 1.95 | 5.37 | 2.05 | 85.16 | 10.70 | 0.94 |
| 1966-1968 | 7.78 | 3.16 | 2.98 | 6.14 | 1.64 | 86.70 | 10.66 | 3.25 |

*Note:* The countries are Bolivia, Chile, Costa Rica, Dominican Republic, Ecuador, El Salvador, Guatemala, Honduras, Nicaragua, Panama, Paraguay, and Peru.

*Source:* ECLA, on the basis of official data.

## APPENDIX TABLE 41

### Latin America: Relative Burden of Service Payments
(millions of dollars at 1960 prices)

| Year or Period | Purchasing Power of Exports (A) | Effect of Reduction of Import Coefficient (B) | Gross Inflow of Foreign Capital (C) | Effect of Net Reduction of Import Coefficient (D) (B+C) | Purchasing Power of Exports Plus Effect of Net Reduction of Import Coefficient (E) (A+D) | Total Service Payments (F) | Percentage Relation (G) (F/E) |
|---|---|---|---|---|---|---|---|
| 1950 | 7,668.5 | — | 647.2 | 647.2 | 8,315.7 | 1,471.8 | 17.7 |
| 1951-1953 | 7,578.4 | -249.0 | 1,217.0 | 968.0 | 8,546.4 | 1,440.4 | 16.9 |
| 1954-1956 | 8,687.6 | 237.3 | 1,606.0 | 1,843.3 | 10,530.9 | 1,806.3 | 17.2 |
| 1957-1959 | 9,047.8 | 511.4 | 2,745.0 | 3,256.4 | 12,304.2 | 2,470.7 | 20.1 |
| 1960-1962 | 9,562.3 | 1,913.4 | 3,178.8 | 5,092.2 | 14,654.5 | 3,161.8 | 21.6 |
| 1963-1965 | 10,747.5 | 3,196.3 | 3,145.0 | 6,341.3 | 17,088.8 | 3,689.0 | 21.6 |
| 1966-1968 | 12,015.7 | 3,312.7 | 3,825.8 | 7,138.5 | 10,154.2 | 4,227.2 | 22.1 |

# APPENDIX TABLE 42

## Countries in Which Import Coefficient Decreased: Relative Burden of Service Payments
### (millions of dollars at 1960 prices)

| Year or Period | Purchasing Power of Exports (A) | Effect of Reduction of Import Coefficient (B) | Gross Inflow of Foreign Capital (C) | Effect of Net Reduction of Import Coefficient (D) (B+C) | Purchasing Power of Exports Plus Effect of Net Reduction of Import Coefficient (E) (A+D) | Total Service Payments (F) | Percentage Relation (G) (F/E) |
|---|---|---|---|---|---|---|---|
| 1950 | 6,228.5 | — | 538.5 | 538.5 | 6,767.0 | 1,211.4 | 17.9 |
| 1951-1953 | 5,987.4 | -57.9 | 1,010.9 | 953.0 | 6,940.4 | 1,209.8 | 17.4 |
| 1954-1956 | 6,867.4 | 532.2 | 1,309.2 | 1,841.4 | 8,708.8 | 1,508.3 | 17.3 |
| 1957-1959 | 7,182.7 | 872.4 | 2,163.8 | 3,036.2 | 10,218.9 | 2,095.8 | 20.5 |
| 1960-1962 | 7,326.1 | 2,372.0 | 2,429.7 | 4,801.7 | 12,127.8 | 2,648.1 | 21.8 |
| 1963-1965 | 7,898.2 | 3,977.6 | 2,090.5 | 6,068.1 | 13,966.3 | 2,928.9 | 21.0 |
| 1966-1968 | 8,269.5 | 4,617.4 | 2,539.4 | 7,156.8 | 15,426.3 | 3,208.3 | 20.8 |

*Note:* The countries are Argentina, Brazil, Colombia, Mexico, Uruguay, and Venezuela.

## APPENDIX TABLE 43

### Other Countries: Relative Burden of Service Payments
(millions of dollars at 1960 prices)

| Year or Period | Purchasing Power of Exports (A) | Effect of Reduction of Import Coefficient (B) | Gross Inflow of Foreign Capital (C) | Effect of Net Reduction of Import Coefficient (D) (B+C) | Purchasing Power of Exports Plus Effect of Net Reduction of Import Coefficient (E) (A+D) | Total Service Payments (F) | Percentage Relation (G) (F/E) |
|---|---|---|---|---|---|---|---|
| 1950 | 1,440.1 | — | 110.8 | 110.8 | 1,550.9 | 258.6 | 16.7 |
| 1951-1953 | 1,591.0 | -190.7 | 205.2 | 14.5 | 1,605.5 | 228.4 | 14.2 |
| 1954-1956 | 1,820.2 | -299.9 | 297.0 | -2.9 | 1,817.3 | 298.6 | 16.4 |
| 1957-1959 | 1,865.1 | -373.6 | 581.5 | 207.9 | 2,073.0 | 376.8 | 18.2 |
| 1960-1962 | 2,236.2 | -480.0 | 747.4 | 267.4 | 2,503.6 | 511.4 | 20.4 |
| 1963-1965 | 2,849.3 | -803.3 | 1,057.4 | 254.1 | 3,103.4 | 763.7 | 24.6 |
| 1966-1968 | 3,746.2 | -1,324.3 | 1,289.8 | -34.5 | 3,711.7 | 1,017.7 | 27.4 |

*Note:* The countries are Bolivia, Chile, Costa Rica, Dominican Republic, Ecuador, El Salvador, Guatemala, Honduras, Nicaragua, Panama, Paraguay, and Peru.

# APPENDIX FIGURES

# APPENDIX FIGURE 1

## Growth of Countries Considered
(indexes 1963 = 100)

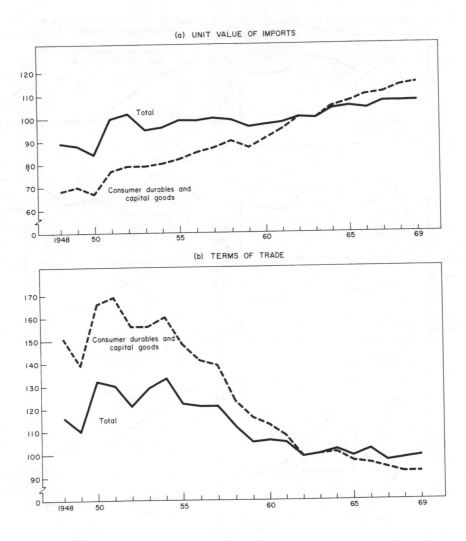

(a) UNIT VALUE OF IMPORTS

(b) TERMS OF TRADE

# APPENDIX FIGURE 2

## Brazil
### (percentages of product)

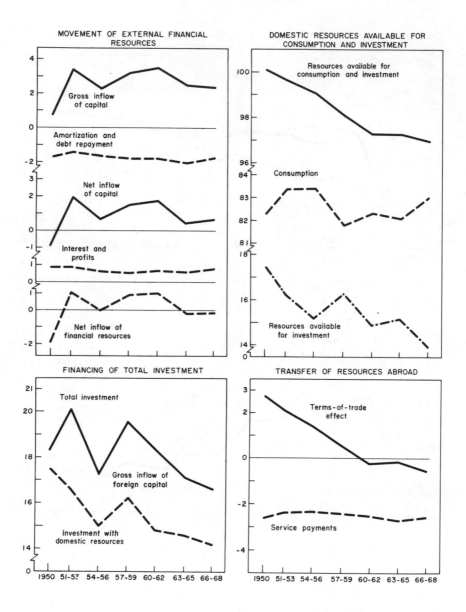

MOVEMENT OF EXTERNAL FINANCIAL RESOURCES

Gross inflow of capital

Amortization and debt repayment

Net inflow of capital

Interest and profits

Net inflow of financial resources

DOMESTIC RESOURCES AVAILABLE FOR CONSUMPTION AND INVESTMENT

Resources available for consumption and investment

Consumption

Resources available for investment

FINANCING OF TOTAL INVESTMENT

Total investment

Gross inflow of foreign capital

Investment with domestic resources

TRANSFER OF RESOURCES ABROAD

Terms-of-trade effect

Service payments

1950  51-53  54-56  57-59  60-62  63-65  66-68

282

# APPENDIX FIGURE 3

## Mexico
### (percentages of product)

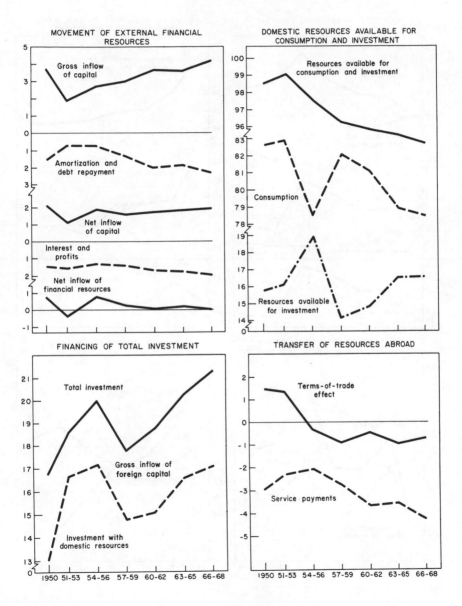

# APPENDIX FIGURE 4

## Argentina
## (percentages of product)

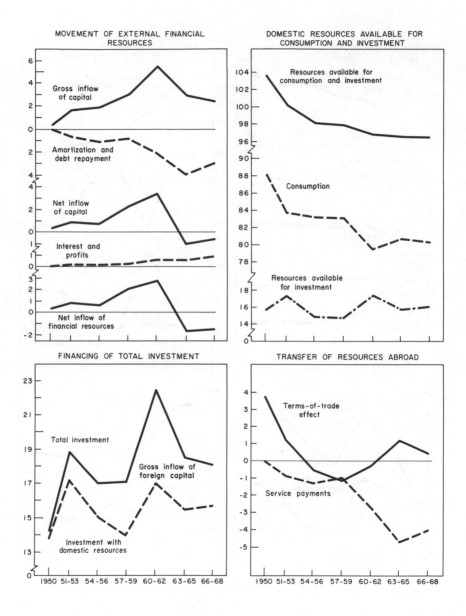

MOVEMENT OF EXTERNAL FINANCIAL RESOURCES

DOMESTIC RESOURCES AVAILABLE FOR CONSUMPTION AND INVESTMENT

FINANCING OF TOTAL INVESTMENT

TRANSFER OF RESOURCES ABROAD

# APPENDIX FIGURE 5

## Uruguay
### (percentages of product)

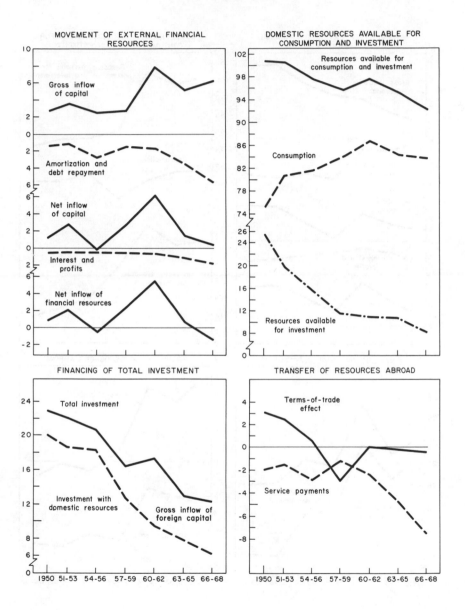

MOVEMENT OF EXTERNAL FINANCIAL
RESOURCES

DOMESTIC RESOURCES AVAILABLE FOR
CONSUMPTION AND INVESTMENT

FINANCING OF TOTAL INVESTMENT

TRANSFER OF RESOURCES ABROAD

# APPENDIX FIGURE 6

## Colombia
### (percentages of product)

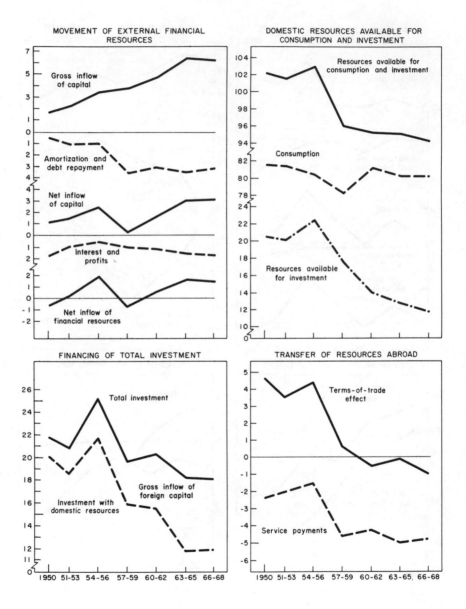

MOVEMENT OF EXTERNAL FINANCIAL RESOURCES

Gross inflow of capital

Amortization and debt repayment

Net inflow of capital

Interest and profits

Net inflow of financial resources

DOMESTIC RESOURCES AVAILABLE FOR CONSUMPTION AND INVESTMENT

Resources available for consumption and investment

Consumption

Resources available for investment

FINANCING OF TOTAL INVESTMENT

Total investment

Gross inflow of foreign capital

Investment with domestic resources

TRANSFER OF RESOURCES ABROAD

Terms-of-trade effect

Service payments

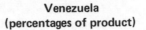

## Venezuela
### (percentages of product)

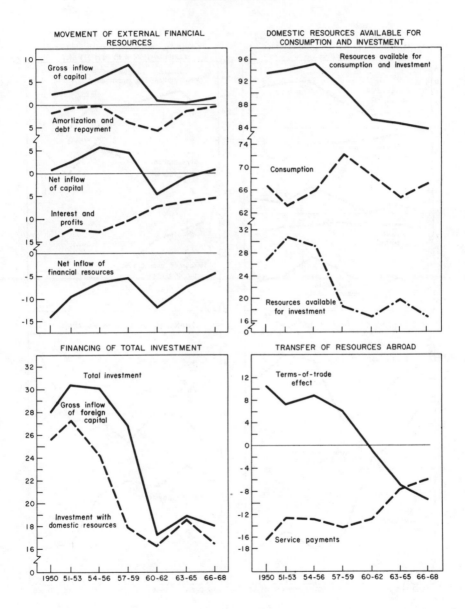

# APPENDIX FIGURE 8

## Chile
### (percentages of product)

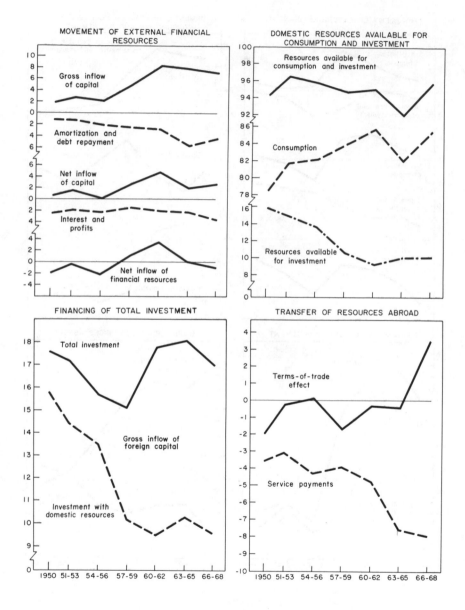

# APPENDIX FIGURE 9

## Peru
### (percentages of product)

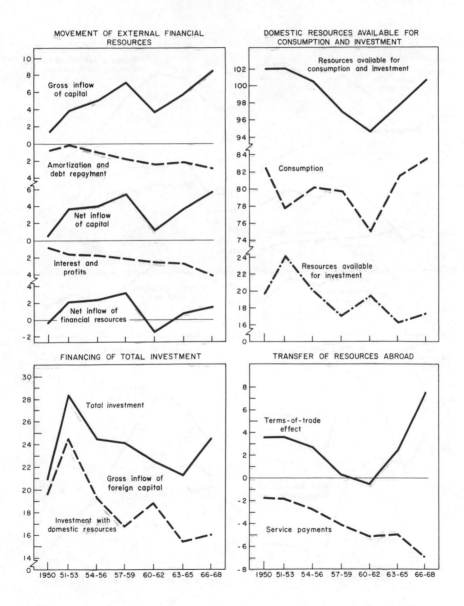

MOVEMENT OF EXTERNAL FINANCIAL RESOURCES

Gross inflow of capital

Amortization and debt repayment

Net inflow of capital

Interest and profits

Net inflow of financial resources

DOMESTIC RESOURCES AVAILABLE FOR CONSUMPTION AND INVESTMENT

Resources available for consumption and investment

Consumption

Resources available for investment

FINANCING OF TOTAL INVESTMENT

Total investment

Gross inflow of foreign capital

Investment with domestic resources

TRANSFER OF RESOURCES ABROAD

Terms-of-trade effect

Service payments

1950  51-53  54-56  57-59  60-62  63-65  66-68

# APPENDIX FIGURE 10

## Guatemala
### (percentages of product)

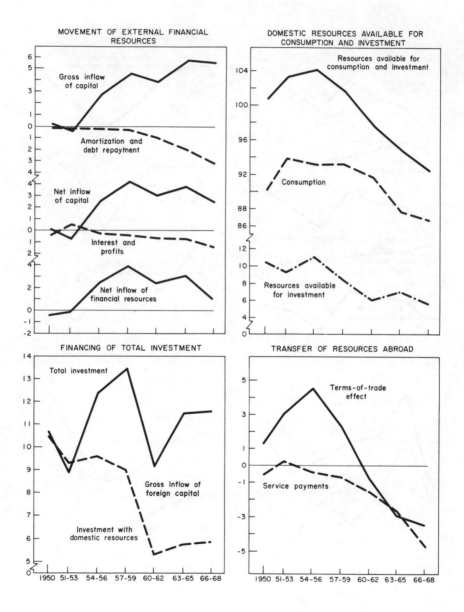

MOVEMENT OF EXTERNAL FINANCIAL
RESOURCES

Gross inflow
of capital

Amortization and
debt repayment

Net inflow
of capital

Interest and
profits

Net inflow of
financial resources

DOMESTIC RESOURCES AVAILABLE FOR
CONSUMPTION AND INVESTMENT

Resources available for
consumption and investment

Consumption

Resources available
for investment

FINANCING OF TOTAL INVESTMENT

Total investment

Gross inflow of
foreign capital

Investment with
domestic resources

TRANSFER OF RESOURCES ABROAD

Terms-of-trade
effect

Service payments

1950  51-53  54-56  57-59  60-62  63-65  66-68

# APPENDIX FIGURE 11

## Countries in Which the Import
## Coefficient Decreased, Including Venezuela
## (percentages of product)

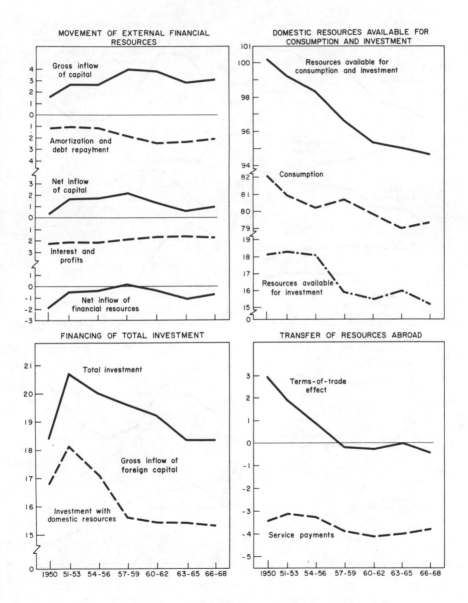

MOVEMENT OF EXTERNAL FINANCIAL RESOURCES

DOMESTIC RESOURCES AVAILABLE FOR CONSUMPTION AND INVESTMENT

FINANCING OF TOTAL INVESTMENT

TRANSFER OF RESOURCES ABROAD

# APPENDIX FIGURE 12

## Countries in Which the Import
## Coefficient Increased
## (percentages of product)

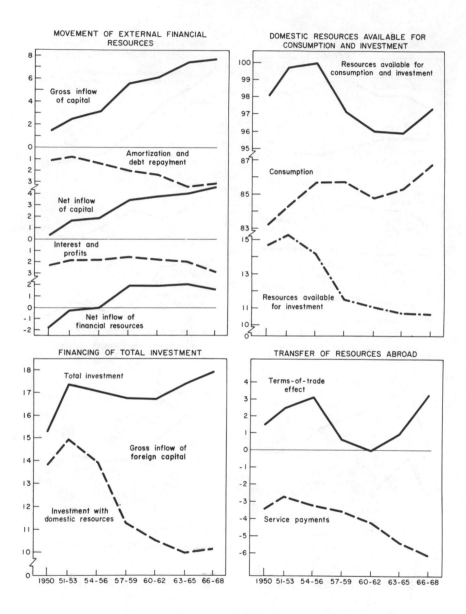

# APPENDIX FIGURE 13

## Relative Burden of Financial
## Service Payments
### (financial service payments as a percentage
### of purchasing power of exports)

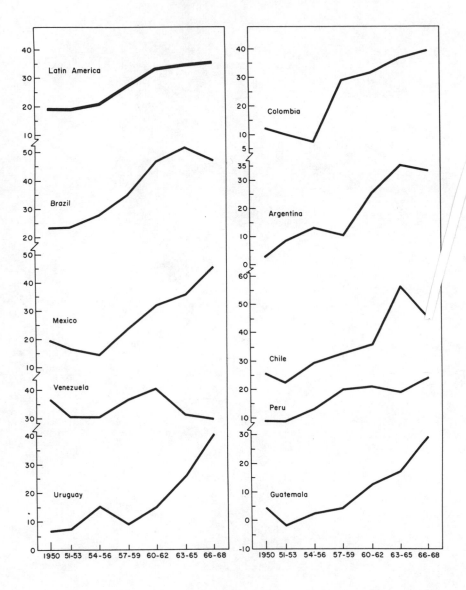

## ABOUT THE AUTHOR

Raúl Prebisch is Director-General of the Latin American Institute for Economic and Social Planning and former Executive Secretary of the United Nations Economic Commission for Latin America (ECLA) with headquarters at Santiago, Chile.

From 1925 to 1927, he was Deputy Director of the Department of Statistics in Argentina and, from 1927 to 1930, Director of Economic Research for the National Bank of Argentina. He was Argentina's Under-Secretary of Finance from 1930 to 1932, and served from 1933 to 1935 as Adviser to the Ministers of Finance and Agriculture.

Dr. Prebisch was organizer and first Director-General of the Central Bank of the Republic of Argentina (1935-1943). Upon his retirement from the Argentine Central Bank, he devoted his time to research and to his university post.

In 1948 he then joined the Secretariat of the United Nations Economic Commission for Latin America and was appointed its Executive Secretary in 1950. He relinquished that post in 1963.

At the close of 1955, Dr. Prebisch was appointed to his former chair of political economics at the University of Buenos Aires, on an honorary basis. He was also made an honorary member of the Faculty of Economics of the University of Chile at Santiago; the Universities of San Andrés, La Paz, Bolivia and San Marcos, Lima, Peru. He has been given honorary doctorates by Columbia University, New York, Universidad de los Andes, Colombia, and the University of Punjab, India.

In May, 1962, Dr. Prebisch was appointed Director-General of the Latin American Institute for Economic and Social Planning, established in Santiago (Chile) under the aegis of the United Nations Economic Commission for Latin America, and with financial assistance from the United Nations Special Fund and the Inter-American Development Bank.

After his appointment in 1963 as Secretary-General of the United Nations Conference on Trade and Development, Dr. Prebisch visited a number of geographic areas for regional discussions of trade problems and conferred with a number of individual governments on questions relating to the Conference.

The Nineteenth Session of the U.N. General Assembly approved the creation of the Conference on Trade and Development (UNCTAD) as a permanent organ of the General Assembly, and unanimously confirmed the appointment of Dr. Prebisch as Secretary-General of UNCTAD.

When his activities with UNCTAD ended in 1969, Dr. Prebisch reassumed his functions as Director-General of the Latin American Institute for Economic and Social Planning. In that capacity he acts as a Special Advisor in Washington to the President of the Inter-American Development Bank, and to the President of the Inter-American Committee of the Alliance for Progress. Additionally, at the request of the Secretary-General U Thant, Dr. Prebisch serves as advisor to the United Nations Secretary-General and to the Under-Secretary-General of the Department of Economic and Social Affairs on activities pertaining to the Second Development Decade.